MIKE MEYERS' CERTIFICATION
Passport ★

Network+ ™

NIGEL KENDRICK
MIKE MEYERS

 OSBORNE

New York • Chicago • San Francisco
Lisbon • London • Madrid • Mexico City
Milan • New Delhi • San Juan
Seoul • Singapore • Sydney • Toronto

McGraw-Hill/Osborne
2600 Tenth Street
Berkeley, California 94710
U.S.A.

To arrange bulk purchase discounts for sales promotions, premiums, or fund-raisers, please contact McGraw-Hill/Osborne at the above address. For information on translations or book distributors outside the U.S.A., please see the International Contact Information page immediately following the index of this book.

Mike Meyers' Network+ Certification Passport

1 2 3 4 5 6 7 8 9 0   DOC DOC   0 1 9 8 7 6 5 4 3 2

Book p/n 0-07-219589-4 and CD p/n 0-07-219588-6
parts of
ISBN 0-07-219523-1

Publisher	**Acquisitions Coordinator**	**Indexer**
Brandon A. Nordin	Jessica Wilson	Irv Hershman
Vice President &	**Technical Editor**	**Design and Production**
Associate Publisher	Kevin Vaccaro	epic
Scott Rogers		
	Copy Editors	**Illustrators**
Acquisitions Editor	Dennis Weaver	Michael Mueller
Michael Sprague	Judy Ziajka	Lyssa Sieben-Wald
Project Editor	**Proofreaders**	**Cover Series Design**
Katie Conley	Carroll Proffitt	Ted Holladay
	Linda Medoff	

This book was composed with QuarkXPress™.

Dedication

This book is dedicated to everyone who's ever answered—or aspires to answer—that universal distress call: "Hey, the network's down!"

Acknowledgments

We would like to take a moment to acknowledge the many folks who helped make this book possible.

To our families, for their patience and support throughout yet another big project.

To Scott Jernigan, editor extraordinaire, who kept the writers honest and made this book the polished gem we knew it could be.

To Cary Dier, who did a marvelous job of blending the voices of East Texas and West Sussex so spot-on purtily.

To the folks at McGraw-Hill/Osborne and Epic, for their wonderful input, encouragement, and threats of bodily harm: Michael Sprague, Jessica Wilson, Katie Conley, Michal Mueller, and Lyssa Sieben-Wald.

And to the Total Seminars HQ team in Houston—Dudley, Janelle, Roger, Amber, Martin, Cindy, Kathy, John H., John D., David, and Bambi: Thanks for another fine effort! I just knew that being under the watchful, unblinking, and thoroughly unnatural eye of Icarus (my pet formerly-living duck) would make everybody so much more productive and cheerful!

Contents

3 Network Topologies and Standards 49

5 Protocols and Protocol Suites 115

Check-In

May I See Your Passport?

What do you mean, you don't have a passport? Why, it's sitting right in your hands, even as you read! This book is your passport to a very special place. You're about to begin a journey, my friend: a journey toward that magical place called certification! You don't need a ticket, you don't need a suitcase—just snuggle up and read this passport. It's all you need to get there. Are you ready? Well then, let's go!

Your Travel Agent: Mike Meyers

Hello! I'm Mike Meyers, president of Total Seminars and author of a number of popular certification books. On any given day, you'll find me stringing network cable, setting up a web site, or writing code. I love every aspect of this book you hold in your hands. It's part of a powerful new book series called the *Mike Meyers' Certification Passports.* Every book in this series combines easy readability with a condensed format—in other words, the kind of book I always wanted when I went for my own certifications. Putting a large amount of information in an accessible format is certainly a challenge, but I think we've achieved our goal, and I'm confident you'll agree.

I designed this series to do one thing and only one thing: to get you the information you need to achieve your certification. You won't find any fluff in here. Nigel and I packed every page with nothing but the real nitty-gritty of the Network+ Certification exam. Every page has 100 percent pure concentrate of certification knowledge! But we didn't forget to make the book readable, so I hope you also enjoy the casual, friendly style.

My personal e-mail address is mikem@totalsem.com, and Nigel's e-mail address is nkendrick@skillmarque.com. Please feel free to contact either of us directly if you have any questions, complaints, or compliments.

Your Destination: Network+ Certification

This book is your passport to CompTIA's Network+ Certification, the vendor-neutral industry-standard certification for basic networking skills. Network+ Certification can be your ticket to a career in all-around networking or simply an excellent step in your certification pathway. This book is your passport to success on the Network+ Certification exam.

Your Guides: Mike Meyers and Nigel Kendrick

You get a pair of tour guides for this book, both me and Nigel Kendrick (I'm the one holding up the red umbrella—see?). I've written numerous computer certification books—including the *All-in-One Network+ Certification Exam Guide* and the best-selling *All-in-One A+ Certification Exam Guide*. More to the point, I've been working on PCs and teaching others how to make, fix, and network them for a *very* long time, and I love it! When I'm not lecturing or writing about PCs, I'm working on PCs or spanking my friend Scott in *Half Life* or *Team Fortress*—on the PC, naturally!

In 1982, Nigel was working as a Junior Electronics Engineer when his boss asked him to go down to the stores and bring back a shipment of these new-fangled devices called IBM Personal Computers, set them up, and then show the other engineers how to use them. Nigel spent the next few years looking after the company's growing (pioneering!) PC network, before joining a systems integration company as its technical support manager, with specific responsibilities for the Help Desk, Networking, and PC Manufacturing divisions.

Nigel now runs his own training and courseware development company in West Sussex, on the South Coast of England, specializing in technical IT, Call Center, and Help Desk consultancy, training, and courseware development. Nigel has worked for many training companies around the UK and the rest of the world presenting end-user and "train the trainer" courses as well as developing customized training material. Now writing for Total Seminars, Nigel's short-term ambition is to become as wacky as the rest of the team.

Why the Travel Theme?

The steps in gaining a certification parallel closely the steps in planning and taking a trip. All of the elements are the same: preparation, an itinerary, a route, even mishaps along the way. Let me show you how it all works.

This book is divided into 12 chapters. Each chapter begins with an *Itinerary* section that lists the objectives covered in that chapter, and an *ETA* section to give you an idea of the time involved in learning the skills in that chapter. Each chapter is organized by the objectives, which are either drawn from those officially stated by the certifying body, or reflect our expert take on the best way to approach the topics. Also, each chapter contains a number of helpful items to highlight points of interest:

Exam Tip
Points out critical topics you're likely to see on the actual exam.

Travel Assistance
Lists additional sources, such as books and web sites, to give you more information.

Local Lingo
Describes special terms in detail in a way you can easily understand.

Travel Advisory
Warns you of common pitfalls, misconceptions, and downright physical peril!

The end of each chapter gives you two handy tools. The *Checkpoint* reviews each objective covered in the chapter with a handy synopsis—a great way to review quickly—and end-of-chapter *Review Questions* (and answers) test your newly acquired skills.

But the fun doesn't stop there! After you've read the book, pull out the CD and take advantage of the free practice questions! Use the full practice exam to hone your skills, and keep the book handy to check your answers.

If you want even more practice, log onto http://www.osborne.com/passport, and for a nominal fee, you can get additional high-quality practice questions.

When you find yourself acing the practice questions, you're ready to take the exam. Go get certified!

The End of the Trail

The IT industry changes and grows constantly, *and so should you*. Finishing one certification is only one step in an ongoing process of gaining more and more certifications to match your constantly changing and growing skills. Read Appendix B, "Career Flight Path," at the end of the book to find out where this certification fits into your personal certification goals. Remember, in the IT business, if you're not moving forward, you're way behind!

Good luck on your certification! Stay in touch!

Mike Meyers
Series Editor
Mike Meyers' Certification Passport

Network
Fundamentals

	NEWBIE	SOME EXPERIENCE	EXPERT
ETA	4 hours	2 hours	1 hour

1

This chapter takes you gently into the wonderful world of networking so that you can read the following chapters with some fundamental knowledge already in place. If you think you already have enough basic network experience, you can skip this chapter, but then again, a little refresher on the basics (*especially* the OSI seven-layer model) may not be a bad idea—and the chapter is not long!

Big or small, networks all serve the same purpose: to share things, whether it's disk space on a server, a printer, or an e-mail system. Networks enable more than one user to access shared resources. Back in the late 1980s, the average size of a network was often quoted to be eight users, and the main reason for the original growth in PC networking was to share expensive laser printers—sometimes just *one per company*! Today, we see networks that span the globe as well as humble two-machine setups for research purposes (otherwise known as death-match gaming). Every desktop operating system (such as Windows 9*x*/2000/XP) has built-in networking capabilities, which means that you can network nearly every PC today, without resorting to expensive software to make the network work.

So what's involved? Well, you'll probably need some equipment to link together, and since we're focusing on the Network+ exam, we'll do the same as the exam authors and concentrate on PC networking. Ready…?

Objective 1.01

Overview of Network Hardware

We need to begin with some hardware on our network (see Figure 1-1), the most obvious example of which is a PC. There's usually no problem linking together supposedly incompatible systems. For example, it's quite feasible to work on a PC running Windows 2000 while your data and programs are stored on a corporate minicomputer running a different operating system, such as UNIX or Linux or one of their close relatives. This is real corporate networking, and the fact that you are using a non-PC platform to store your data is handled by the networking software and hardware. All you see, for example, is another drive letter on your computer—maybe W: for word processing—and that's it!

Clients and Servers

Networks have two categories of computers: those that access the networked resources (clients) and those that provide the resources (servers).

FIGURE 1-1   A typical pile of networked hardware

Clients

Any PC or other computer system that makes use of network resources is a *client*. In the old days, we might have called them workstations, but the correct, modern term is client. Some may say *terminal*, but that really refers to a screen and keyboard-only setup (no processing power, no Windows!) used for working with mainframes and minicomputers that do all the thinking for you.

Local Lingo
client   A computer system that makes use of shared network resources.

Almost any PC can be a client, provided that you can somehow attach it to the network and run the software needed to get it communicating. Networking a PC won't make it more powerful, but will allow it to use resources situated elsewhere in the building, or perhaps halfway round the world.

Servers

Servers manage the network's shared resources. A small network may have only one server, but a corporate setup may have dozens, each performing a specific task. For example, one server may hold the network's disk space, and another may manage the printer. A third server may provide access to the Internet while also acting as a firewall to keep out unwanted hackers trying to probe around your network. Ultimately, the number of servers on a network depends on the workload the network is going to face and whether one server can cope. Later chapters will discuss how networks behave under load and what can be done to keep things running smoothly.

Local Lingo

server   A computer system that provides and manages shared network resources.

Servers have a sense of duty and will try to protect your resources from unwanted access. Every major network operating system (NOS), such as Microsoft Windows NT Server, Novell NetWare, UNIX, Linux, and other variants will expect every user trying to access their resources to provide a valid user name and password. Other common features include the ability to restrict a specific user's network access to one or more machines or to only during certain days or times.

Exam Tip

Purists may argue that UNIX and Linux are not network operating systems but multiuser operating systems—originally used via a dumb terminal and with centralized storage and printing—that now also happen to support network interconnectivity to client PCs and other servers. Fair enough, but they are certainly networkable and, especially in the case of Linux, can be configured to present themselves on a network as if they are servers.

Client/Server Networks

For most medium to large business networks (it's difficult to give a figure but, say, a system with more than 10 clients), a dedicated server is usually the norm, giving us what's referred to as a *client/server* or *server-based* network (see Figure 1-2). The main point here is that the server has a specific role to play (it's a server!) and will be tucked away safely (maybe in a computer room) and left to get on with its job—you won't find someone sitting at the server running Microsoft Word or Quake III. The only time the server will see user activity at the keyboard is when an authorized person performs some administrative task, such as installing a program update, running a tape backup program, or perhaps checking the server's log files when an unexpected event occurs.

OK, so you have a PC on your desk; is it a client or a server? Ha, trick question! You can't tell just by looking—it could be either. Read on, and all will be revealed.

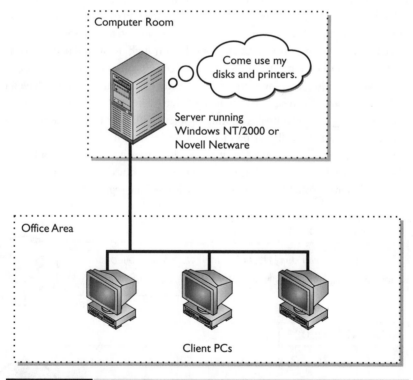

Computer Room

Come use my disks and printers.

Server running Windows NT/2000 or Novell Netware

Office Area

Client PCs

FIGURE 1-2   Some clients and a server

Peer-to-Peer Networks

Although traditional networking has always involved dedicated servers, you could almost always find specialized software to enable clients to share certain resources. Novell Personal NetWare, for example, enabled DOS-based clients to share disk space and printers. Since Microsoft introduced Windows for Workgroups, with its built-in server capabilities, all subsequent desktop computer operating systems— including Windows NT Workstation, 95, 98, 2000, ME, and XP—have supported some form of client-based sharing. These products enable machines to act as clients or servers, or as both at the same time. Every machine is the same in this respect, and we say that they are all peers (equals) because you don't need a dedicated server. Too good to be true? Yes and no!

So-called peer-to-peer networking (see Figure 1-3) is ideal for small offices or groups of people who need to share a printer or two (you can do this and still be part of a bigger client/server network), but running a PC as both a client and a server is hard work, and the system will slow down rapidly as other clients access its shared resources. There are other issues with peer-to-peer networking as well. What happens if someone switches off the PC at the end of the day while others are still accessing it? Security on such a network is not too great either. Although it is true that you can control access to your disk through the shared network connection, if your PC is in the middle of the office and someone wants your data, that person can just walk over and get it directly from your PC (if you haven't locked it). That's not so easy to do when you have a dedicated server in a secure computer room. Data control is another problem with peer-to-peer networking if you have several PCs all sharing their disk space. Since it's easy to lose track of where something has been saved, multiple copies of the same document or file are virtually inevitable. Using a dedicated server provides one central point for storage—and there's probably someone tasked with making regular backups, too.

Exam Tip
Peer-to-peer networking is ideal for small workgroups, but offers limited security and is easily disrupted by computer shutdowns.

Local Lingo
peer-to-peer networking Sharing resources among networked client systems which can also act as servers, so no dedicated server is needed.

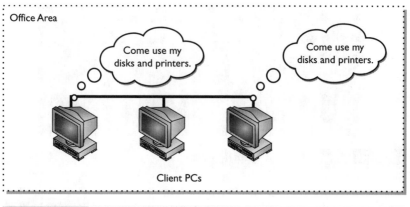

FIGURE 1-3 A peer-to-peer network

Linking It All Together

Our network will not work very well unless we have some way of getting data from the server to the clients. We need a communication channel and a way of connecting our computers to it—in essence, the core network components themselves. Later chapters will elaborate, but the basics are as follows.

Network Wiring (and the Rest)

The vast majority of the network that you see will be in the form of copper cabling, snaking from the back of your PC down the back of the desk to a socket in the floor or wall, or perhaps just on into the distance somewhere. There are a number of network wiring types, each with its own characteristics, speed, length limitations, and restrictions. You may find that your network uses one type of wiring in one area and something completely different in another area, depending on the age of the installation and the cable type chosen to match the requirements at the time. Networks can also use other forms of "wiring" such as optical fiber, infrared, and wireless, for starters. Clearly, some of these wiring types don't use wire at all, so we use the term *network media* to encompass all varieties. Figure 1-4 shows one type of network wiring called unshielded twisted pair, or UTP. There's more about network media in Chapter 2.

Network Interface Cards (NICs)

A NIC is the plug-in (or built-in) interface between your computer system and the network media. Every client and server must have at least one NIC (yes, a system

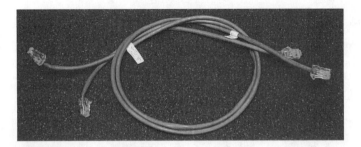

FIGURE 1-4   UTP wiring (patch leads)

can have more than one under some circumstances), and the NIC must be compatible with your computer system, the network media, and the way in which the network passes information. If it isn't, your PC isn't going to do much networking! Although some modern PCs have built-in NICs, you still may need a regular, plug-in NIC if, for example, the onboard NIC develops a fault, and it's too expensive to have the whole system board repaired or replaced. Figure 1-5 shows a typical NIC.

Network Equipment

A network often needs to grow beyond one or more limiting factors. For example, some network cable types can support only a certain number of machines on a single length of cable, or only a certain length of cable per network segment. Or maybe you need to join your network to another network at a remote site. For

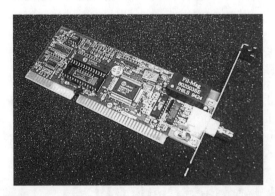

FIGURE 1-5   A typical NIC

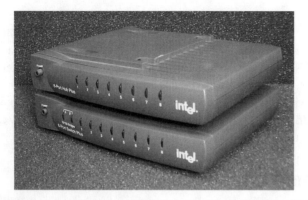

FIGURE 1-6   A network hub and switch

most problems of this type, the solution usually involves adding modules or pieces of equipment that enable your network to handle more machines or greater distances. These devices have names such as repeater, hub, switch (see Figure 1-6), bridge, and router. As you'll see in Chapter 4, you can choose among many devices to help solve your problems, but there will always be one that's more suitable than the others (probably for cost reasons). We'll explore later what these devices are and what they do.

Objective 1.02

Overview of Network Software

OK, the network's in place, and you've bought the hardware and installed the network cabling. Now you're reaching for the software...

We've already mentioned the mainstream, server-based networking products such as Microsoft Windows NT Server and Novell NetWare, and we've told you about the peer-to-peer functionality built into most desktop operating systems. This section expands on these discussions and describes the component parts that must be installed and configured correctly to make your computer system work properly on a network, whether it's as a client, a server, or a peer-to-peer machine. In many cases, the basic installation of these software components is automatic, and everything you need is actually supplied with your operating system. For example, Windows 9*x* or 2000/XP can detect that you've added a NIC and install all the right drivers—the amount of input required from you may be minimal.

NIC Driver

Nothing's going to happen if you can't send and receive data through the network. The NIC is connected to the network media, and the server or client software probably comes supplied with suitable drivers. If it doesn't, just reach for the disk supplied with the NIC or perhaps visit the manufacturer's web site to download a suitable driver. A visit to the web site is generally a good idea in any case, just to make sure that you are using the latest driver.

Protocol Driver

Once you have the right NIC driver installed, you need to consider the language—or *protocol*—that the network will use to convey the data. Over the years, various protocols have been developed, and you need to ensure that the client and server PCs (yes, and peer-to-peer systems) all speak the same language. If they don't, you won't be able to see some or all of the resources potentially available on the network. To complicate matters, you may need to ensure that the systems support more than one protocol—this is true when you have a mix of systems services on the network, and there's no common protocol that fits them all. The main communication protocols referred to on the Network+ exam are NetBEUI, IPX/SPX, and TCP/IP, and there's much more about these in Chapter 5.

Local Lingo
protocol   A standardized way of performing a specific action, such as communicating across a network or exchanging information.

Client and Server Software

If you're installing one of the major network operating systems (NOSs), then a lot of the files copied from the installation CD represent parts of the core NOS—the *server software*. On the other hand, if you're working on a client PC running, say, Windows 98 SE, then the client and server software services are actually just modules that need to be enabled and configured using the Network applet in the Control Panel. And, as we said before, you might find that most of this is done automatically anyway. Did you notice that we mentioned "Windows 98 SE" and then "server software"? Surely Windows 98 SE is used for *client* PCs and not servers? True, but don't forget that to be a peer-to-peer machine, a client PC also needs to act as a server, so Windows 98 SE (and 95, 2000, ME, and so on) comes with a *File and Printer Sharing* service module.

Redirector

One important role played by the client software is to provide an interface between the resources of the network and the functions of the host PC's operating system. This means, for example, enabling a network storage location to appear as a driver letter (say, W:), or a shared network printer to be accessed from a PC by printing to LPT2, even if the PC doesn't actually have a physical second parallel port. In networking terms, this feature is called *redirection* (Novell also uses the term "requester"). You simply refer to a resource by a drive letter or port that's not alien to the operating system, and before the OS has a chance to realize that W: or LPT2 doesn't actually exist, the client software has already stepped in and redirected the request to the relevant network resource.

Exam Tip	
Client software is also known as redirector or requestor software.	

Now That We Are Whole...

To summarize, there are three main software components that must be installed and configured correctly to enable a PC to run on a network (see Figure 1-7):

- NIC driver
- Protocol driver(s)
- Client/server services

Once you have these core components in place, the operating system and applications can make use of (or provide, in the case of a server) network resources.

If you look at what's been covered to this point, you'll notice that the focus has moved from the media, to the network card, to protocols, to the client/server software, and then to the operating system and applications—a clear progression in layers of functionality.

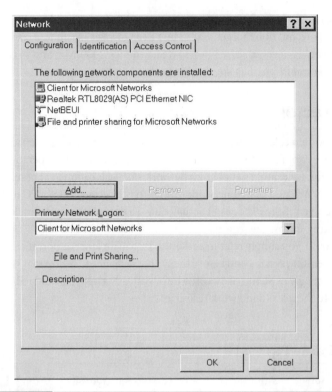

FIGURE 1-7   A Windows 9x machine with a client driver, NIC driver, protocol, and file and printer sharing service installed

Strangely enough (almost as if we'd planned it!), there is an industry standard way of describing how networks and their hardware and software function with reference to a model that has seven layers of generic functionality: the so-called OSI seven-layer model, which will be discussed in this book quite soon. But first...

Objective 1.03   Data Packets

The fundamentals of computing are all about data: moving data, storing data, processing data, and transmitting and receiving data. Networks rely on data, too, and so, before we move on, we need to talk about the facts of (data) life.

Consider a data file: it can be small, like a 200-byte text file, or big, like a 20-megabyte database. In either case, we want to be confident that when we click Save, our data makes its way safely to the server. In addition to application data, our networked PC is also going to send data codes with special meaning to our servers—instructions such as: "Log me in, my user name is...," "Here's my password...," "Send this to SALES_LASER02." (In reality, these requests won't be encoded in plain English, but in binary data sequences that are understood by the NOS.)

We know that all of this data is going to travel through our network media, but we need to understand a little about *how* this is accomplished for various other principles in this book to make sense. So here's a breakdown of how it works:

- **Networks carry data in packets**   The data in our 20-megabyte database is just a series of binary ones and zeroes. If we just throw all this data onto the network, no other machine is going to know what it is, where it came from, or where it needs to go. We need order—we need *packets*!

  A packet (or *frame*) contains some or all of the data we want to send across our network. If we're sending only a few bytes, such as our 200-byte text file, then it might all fit in one packet, but our database certainly won't. Because of the way that networks operate, they can carry only data packets that are between certain sizes, with typical packet sizes ranging from 1,500 to 4,000 bytes, according to the network technology being used.

  Think of a packet as an envelope into which you can stuff just so much paper. It's a carrying mechanism in a standardized format that's recognizable by every device on the network.

- **Packets need addresses**   You probably wouldn't post a letter without writing an address on the front of the envelope, and we certainly won't put a packet of data on a network without stating where it's supposed to go. In fact, a data packet contains both the recipient's and the sender's addresses so that the recipient knows where the packet came from, or in case there's a problem, how to contact the sender.

- **How big is that packet?**   A packet can contain any amount of data within predefined limits. Every data packet includes a note of how much data it actually contains. Among other things, this aids in error checking because the recipient can determine whether the packet that has just been received is complete.

- **What protocol is this packet using?**   We already know the names of three network protocols: NetBEUI, IPX/SPX, and TCP/IP. Every basic network packet includes a protocol ID field to help devices on the network determine how to decode and understand the contents of the packet. This field also makes it easier for network devices to pay attention only to packets formatted using a protocol they support.

- **That packet looks unwell!** It's a hard slog through all the media from your PC to the destination device, and data packets can be corrupted along the way by electrical interference, loose connectors, power glitches, and a host of other events. To help detect dodgy data packets, each packet includes a cyclic redundancy check (CRC) value that's computed by the sending device using the data in the packet. The CRC value is the result of a complex binary mathematical calculation on the data that is performed by both the sender and the recipient of the packet. If the CRC in the packet and the locally generated CRC don't match, then something's wrong, and the recipient will ask for the packet to be resent.

Figure 1-8 shows the format of a basic data packet.

Packet Summary

Data packets contain important pieces of information. The main ones are listed here:

- The sender's address
- The recipient's address
- A protocol ID
- A data length field
- The data
- A CRC value

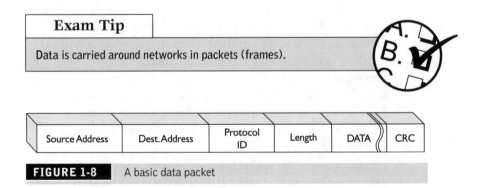

> **Exam Tip**
>
> Data is carried around networks in packets (frames).

Source Address	Dest. Address	Protocol ID	Length	DATA	CRC

FIGURE 1-8 A basic data packet

The OSI Seven-Layer Model

Objective 1.04

This is the part of the course that strikes fear into many a network technician, but we're pretty confident that when you finish this section, you'll wonder what all the fuss is about! Honest!

The Open Systems Interconnect (OSI) seven-layer model was developed by a standards organization called ISO. Contrary to popular belief, ISO is not an abbreviation—it's derived from the Greek word for equal.

ISO wanted a framework into which the major network hardware and software components and protocols could be placed to give every item a common reference point: a means of relating the components and their functionality to each other and a way of standardizing some of the components and protocols.

Exam Tip

The Network+ exam expects you to know the layers by name (especially layers 1 through 4), how they function in relation to each other, and what they represent.

Each layer of the model represents a particular aspect of network functionality. For example, layer 1—the Physical layer—represents electrical signals, connectors, and media types and the way that data is placed on the network media.

For a simple example of how layers work, imagine that you're designing your own range of NICs, and you've gotten to the stage where you're choosing what connector type to use for the media and card interface. Off you trot to your local electronics store, where a simple, four-pin audio connector catches your eye. You finish your card design and send it to the manufacturer, but when the product hits the stores, it doesn't sell. That's because no one else uses that four-pin connector type on their NIC or media, and so no one can hook your cards onto their network. In addition, those who have tried to interface to your card were a bit shocked (literally!) to discover that your data signals use a 120-volt reference for binary 1 (in the real world, data signals on a network cable are a fraction of a volt).

What went wrong? You should have used a media connector type and an electrical signaling system that conform to the relevant OSI physical layer standards. Also, don't be surprised if you get sued by that technician with the smoking screwdriver and singed hair!

As well as helping to standardize the design elements of network components, the OSI model helps position and standardize network protocols with reference to one another. As you'll see, this is important because more than one protocol or action is needed to get your data onto a network (or, indeed, to do the reverse and pick up data from a network). For example, the "protocol" TCP/IP, in fact, refers to two protocols, TCP and IP, and these two protocols don't work alone. What do they do? Chapter 5 is where you'll find out.

To summarize, the OSI seven-layer model is a theoretical representation of how a networked device functions and helps us understand the interrelationships among hardware, software, protocols, and applications. Many network technicians refer to network devices by their positions in the model; for example, a repeater (a device mentioned earlier) is a layer 1 (Physical layer) device.

The Layers and What They Represent

Here's a run through the layers and an overview of their tasks and responsibilities. Figure 1-9 summarizes the layers and their functions.

Layer 1: Physical Layer

Layer 1 is responsible for defining the network standards relating to electrical signals, connectors, and media types and the way that data is placed on the network media.

Layer 2: Data Link Layer

Layer 2 is responsible for gathering together and completing all of the elements that make up a data packet and putting the whole thing together so that it can be passed to a Physical layer device and on to the network. The Data Link layer assembles outgoing packets and generates the CRC. For incoming packets, it checks the data for validity by comparing its locally generated CRC value with that sent in the packet. The Data Link layer also determines whether it is possible or permissible at any instant to try and send data to the network. At any instant, another computer

Layer	Functionality
7. Application	Network services, authentication
6. Presentation	Translation, encryption
5. Session	Connections, sessions
4. Transport	Fragmentation, defragmentation, reliable data delivery, error correction/management, flow control
3. Network	Addressing, routing
2. Data Link	Packets/Frame, CRC generation/checking, network access
1. Physical	Media, connectors, electrical signals

FIGURE 1-9   The OSI seven-layer model

may already be using the network. If you transmit data at the same time, both packets will become corrupted.

Layer 3: Network Layer

Layer 3 understands addressing—how to find the ultimate destination address for a data packet—and routing, to make sure the packet ends up in the right place.

Layer 4: Transport Layer

If the data being sent is bigger than the allowable packet size, the Transport layer breaks the data into smaller, manageable chunks that will fit inside two or more packets. Breaking up data into smaller chunks is also known as *fragmentation*. The Transport layer is also responsible for confirming whether transmitted packets have reached their destination intact (or at all) and retransmitting them if they haven't (error correction/management). For incoming packets, the Transport layer reassembles the fragmented data (performs defragmentation), carefully ensuring that received packets are processed in the right order. The Transport layer also manages the flow of data to ensure that packets are sent at a pace that's suitable for the receiving device and for general network conditions. Sending data too quickly is like speaking too fast: you may have to keep repeating yourself to get the message understood, which is actually counterproductive.

Layer 5: Session Layer

Layer 5 sets up, manages, and terminates the data connections (called *sessions*) between networked devices. These sessions enable networked systems to exchange information.

Layer 6: Presentation Layer

Layer 6 is responsible for managing and translating information by catering to differences in the ways some computer systems store and manage their data. Presentation layer protocols are also responsible for data encryption.

Layer 7: Application Layer

Layer 7 represents the network-related program code and functions running on a computer system. This program code provides network support for the main applications being run, such as the redirector software discussed earlier, allowing a shared network location to appear on a machine as drive W: and providing services such as login authentication. Some application layer functions do exist as user-executable programs. Some file transfer and e-mail applications, for example, exist entirely on this layer.

Using the Seven-Layer Model

The seven-layer model is only a theoretical representation of how networks function. Although knowing it inside out won't change your life, it should help you pass the Network+ exam. The conceptual use of the model assumes that an event on one computer system (for example, a user pressing ENTER on a login screen) creates some data that sets off a chain of events. The data runs down through the layers on the sending machine and then leaves the system in a data packet, which travels across the network and then up through the layers on the receiving machine, until the data arrives intact at the application layer and causes something to happen. Later chapters in this book point out where certain key protocols and hardware fit into the model, and this can be useful stuff to know for both the Network+ exam and real life. Be prepared for a shock, however, because some network arrangements and protocols don't fit exactly into the model and, under some circumstances, not all of the layers are actually used. Does this matter? Well, as long as your data gets from point A to point B successfully, probably not.

Objective 1.05   Real-World Networking

Enough theory! Let's get back to the real world. You've a few more terms to absorb before you're ready to be let loose on the next chapter.

Network Size

You may have heard the terms LAN and WAN before, but did you know that there's a whole bunch of other *AN abbreviations that also describe the general size of a network (see Figure 1-10)? This section lists the main ones in order of size, with the smallest first.

By the way, network technicians often refer to every network they mention as either a LAN or a WAN. In practice this doesn't really matter unless you feel like correcting them just to see how they react.

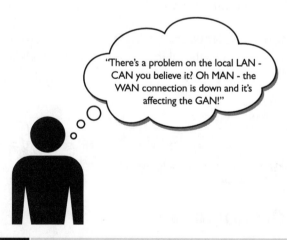

"There's a problem on the local LAN - CAN you believe it? Oh MAN - the WAN connection is down and it's affecting the GAN!"

FIGURE 1-10   Terms to describe network sizes

Local Area Network (LAN)   A LAN is a single network confined to one building or area of a building. There may be links to other locations at the same site, but these will be very localized.

Campus Area Network (CAN)   CAN is a fairly new term, used to describe a group of interconnected LANs within a small geographical area, such as a school campus, university, hospital, or military base.

Metropolitan Area Network (MAN)   The term *MAN* is usually applied to networks that have a sociopolitical boundary; such as a network of district authority offices in a town or city. Sites on a MAN are usually interconnected using fiber-optic cable or some other high-speed digital circuit (rather than standard phone lines, for example), and the MAN itself may well carry voice as well as data traffic.

Wide Area Network (WAN)   A WAN is two or more interconnected LANs spread over a large geographic area, even on different continents. The Internet is the largest WAN in existence.

Global Area Network (GAN)   A GAN is a single network with connection points spread around the world. GANs are used mostly by large corporate organizations and consist of a series of networked, orbiting satellites. Note the subtle difference between a WAN and a GAN: the latter is a single network, not a number of interconnected networks.

Solar System Area Network (SSAN)   A SSAN is a series of interconnected GANs connecting all the habitable planets and planetoids in a single solar system…err…. Well, we'll see one someday!

Travel Advisory

These terms don't exist as official standards, but their use and definitions have become generally accepted over time.

Network Performance

Many factors affect network performance, but here we want to talk about just the basic speed of a standard network, how network speed is measured, and some of the terms related to performance.

Bandwidth

Network data speeds are measured in megabits per second—sometimes abbreviated Mbps. That lowercase *b* is important, because an uppercase *B* would imply mega*bytes*. For a standard corporate network, the speed at which data travels between networked systems will typically range between 4 and 100 Mbps, depending on the network standard used. In real terms, this means that a network link could easily work at about the same pace as a quad-speed CD-ROM drive—hardly blazing a trail, but this illustrates one key point about networking: it's not always about speed; it's about the ability to access shared resources.

So where does this word *bandwidth* come in? Well, the data signal traveling through the network media (usually some form of copper wire) is an electrical signal that's changing voltage rapidly to represent a string of binary data (remember our packets?). Any signal that changes in this cyclic way has a frequency associated with it—measured in Hertz (Hz)—which is known as its *bandwidth*. Your network media is designed to operate across a certain range of frequencies, or bandwidths, and if you try to push data through the network at a faster rate (exceeding your bandwidth), you will quickly discover that the laws of physics are not negotiable!

The bandwidth of the network is closely related to its maximum theoretical speed. So network technicians will often say things like "our network has a bandwidth of 10 megabits per second," when they really mean "our network has a top speed of 10 megabits per second," or "the bandwidth of our network provides a throughput of 10 megabits per second." For the purposes of the Network+ exam, all of these variations are considered to be correct and to mean the same thing.

Local Lingo

bandwidth   A term used to refer to the performance (speed) of a network.

CHECKPOINT

✔ **Objective 1.01: Overview of Network Hardware**   The most obvious pieces of network hardware are the computers on the network. These are divided into client and server systems unless they are desktop systems that are sharing resources, in which case they are known as peer-to-peer systems.

Corporate networks generally use dedicated servers because they offer higher performance, greater stability, and better security than peer-to-peer options. Your network won't be complete without some media such as copper wiring, fiber optics, wireless, or infrared to interconnect your systems, and a Network Interface Card (NIC) to connect your system to the media. Other devices on the network—such as repeaters, hubs, bridges, and routers—enable you to expand the system locally or to other sites.

✔ **Objective 1.02: Overview of Network Software** The major software components of a network are the network operating system (NOS), NIC drivers, protocol drivers, and client/server services. Most of the components needed to get a network up and running are supplied as standard with your NOS or as part of your client operating system (Windows NT/9x/2000/ME/XP, Linux, and so on).

✔ **Objective 1.03: Data Packets** To send a piece of data across a network, it has to be placed in a standard, formatted structure known as a packet or frame. These packets also state the source and destination addresses of the data, the protocol being used, and the amount of data being sent. A cyclic redundancy check (CRC) value is also added to the packet to enable the receiving device to check the packet for errors. If the packet looks faulty, the recipient will ask for it to be resent.

✔ **Objective 1.04: The OSI Seven-Layer Model** The OSI seven-layer model describes how data flows from one networked system to another—it's a theoretical model into which many of the standards, components, and functions of a network fit. The model promotes the use of recognized network standards and helps ensure compatibility between network hardware and software from different manufacturers.

✔ **Objective 1.05: Real-World Networking** Networks come in all shapes and sizes, and there are a number of de facto abbreviations that can be used to describe different types of networks, from small LANs to worldwide GANs. One of the key features of a network is its performance at the desktop (that is, the speed at which the client machines can send and receive data), which is usually measured in megabits per second. Accessing data across a network is not necessarily that fast compared to accessing the same data from a local hard disk, but this is far outweighed by the benefits of being able to share data and resources, such as printers, with a large number of clients. The term bandwidth is often used interchangeably with speed, although the two are not quite the same thing.

REVIEW QUESTIONS

1. What name is given to a computer that can act as both a client and a server? (Select one answer.)

   A. A multitasking computer
   B. A mainframe computer
   C. A peer-to-peer computer
   D. A LAN computer

2. Which of the following statements are *not* true? (Select all that apply.)

   A. A peer-to-peer server is the best choice for a large corporate network.
   B. Client/server networks are more robust that peer-to-peer networks.
   C. Novell NetWare is an example of a peer-to-peer NOS.
   D. Windows 98 SE does not support peer-to-peer networking.

3. You have configured a new client PC and connected it to your LAN. You can see some of the servers on the network, but not all of them. What is the most likely cause? (Select one answer.)

   A. A faulty NIC
   B. Faulty media
   C. A faulty OSI layer
   D. A missing protocol driver

4. Which of the following items is *not* part of a data packet? (Select one answer.)

   A. Media identifier
   B. Data length
   C. Protocol ID
   D. CRC

5. Which layer of the OSI model is responsible for addressing and routing? (Select one answer.)

   A. Transport
   B. Network
   C. Session
   D. Application

6. Which layer of the OSI model can translate data from one format to another? (Select one answer.)

   A. Application
   B. Presentation
   C. Session
   D. Transport

7. At which layer of the OSI model is error correction performed? (Select one answer.)

   A. Data Link
   B. Physical
   C. Transport
   D. Session

8. Layer 3 is the _____ layer of the OSI model. (Select one answer.)

   A. Session
   B. Application
   C. Data Link
   D. Network

9. Which of the following takes place at the Data Link layer? (Select all that apply.)

   A. Packet fragmentation
   B. Data framing
   C. CRC checking
   D. Encryption

10. Which of the following are not common network protocols? (Select two answers.)

    A. IPBEUI
    B. IPX/SPX
    C. NetBEUI
    D. NET/IP

REVIEW ANSWERS

1. **C** A desktop PC acting as a client and a server is said to be a peer-to-peer system.

2. **A** **C** **D** Only statement B is true. Client/server networks are more robust than peer-to-peer networks.

3. **D** We know that we're on the network because we can see *some* resources, so the NIC (A) and media (B) must be okay. Answer C is just meaningless. Because we can't see *some* resources, we probably don't have the required protocol installed—answer D.

4. **A** There's no such field as "media identifier" in a data packet, but all the others are present.

5. **B** The Network layer provides addressing and routing functionality.

6. **B** The Presentation layer (answer B) can translate data.

7. **C** Error correction is performed by the Transport layer.

8. **D** Layer 3 is the Network layer.

9. **B** **C** The Data Link layer puts everything together in a packet and checks incoming CRC information.

10. **A** **D** Only IPX/SPX and NetBEUI (B and C) are true protocols; the others are made-up names.

Network
Media

NEWBIE	SOME EXPERIENCE	EXPERT
2 hours	1 hour	30 minutes

ETA

Welcome to Chapter 2! Since you've made it this far, we'll assume that either you enjoyed Chapter 1 so much that you've decided to continue, or you skipped the first chapter because you feel you're already comfortable with the basics of networking and network terminology. Well, in either case, here's your first test.

People in the know talk about network *media* rather than *cabling*. How come? Well, of course, as you knew all along, it's because some parts of a network's data highway can be made up of materials other than physical cable or fiber. For example, there might be a laser or microwave link between buildings, and perhaps infrared or wireless devices connecting laptops to your main network. Inside the building, you'll find connectors, adapters, wall ports, and other such parts.

Local Lingo

bounded media   Physical network cabling (copper and fiber).

unbounded media   Microwave, wireless, and infrared network links.

As you might imagine, there are a number of different network media types. Some are faster than others, some will work over relatively long distances, and some don't require a physical connection to the main network (ideal for mobile executives and their laptops). This chapter covers all of the major media types and their characteristics, use, and key features.

Exam Tip

Network media and connectors and the electrical signals traveling over them are represented by standards at layer 1 (the Physical layer) of the OSI seven-layer model.

Objective 2.01   Coaxial Cable

Coaxial cable is the kind of cabling used to bring the signal down from a rooftop antenna to a TV set or radio receiver or, in this case, to link together networked devices. "Coax" is the granddaddy of all mainstream network media types and is very much associated with the original designs of the popular Ethernet networking standard, developed in 1973 and still going strong today in a number of forms.

Coaxial cable has a central conducting core surrounded by a protective, insulating layer, an outer metal screen made of a woven copper mesh, a metal-covered plastic or foil or both, and an overall insulating jacket (see Figure 2-1). The metal screen helps protect the data traveling down the central core from being corrupted by external signals, such as radio waves, and other sources of electromagnetic interference (EMI), such as high-current power cables, mobile phones, electric motors, fluorescent tubes, and local electrical storms. The screen also reduces the amount of data signal that can radiate from the cable to become another source of EMI and thus cause problems for other data cables and systems. The cable is referred to as coaxial (or simply coax) because both the center wire and the braided metal shield share a common axis, or centerline.

Local Lingo

crosstalk An unwanted interaction between two electrical signals.

Coax is not used much these days for new network installations and is considered old technology. That said, if you want to link a few PCs together in a small office to share data and perhaps a printer or two, then coax might do—but there are more modern, sexier ways to set up a network.

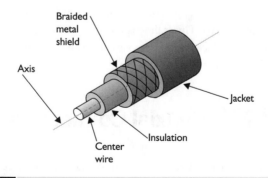

FIGURE 2-1 Coaxial ("coax") cable

TABLE 2.1	Coaxial Cable Types for Networking	
Network Type	**Coax Type**	**Nominal Impedance**
Thin Ethernet	RG-58	50 ohms
Thick Ethernet	RG-8 or RG-11	50 ohms
ARCNet	RG-62	93 ohms

Coaxial Cable Types

There's a mind-boggling number of different types of coax, each one suitable for a specific purpose, such as audio, video, TV, satellite, cable, radio, and, of course, data. Each coax type has its own set of characteristics, closely matched to the type of signal that cable is designed to carry. Using the wrong type for the wrong purpose can mess up the signal traveling down the cable. In the wonderful world of datacommunications, the two coax types most often mixed up are those used for networks based on the Ethernet standard and those used for another "old boy" known as ARCNet. Using even one small length of the wrong coax may cause complete network failure or bizarre problems such as dead spots along the length of the network.

Specific coax types were developed for the Ethernet standard, but a number of radio cables have very similar characteristics, and these so-called *radio-grade (RG)* cables also became associated with Ethernet. Another RG coax type is commonly associated with ARCNet. Table 2-1 shows the RG coax types used for data networking and also shows an often-quoted characteristic known as the cable's nominal impedance (a measure of how much the cable impedes the flow of electric current). As you can see, the nominal impedance of ARCNet coax is different from that of Ethernet coax. This is the main reason why the cable types should not be used in the wrong place. The differences between thick and thin Ethernet are explained in the next chapter.

Objective 2.02 Coaxial Connectors

Both Thin Ethernet and ARCNet use BNC connectors, shown in Figure 2-2, to attach the coax to other devices, such as the Network Interface Cards (NICs)

Coaxial cable fitted with BNC connectors

inside a computer. These twist-and-lock connectors were originally fitted to the coax using wire strippers, a soldering iron, and a wrench, but it's much quicker and easier to use wire strippers, crimp connectors, and a crimping tool. *Crimping* means to bend or squeeze the metal of the connector around the cable to secure it to the cable, which definitely beats the hassle of soldering and using the wrench.

Network devices are connected to Thick Ethernet coax via an adapter box known as a *transceiver*. The transceiver itself clamps directly onto the cable and makes contact with the inner conductor and outer braid using a set of sharp spikes known as *bee-sting* or (plastic fangs ready?) *vampire taps*. Occasionally, you will encounter a transceiver that uses connectors that screw on, known as PL-259s, though these are often associated with radio equipment (antennas, radio ham sets, and so on). PL-259 connectors (the PL stands for plug) screw into SO-259 (socket) connectors. These connectors may also be found at the ends of the coax to attach the bus terminators (covered later in this chapter).

Local Lingo

BNC The origins of the acronym BNC have been lost. Various sources call it a bayonet connector, bayonet navy connector, British Naval Connector, Bayonet Neill Concelman, bayonet nut connector, and so on. You need to know only what a BNC connector is and how to use it. Don't worry about what the acronym stands for!

Objective 2.03 UTP and STP Cable

Many modern networks are constructed using a telephone-type cable known as unshielded twisted pair (UTP). UTP network cables, as shown in Figure 2-3, have four pairs of twisted wires. The twists in the cable pairs reduce crosstalk (remember that?) and also act as a partial shield. As you might have guessed from the name, UTP has no overall metal screen—just the cable pairs inside the covering. UTP cable is popular because it is relatively cheap and simple to install. Better still, the same wiring infrastructure can be used for data and voice/telephony. That means that if UTP cable is installed as part of a building's infrastructure (or as part of a refit), then only one cabling system is required for many of the building's services, except electricity, gas, and water!

Although UTP cable is low cost, it can be used with some fairly high-tech, high-spec, high-price kits to create very sophisticated, high-performance networks.

As the name implies, shielded twisted-pair (STP) cable *does* have a screen covering the wire pairs, and there is also a ground wire (also known as a *drain wire*) running the length of the media. STP is intended for use in electrically noisy environments and is also specified for certain IBM networking requirements, but generally, UTP is more widely used, so we won't spend much time on STP cable in this chapter.

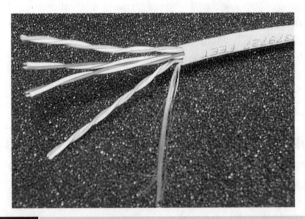

FIGURE 2-3   Four-pair UTP cable

UTP Cable Types

UTP comes in a variety of grades, called categories, numbered Category 1 through Category 5, summarized in Table 2-2. These categories define the maximum supported data speed of the cable, and they have been developed over the years to cater to faster and faster network designs.

Exam Tip

If you do a bit of net surfing, you will probably find references to CAT 5e, CAT 6, and CAT 7 media. Don't worry; these "standards" are not covered by the current exam, partly because they are unofficial and have been created in the field by cabling companies trying to guess what will be needed to cope with future (as yet nonexistent) networking requirements. If you know what CAT 1 through 5 can do, that will be good enough for now.

It might have caught your eye in the Table 2-2 that UTP cable is used for Ethernet networks, but a few paragraphs ago, you learned about Ethernet and *coax* cable. Well, UTP is the way forward, and Ethernet was one of the first networking standards to be reengineered to work on this media type. In addition, most new

TABLE 2.2   UTP Cable Categories

Category	Typical Use
Category 1	Regular analog phone lines; not used for data communications
Category 2	Telephony and alarm systems
Category 3	Ethernet over UTP at 10 megabits per second (10BaseT)
Category 4	Token Ring at 16 megabits per second
Category 5	Ethernet over UTP at 100 megabits per second (100BaseTX) and Gigabit Ethernet (1000BaseT)

cabling installations will use Category 5 (CAT 5) cabling because it supports all current (and planned future) data speeds and standards. In fact, although it is typically associated with data rates up to 100 megabits per second, it can be run at faster speeds. The category level of a piece of cable will normally be written on the cable itself, as shown in Figure 2-4. All cable accessories, such as the wall- or pillar-mounted data ports, must also match the category of the cable being used. Mixing CAT 5 cable with CAT 3 wall sockets, for example, could cause that part of the network (known as a segment) not to work properly. The post-installation network testing should pick up this type of mismatch, but it is better to get things right the first time rather than find out later that you need to replace all of your data outlets!

Patch Cable and Premises Cable

If you've ever picked up a UTP patch lead (the sort of lead that connects a PC to a wall port or that connects pieces of a network kit together in the computer room cabinet) and it felt stiff and inflexible, it's probably made from the wrong type of UTP cable. Just to add yet another twist to the story (pun not intended!), there are two types of UTP cable: the stuff that's used for patch leads and the stuff that's used to wire buildings. To make patch leads flexible and easy to route through wiring cabinets, under desks, and the like, the conductive core of each wire is made from fine strands of copper. But to make *premises* wiring cable more robust and able to withstand some heavy handling as it's (professionally) pulled through trunking and plenum space, the cores are made of solid copper. It's very tempting to use UTP premises wiring cable for patch leads—especially if there are reels of the stuff lying around at the end of a job. If you do, though, you're setting yourself up for a fall, because the crimp connectors in UTP plugs (see the next section) are designed for stranded core cable, and if you use the solid stuff, the squeezing action of the crimp procedure compresses the solid copper core enough to make it brittle and prone to cracking. After a few months in service, it may start to do annoying things like failing intermittently.

FIGURE 2-4   The marking shows this to be Category 5E UTP cable.

Local Lingo

horizontal wiring   Solid core UTP, also called premises wiring, often laid out flat in ducting or in cable trays in the plenum.

plenum   A fancy name for the gap between the real ceiling (or the bottom of the next floor up, if you want) and the suspended tiles.

While we're talking about plenums, if you read the instructions for many pieces of networking hardware, you will notice that they specifically exclude plenum areas in their installation notes. This is because the equipment may give off toxic fumes in the event of a fire that could spread quickly through the plenum area, creating a hazard. Plenum cable (copper and fiber types) has a special, low-toxicity jacket specifically for installation in these areas. Don't use regular (PVC) jacketed cables in the plenum.

Objective 2.04   UTP Connectors

UTP network cabling uses an eight-contact connector type known as an RJ-45, as shown in Figure 2-5 (the RJ stands for registered jack). The pins on the RJ-45 are numbered from 1 to 8, as shown in Figure 2-6, and different pin combinations are used with different networking standards, as covered in the next chapter. One feature of this arrangement is that interconnecting the wrong types of networking equipment is unlikely to have a disastrous effect.

FIGURE 2-5   An RJ-45 connector

FIGURE 2-6   RJ-45 connector pin numbering

Many UTP networking standards use only two of the four UTP cable pairs, but the best practice is always to connect all four pairs at every network connector for compatibility with other, and future, standards. Some sources conclude that it would be possible to use a four-contact connector system known as RJ-11 for UTP networking by using just the two required pairs, but in reality, this configuration would be very unusual.

> **Exam Tip**
>
> In the real world, UTP-based networks use RJ-45 connectors, though it would be possible (but *very* unusual) to design a UTP network using RJ-11 connectors.

UTP Wiring Standards

It probably won't come as a surprise to know that UTP connectors and wiring have a color code and wiring scheme associated with them (just something else for you to remember!). Each wire inside a UTP cable must connect to the proper pin on the connector at each end of the cable. The wires are color-coded to assist in properly matching the ends; each pair of wires has a solid-colored wire and a striped wire: blue/blue-white, orange/orange-white, brown/brown-white, and green/green-white. Because signals sent down pin 1 on one end of a cable must be received on pin 1 on the other end of the cable (and so on), the same wire must connect to pin 1 on both ends. Industry organizations have developed a variety of standard color codes to facilitate installation. The most common spec in use today is known EIA/TIA 568B (for Electronics Industry Association/Telecommunications Industry Association); see Figure 2-7. Using an established color-code scheme ensures that the wires match up correctly at each end of the cable, and also makes specific pairs of wires carry specific signals in a way that minimizes potential problems such as crosstalk. Consistency also makes troubleshooting and repair easier.

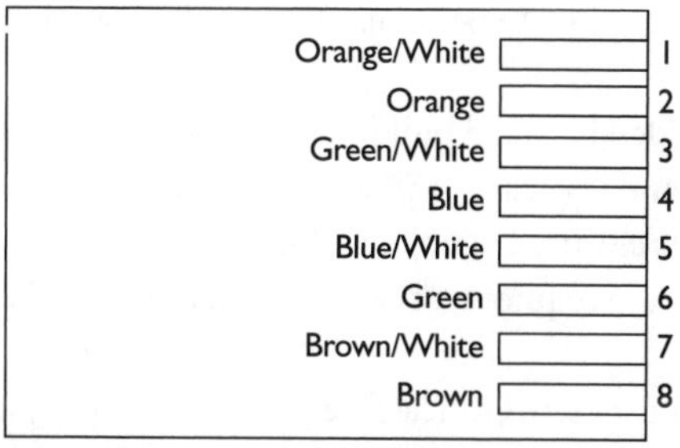

Orange/White		I
Orange		2
Green/White		3
Blue		4
Blue/White		5
Green		6
Brown/White		7
Brown		8

FIGURE 2-7 The EIA/TIA 568B standard

UTP Testing

Because UTP cable doesn't have an overall screen, it is much more susceptible to EMI and crosstalk compared to coax. Because of this, there are some very specific requirements for the installation of UTP cabling. For example, just like coax, it should not be routed near light fittings in the plenum, be run parallel to heavy power cables, or be run over and squashed on a regular basis by your office chair! But in the case of UTP cable, the way the wires are attached to the wall plates and the number of sharp bends in a horizontal run can adversely affect performance. Professional installers will test every single run (segment) of UTP cabling to satisfy themselves, and their customer, that the job has been done right using a special testing kit that measures the overall length of each segment, checks various electrical characteristics, and detects possible crosstalk (with fancy names such as near-end crosstalk and far-end crosstalk) between the wire pairs. Cable segments that fail to meet the required specs may not work properly at the intended (or future) data speeds and may have to be rejoined to the wall plates or, worse case, rerouted or replaced. Once everything has been sorted out, the printed test results are often presented to the customer as part of the network installation completion sign-off process.

Objective 2.05 # Optical Fiber

Optical fiber is relatively expensive to purchase and install because it requires specialist handling and connection techniques. For this reason alone, fiber is not usually installed for desktop network connection unless there is good justification. In general, fiber will be used where one or more of the following apply:

- Long distances need to be covered, up to the maximum segment distance of 2 km.
- A link is needed between buildings, and other options, such as microwave and laser, are impractical (no line of sight, for example), too expensive, or electrically unworkable.
- High speeds are required, or a significant amount of data needs to be carried.
- Security is a concern. Optical fibers don't radiate signals that can be picked up by listening equipment, and it is difficult to tap a fiber without being detected.
- The general environment is electrically unfriendly to data—that is, full of EMI, such as in a factory or in a radio/TV/radar transmitter room.
- Any potential for an electrical spark must be eliminated, such as in a laboratory using flammable gases and other volatile chemicals.

The Network+ exam doesn't concentrate much on fiber, but you should note a few key points.

Data can be sent down an optical fiber cable as either infrared or laser light, according to the system in use and the maximum distances involved. Each type of system requires a specific type of media; infrared LED systems use so-called *multimode* fiber, whereas laser-diode-based systems (mainly used for high-speed, long-haul data and telecom links) use *single-mode* (*monomode*) cable.

Travel Advisory

Infrared and laser diode light sources can cause eye damage if stared at directly, so never look down a fiber cable to see if it's working. Professional testing kits use optical sensors and/or cameras. If you don't have the proper equipment available, test for faults by replacing suspect fiber leads with known good ones.

An optical fiber cable has three components: the fiber itself; the cladding, which actually makes the light reflect down the fiber; and the insulating jacket. Fiber cabling is specified by its mode of operation and a two-number designator representing the core and cladding diameter in microns (μm, or millionths of a meter). The most common size used for general networking is multimode 62.5/125 μm. Almost all fiber networking standards require two fibers, and a pair are often connected together as duplex optical fiber cabling (Figure 2-8).

FIGURE 2-8   Duplex optical fiber cable

Objective 2.06   Optical Fiber Connectors

Because they are optical, rather than electrical, fiber cables have their own series of connector types. You cannot, for example, whack a BNC connector onto a piece of fiber (well, you probably *could*, but it won't impress anyone!). The two most common types of fiber-optic connectors are the *ST* (twist and lock) and *SC* (push fit) types (see Figure 2-9), but you may also come across an FDDI duplex

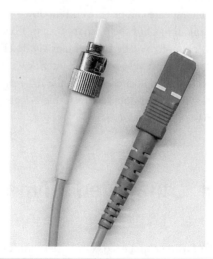

FIGURE 2-9   ST and SC fiber connectors

TABLE 2.3	Common Optical Fiber Networking Standards	
Standard	**Description**	**Speed**
10BaseFL	Ethernet over fiber	10 megabits per sec
100BaseFX	Ethernet over fiber	100 megabits per sec
FDDI	Fiber Distributed Data Interface	100 megabits per sec

connector. The Fiber Distributed Data Interface, or FDDI, topology can sometimes be found linking servers and other high-performance systems in some computer rooms; you'll learn more about the FDDI topology in the next chapter. ST connectors *do* look a bit BNC-ish, but be careful because, unlike a BNC connector, which can be impaled on its socket and twisted with total abandon until the locking guides engage with the fixing lugs, ST connectors have a keying mechanism to stop just this kind of youthful exuberance. If you do get carried away, you can snap the ceramic connector body—so easy does it!

Uses for Fiber

Although science programs often delight in telling you how many times a second the entire works of Shakespeare can be transmitted down a single fiber across a transatlantic phone link, that's not the primary use for fiber cable. Most of the fiber you are likely to encounter will be 10BaseFL or 100BaseFX, running at 10 or 100 megabits per second respectively, providing interlocation links on Ethernet-based networks. You will also find fiber cable, using the 100-megabit FDDI standard, interconnecting systems in a computer room. Table 2-3 gives descriptions and speeds for the three basic fiber optic standards.

 **Objective 2.07** **Other Media Types**

Don't even think of using copper (coax or UTP) solutions for interbuilding links because differences in the neutral-to-earth voltage (a small voltage which develops at the point where an electrical system is grounded) of two build-ings can cause major data corruption problems as well as a possibly dangerous voltage difference between ends of the medium. The problem in this situation is caused by the ground materials—the water and minerals in the soil between the buildings—which act like the chemicals in a battery. When you string a piece of wire between the two poles of the battery (in this case, the buildings), a current flows between the poles, messing up the data and causing a voltage difference to build up, as shown in Figure 2-10. A few years ago, one member of the Total Seminars writing team encountered such a phenomenon, and the measured volt-age between two points on the coax installation was just over 70 volts!

When a common grounding point cannot be established or guaranteed, the only way to link two buildings is by using fiber because it uses photons rather than electrons to carry the signal, providing no electrical connection. You can also use a wireless or laser link between buildings.

Wireless Links

Wireless media and its components fall into two broad categories: interbuilding links and cellular systems for inner areas of office space. Interbuilding links can extend your network by up to perhaps 1.5 km over a line-of-sight microwave link. Although the unit cost for such a microwave link seems high, it's likely to be a lot cheaper than digging a trench and installing fiber—an option that may not be available in your local business neighborhood anyway.

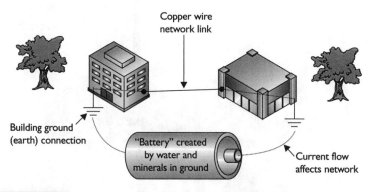

FIGURE 2-10   The use of copper media to link between buildings can create a battery effect.

Office-based cellular radio links are currently all the rage and can be used to link PCs and laptop computers to a main network through the installation of a localized transmitter/receiver unit (transceiver), officially known as an access point (AP), which transmits and receives signals to and from the wireless network adapters (Figure 2-11). By installing a number of strategically placed transceivers, coverage over a wide area of floor space can be achieved. The main drawbacks of wireless links are cost, security, and speed. Speedwise, things aren't too bad, but when you consider that mainstream, copper-based network solutions can give you speeds up to 100 megabits per second, wireless at 1 megabit per second is going to be acceptable only if it is the only practical solution. As for security, stories abound of techno-addicts (and investigative journalists!) driving around with makeshift "Mission Impossible" antennae on their cars, tapping into corporate wireless networks and surfing the net for free. Certainly, it seems that current wireless standards may need to have their encryption systems reappraised, but provided that you pay proper attention to your server's access security (user name and password), then this might be only a minor irritation. After all, if corporate spies want to see what's flying around your network, they can always tune in to the signals being radiated by your coax and UTP wiring!

Laser Links

Lasers are also an option for point-to-point links, but setup is a little trickier, and laser systems can suffer from weather-related problems (bright sun, rain, and fog)

FIGURE 2-11   Wireless networking equipment for the office

as well as loss of signal as the high-power laser emitter ages. In any case, laser (and microwave) systems require a line-of-sight path between the transmitter and receiver, so the possible effect of intermediate obstacles needs to be assessed.

✔ **Objective 2.01: Coaxial Cable**   Coax cable is the classic example of bounded network media. Coax cable consists of an inner core and an over-all metal screen, plus layers of insulation. The screen gives the cable a degree of protection against electromagnetic interference, but still, like most cop-per-based media, it should be kept away from sources of interference. A wide number of coax cable types are available, but specific types must be used for networking—not just any coax will do. The two networking stan-dards most closely associated with coax are Ethernet and ARCNet, although other media types have generally superceded coax in network designs, and ARCNet installations, in particular, are now quite rare.

✔ **Objective 2.02: Coaxial Connectors**   Wherever there's coax, there are BNC connectors. They originally were soldered and bolted to the cable, but now they are almost universally fitted by crimping (compression). Thick Ethernet installations may use PL-259 plugs and SO-259 sockets, a connec-tor type originally developed for radio use.

✔ **Objective 2.03: UTP and STP Cable**   The vast majority of network instal-lations are now constructed using unshielded twisted-pair (UTP) cable, a four-pair cable originally intended for telephone circuits but enhanced to carry data. Over time, various categories of UTP cable have been developed, each capable of operating at faster data rates than its predecessor. There are two general types of UTP wiring: patch cable uses stranded copper to make the wiring flexible, and premises cable (so-called horizontal cable) uses a solid core to give the wiring more strength to withstand rougher handling as it is installed in ducting and cable trays. Mixing the cable types—for example, using horizontal cable for patch leads—can lead to reliability problems.

✔ **Objective 2.04: UTP Connectors**   Most UTP installations use RJ-45 con-nectors and wall ports. RJ-45 connectors have eight contacts to match the four pairs of wires in the UTP cable. The cable pairs are color-coded to make it easier to follow a standard wiring pattern when connecting media or fitting the cable to wall ports. Various wiring standards stating which pair of wires should be fixed to which connectors have appeared over the years, but the most commonly used standard is EIA/TIA 568B. Because UTP cable is not screened, it must be installed well away from other sources of electrical interference, and most installations are thoroughly tested to make sure they meet basic functional criteria. A screened version of UTP—called STP—is available, but it is much more expensive and not installed unless local conditions demand a high level of screening.

✔ **Objective 2.05: Optical Fiber**   Optical fiber cabling is much more expensive to install than copper alternatives, but it offers several advantages, including greater maximum distance and greater security. It can also be used between buildings at different ground (earth) potentials and in electrically noisy or hazardous environments (no danger from sparks). There are two main types of optical fiber: monomode and multimode, the latter being the most commonly used type for general networking. Optical fiber is specified according to the core (fiber) and cladding diameter (in microns), the most common size being 62.5/125.

✔ **Objective 2.06: Optical Fiber Connectors**   Optical fiber has its own set of connectors because it's an optical system, not electrical. The most common connector types are known as ST (a twist-and-lock connector) and SC (a push-fit connector). Optical fiber connectors should always be handled with care as they can be broken fairly easily.

✔ **Objective 2.07: Other Media Types**   Wireless networking solutions exist for both point-to-point building links and general intraoffice connectivity. Office-based solutions are becoming increasingly popular, especially since key technical issues have been formalized with the IEEE 802.11 and 802.11b standards, allowing different manufacturers to produce compatible equipment and increasing competition in the marketplace. Wireless networks operate in the office by means of one or more cells, each connecting users to the main network via an access point (AP). Wireless network security is fairly good—it's difficult to intercept a specific signal—but there are concerns about the ease with which unauthorized wireless devices can attach to APs and access unsecured network systems and resources, such as Internet gateways. Laser-based systems can also be used for interbuilding links, but they can be relatively expensive, and setup can be a bit more complex compared to a microwave solution.

REVIEW QUESTIONS

1. Which of the following connector types is associated with coax cable? (Select one answer.)

   A. RJ-45
   B. BNC
   C. ST
   D. RG-58

2. Which of the following UTP cable categories is suitable for data transmission at 10 megabits per second? (Select one answer.)

   A. CAT 3
   B. CAT 4
   C. CAT 5
   D. All of the above

3. You have been tasked with installing a network link between two buildings approximately 250 meters apart. Which of the following media types is unlikely to be suitable? (Select one answer.)

   A. Microwave
   B. Laser
   C. Fiber
   D. Thick Ethernet

4. Which of the following connector types is associated with UTP cable? (Select one answer.)

   A. RJ-45
   B. BNC
   C. SC
   D. NBC

5. What name is given to the problem caused when signals from adjacent cables interfere with each other? (Select one answer.)

   A. Talkback
   B. Crossover
   C. Backchat
   D. Crosstalk

6. Which of the following names describes a type of Thick Ethernet transceiver connection? (Select one answer.)

   A. FDDI clamp
   B. Nettle sting
   C. Vampire tap
   D. TE tap

7. You notice that the computer in your office can't connect to the network when you switch on the room lights, but with the lights off it works fine. What is most likely to be the problem? (Select one answer.)

   A. There is a voltage drop when the lights are turned on.
   B. There is a loose BNC connector.
   C. There is light entering a nearby fiber cable.
   D. The cabling system is faulty.

8. What layer of the OSI model does an RJ-45 connector represent? (Select one answer.)

   A. Physical
   B. Data Link
   C. Network
   D. Session

9. Which of the following media types is used for Thin Ethernet-based networks? (Select one answer.)

   A. Cat 3
   B. RG-58
   C. RG-45
   D. 62.5/125

10. You have been tasked with providing network connections for a group of sales reps who regularly bring their laptop computers into the office. Which of the following media types would most likely provide the best solution? (Choose two answers.)

    A. FDDI
    B. UTP
    C. Wireless
    D. 100BaseFX

REVIEW ANSWERS

1. **B** BNC connectors are associated with coax.

2. **D** CAT 3 (answer A) is most often associated with this data speed, but CAT4 and 5 cabling can also run at this speed.

3. **D** Using copper-based media for interbuilding links can lead to electrical problems.

4. **A** RJ-45 connectors are associated with UTP cable.

5. **D** Crosstalk between adjacent cables causes interference.

6. **C** Vampire taps are used to connect transceivers to Thick Ethernet cable.

7. **D** Since applying power to the lighting circuit seems to cause the problem, it is likely that the network media is located too close to the light fitting or wiring in the plenum.

8. **A** Connectors are physical layer devices.

9. **B** RG-58 coax is used for Thin Ethernet networks.

10. **B** **C** UTP and wireless are the best choices. Using fiber (answers A and D) would be very expensive.

Network
Topologies and
Standards

	NEWBIE	SOME EXPERIENCE	EXPERT
ETA	4 hours	2 hours	1 hour

49

Topology is a general description of how the network media connects all the devices on the network together—in other words, the physical layout of the network. Topologies are mostly concerned with the physical cabling (copper and fiber) and wireless technologies, but other networking pieces, such as hubs and repeaters to link various sections of the network together, are also needed to make things work. Particular network topologies are very much associated with specific networking standards that describe how the network sends data between devices, the type of media to be used, the maximum network speed (also known as *bandwidth*), and the number of devices (nodes) that can be attached to the network. This information often turns up in Network+ exam questions, so pay attention here; there's a lot to take in, and it's all important stuff.

Exam Tip

All of the simple components (media, connectors, and so on) that make up a network's topology represent physical layer devices in the OSI model.

Objective 3.01   # The Bus Topology and Ethernet

If you can imagine your laundry hanging on a long, straight clothes line, then you have a pretty good idea of how a bus topology network is constructed, with everything hanging off one long run of cable, as shown in Figure 3-1. Since (networking) time immemorial, the bus topology has been associated with one network design in particular—Ethernet—and, of course, the Network+ exam wants you to prove that you also know the association.

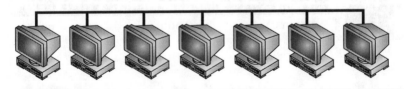

FIGURE 3-1   Bus topology: everything attached to the one cable

Ethernet Overview

We have a company called Xerox to thank for Ethernet. Ethernet was launched in 1973 (into the pre-PC world) and used a single piece of coaxial cable to interconnect several computers, allowing them to transfer data at up to 3 megabits per second. While slow by today's standards, this early design of Ethernet provided the foundation for all later versions.

Ethernet remained a largely in-house technology until 1979, when Xerox decided to look for partners to help promote Ethernet as an industry standard. Working with Digital Equipment Corporation (DEC) and Intel, the company published what became the Digital-Intel-Xerox (DIX) networking standard. It described a bus topology network using coaxial cable that allowed multiple computing systems and other devices to communicate with each other at 10 megabits per second.

Local Lingo

segment   A run of cable (media) linking one or more nodes on a network.

How Ethernet Works

Any network design must consider a number of key elements: the type of media used, how to send data across the wire, how to identify the sending and receiving computers, and how to determine which computer should use the shared cable next.

We already know from Chapter 2 that classic Ethernet networks use coax cable and modern versions use UTP, but in either case, the way the data is sent across the wire remains basically the same, using a process called CSMA/CD.

CSMA/CD

Ethernet networks use a system called *Carrier Sense, Multiple Access/Collision Detection (CSMA/CD)* to determine which computer should use the shared cable at a given moment. *Carrier sense* means that each machine on the network, referred to as a *node*, examines the cable before sending a data packet (see Figure 3-2). If another machine is using the network, the node will detect traffic and wait

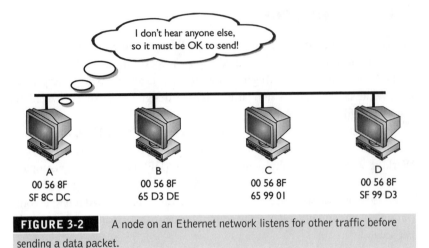

FIGURE 3-2 A node on an Ethernet network listens for other traffic before sending a data packet.

until the cable is free. If it detects no traffic, the node will send its data packet. Carrier sense is analogous to the process you use to get an outside phone line in a large office building. If you have a call to make, you pick up the phone, press a button, and listen. If you hear a dial tone (that is, if the line is free), then you make your call. If you hear a busy signal (that is, if someone else is already using the line), you wait your turn.

Multiple Access means that all machines have equal access to the wire. If the line is free, an Ethernet node does not have to get approval to use the wire—it just uses it. From the point of view of Ethernet, it does not matter what function the node is performing. It could be a desktop system running Windows 95 or a high-end file server. As far as Ethernet is concerned, a node is just a node, and access to the cable is assigned on a strictly first-come, first-served basis. But what happens if two machines listen to the cable and simultaneously determine that it is currently free? They both try to send.

When two computers try to use the cable simultaneously, a *collision* occurs, and both of the transmissions are lost (see Figure 3-3). A collision resembles the effect of two people talking simultaneously: because the listener hears the mixture of the two voices, the listener cannot understand either one.

If a collision occurs, both machines detect the collision by listening to their own transmissions. They compare their own transmissions with the transmission they are receiving over the cable and can determine whether another node has transmitted at the same time, as shown in Figure 3-4. If the nodes detect a collision, both nodes immediately stop transmitting and wait for a short, random period of time before retrying.

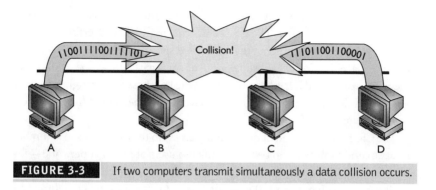

FIGURE 3-3   If two computers transmit simultaneously a data collision occurs.

CSMA/CD has the benefit of being very simple to implement in hardware, and this helps to make Ethernet NICs relatively cheap. The Token Ring method of determining access to a shared cable, discussed later in this chapter, requires much more sophisticated programming algorithms.

That simplicity comes at a price; an Ethernet node will waste some amount of its time dealing with collisions instead of sending data. As you add more devices to the network and cause it to grow—for example, by installing new, data-intensive applications for all users on the network—the number of collisions on the network will increase as the machines generate more packets to access the central

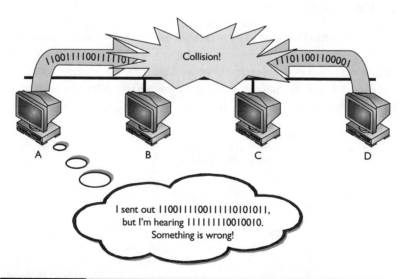

FIGURE 3-4   An Ethernet node can detect when its data has been corrupted by a collision.

database. Every Ethernet network wastes some amount of its available bandwidth dealing with these collisions. The typical Ethernet network is advertised to run at either 10 Mbps or 100 Mbps, but that advertised speed assumes that no collisions ever take place! In reality, collisions are a normal part of the operation of an Ethernet network, and it has been stated that the best possible throughput, under typical conditions, will never be greater than about 70 percent of the theoretical maximum bandwidth.

The CSMA/CD method of determining access to the cable leads to a number of classic conditions that can be very familiar to users of Ethernet networks—for example, network slowdowns at specific times of the day, such as perhaps 9 A.M. on Monday morning when 100 users sit down at just about the same time and type their names and passwords to log into the Ethernet network. Virtually every station on the network then contends for the use of the cable at the same time, causing massive collisions and attempted retransmissions. It is unlikely that the end users will receive any kind of error message as a result of such high levels of traffic. Instead, they will just notice that the network is running slowly, and the Ethernet NICs will continue to retry transmission until they eventually send their data packets successfully. Only if the collisions become so severe that a packet cannot be sent after 16 retries will the sending station give up, with an error message sent to the user.

Termination

Bus-based Ethernet networks (such as those using coax cabling) will function properly only if both ends of the network bus are fitted with terminating *resistors*. Without one or more of these terminators in place, some of the energy in the electrical signals that make up the data packets bounces back up the wire, a phenomenon known as *reflection*, as shown in Figure 3-5.

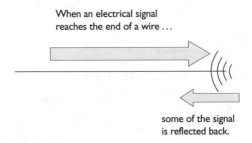

When an electrical signal
reaches the end of a wire ...

some of the signal
is reflected back.

FIGURE 3-5   When a signal hits the end of an unterminated wire, some of its energy reflects back along the wire.

To all other nodes on the network, these reflections look like a mass of data and collisions being generated by other devices, and so they will wait for the network to become clear before transmitting, but the reflections quickly build up to a point where the network looks permanently busy, and so very soon all devices enter a permanent wait mode (see Figure 3-6). The terminating resistor (see Figure 3-7) absorbs the reflections and allows the segment to function properly.

Cable Breaks

A cable break on a bus topology network will, in effect, create two incorrectly terminated sections, and this will cause multiple reflections in both directions, making all stations on the network go into perpetual wait mode (see Figure 3-8). This stops the entire broken cable run from working. Because just one break can affect the entire segment and all machines on it, bus-based networks are said to have a *single point of failure*.

Ethernet Standards

In the early 1980s, the *Institute of Electrical and Electronics Engineers (IEEE)*, an organization that defines industrywide standards in the fields of electronics and computing, adopted the DIX Ethernet standard as a general standard for networking. The IEEE working group, or committee, responsible for general networking standards is known as the 802 committee, and Ethernet became IEEE

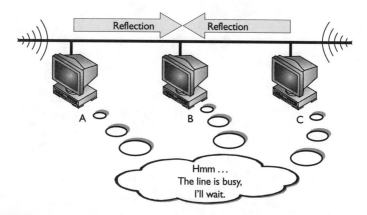

FIGURE 3-6   Reflections cause the network to look permanently busy.

FIGURE 3-7   Thin Ethernet (10Base2) BNC terminators house the
terminating resistors.

standard 802.3. As you will soon discover, the 802 committee and its subcommittees and working groups are responsible for many of the network standards you will encounter and, thus, many of the facts you have to remember for the Network+ exam!

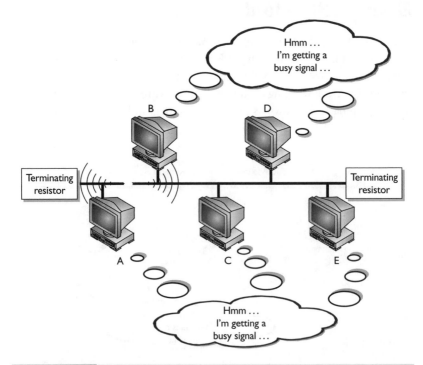

FIGURE 3-8   Reflections caused by a cable break disrupt the entire network.

IEEE 802.3

The term *Ethernet* is now used to refer to any network based on the IEEE 802.3 standard. If you want to be totally accurate, IEEE 802.3 and the original Ethernet spec are not quite identical—for example, the original Ethernet standard makes reference to the use of only coax cable for the network media, whereas 802.3 allows for the use of other types (which is just as well, with all those UTP installations out there!). In practice, it is almost universally accepted that the terms "Ethernet" and "IEEE 802.3" can be used interchangeably

Ethernet on the Bus

Two main standards exist for creating a bus-based Ethernet network, with wonderfully descriptive names: 10Base5 and 10Base2. The IEEE coined these two terms, and they each describe three key features of the network, as shown in Figure 3-9:

- **Speed**   The 10 signifies an Ethernet network that runs at 10 megabits per second.
- **Signal type**   Base signifies that 10Base5 uses baseband signaling, meaning that there is just one signal on the cable at any time, as opposed to a broadband system (such as cable TV coax), which can have multiple signals on the cable.
- **Distance**   The 5 indicates that 10Base5 cables may not be longer than 500 meters. The 2 in 10Base2 is the distance rounded up from 185 meters.

Exam Tip
The other key feature of all Ethernet-type networks is that they support a theoretical maximum of 1,024 nodes.

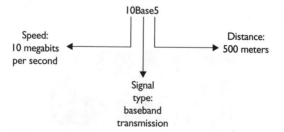

FIGURE 3-9   The term "10Base5" tells us three things about the network.

10Base5

10Base5 describes an Ethernet network that looks very much like the original DIX implementation. 10Base5 coax is often referred to as Thick Ethernet, or ThickNet, because of the relatively large diameter of the cable (see Figure 3-10).

ThickNet has the heaviest shielding of any cabling commonly used for 10-mbps Ethernet, making it an excellent choice for high-interference environments. The thick copper core also reduces signal degradation over the length of the cable, contributing to the 500-meter maximum segment distance. While 10Base5 represented a revolutionary cabling system when originally introduced, its high cost and difficult installation limit its use today. New installations incorporate 10Base5 only in situations that require its heavy shielding or generous distance limitation.

Although not mandatory, proper ThickNet cable is almost always yellow, and because of this and its rigidity, it is occasionally referred to as "yellow cable" or "frozen yellow garden hose." Some confusion has also been caused by the availability of *blue* ThickNet coax—some techs are convinced that blue coax is exterior-grade stuff, and that it will quite happily sit in puddles of water on rooftops between networked locations (presumably, someone worked out the idea that blue = water = outside). In reality, *all* forms of standard network coax are for *interior* use only, and external runs need suitable protection from the elements; otherwise, you'll eventually experience the thrill of water dripping from your coax connectors.

Connecting to the Coax

10Base5 installations use the ThickNet coax as a backbone to carry data around the area covered by the network, but the coax itself is usually hidden away in the ceiling void (plenum) or in trunking, partly because it's quite bulky and stiff and would be a pain to install at desktop level. Devices (nodes) are connected to the coax via a transceiver box, as discussed in Chapter 1. The connection between a node and transceiver uses a multicore cable fitted with 15-pin male DB connectors. These cable assemblies are formally known as *attachment unit interface (AUI)* drop cables and connectors.

FIGURE 3-10   Thick Ethernet coax—note the black band.

Travel Advisory

AUI connectors on network interface cards are identical to PC joystick/MIDI connectors, so be careful: connecting the wrong device to your network or sound/midi/game card may damage something!

Cable Length and Other Limitations

AUI drop cables can be any length up to 50 meters, but the external ThickNet transceivers must be placed an absolute minimum of 2.5 meters apart, as shown in Figure 3-11. Remember that black band in Figure 3-10? Those bands are printed every 2.5 meters along the coax and help technicians space the connections properly when installing the cable. Figure 3-12 shows the connection between a 10Base5 transceiver and a NIC. Up to 100 nodes (transceivers) can be connected to a ThickNet segment.

10Base5 Summary

Here are the key features that distinguish 10Base5 cabling:

- Speed of 10 megabits per second
- Baseband signal type
- Distance of 500 meters per segment
- 100 nodes per segment maximum
- 2.5-meter intervals between nodes
- Cables marked with a black band every 2.5 meters to ease installation
- Expensive cost per foot compared to other cabling systems
- Also known as Thick Ethernet, ThickNet, yellow cable, or frozen yellow garden hose

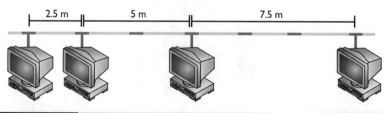

FIGURE 3-11 ThickNet transceivers must be connected to the cable only at 2.5-meter intervals.

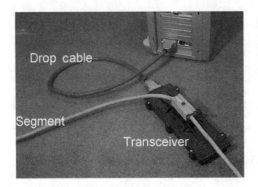

FIGURE 3-12   A 10Base5 transceiver and drop cable

Although some organizations continue to use 10Base5 cabling, most new 10-Mbps installations use either 10Base2 (discussed next) or 10BaseT (discussed later).

10Base2

10Base2 offers a cheap and quick way to network a small number of computers using coaxial cable and Ethernet. 10Base2 is much easier to install and much less expensive than 10Base5. It uses a thinner coax cable, which limits overall segment length (to 185 meters, remember?), and you can only fit 30 nodes on a single segment, but these limitations can be overcome by extending the network as described later.

10Base2 NICs include an integrated transceiver so there's no external box to clamp to the (much thinner) coax. Instead, the coax arrives and leaves the NIC via a BNC T-connector, as shown in Figure 3-13.

FIGURE 3-13   A BNC T-connector

The 10Base2's transceiver spacing requirements are also much simpler. The only rule is that they must be at least 0.5 meter apart, and they don't need to be spaced at specific intervals. Because the transceiver is integrated into the NIC, for "transceiver spacing" you can substitute the words "T-connector spacing" or just "node spacing."

Each end machine on the network has a coax cable arriving at its T-connector (see Figure 3-14) and a BNC terminator taking the place of the other cable (see Figure 3-15).

10Base2 Summary

Here are the key features that distinguish 10Base2 cabling:

- 10 megabits per second
- Baseband signal
- 185 meters per segment
- 30 maximum nodes per segment
- Nodes must be spaced at least 0.5 meter apart
- Inexpensive cost per foot compared to 10Base5
- Known as Thin Ethernet, ThinNet, Cheapernet

Historically, 10Base2 probably once represented the greatest installed base among *all* network types, and there's still a lot of these networks out there, but newer standards, such as 10BaseT and 100BaseTX, offer the same, or better, performance, with greater expansion options and improved reliability such as no single point of failure.

FIGURE 3-14   A BNC T-connector on the back of a NIC with two coax cables attached

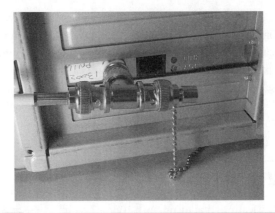

FIGURE 3-15 A BNC T-connector with one cable and a terminator attached

Objective 3.02 The Star Bus Topology

Newer Ethernet standards are based on a hybrid topology known as *star bus*, or *star-wired bus*. Star bus networks use a physical star topology that provides improved stability, and a logical bus that maintains compatibility with existing Ethernet standards.

Physical Star

In a star topology, all nodes connect to a central wiring point, as shown in Figure 3-16. The key advantage of the star topology is that a break in a cable affects only the machine connected to that cable. In Figure 3-17, machine C cannot communicate with any other node, but machines A, B, D, E, and F communicate with each other just fine.

Although the star topology provides a more robust, fault-tolerant cabling system than bus topology, pure star topologies aren't used for modern computer networks.

Logical Bus

In the real world, star topology networks use multiport hubs to link together groups of machines (see Figure 3-18). The way that these hubs pass data between their ports represents the logical (bus) part of the star bus partnership; in effect,

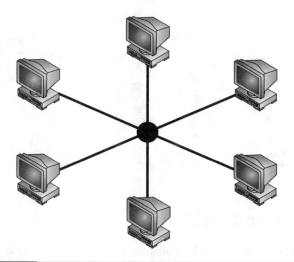

FIGURE 3-16   A star topology

each hub behaves like a terminated Ethernet segment, with each port becoming a
node on that segment. The nodes share the segment according to the same
CSMA/CD rules used for 10Base2 and 10Base5. Using the star bus topology maintains compatibility with previous Ethernet standards, but provides the stability of
a star topology; if a cable gets cut, only one node drops off the network.

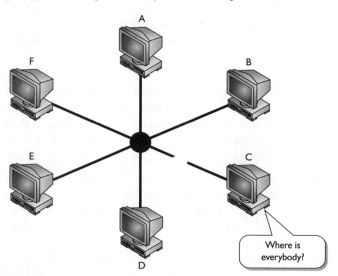

FIGURE 3-17   In a star topology, a broken cable affects only the machine
connected to it.

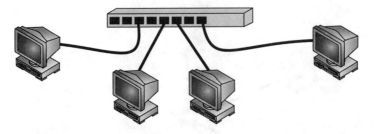

FIGURE 3-18 A 10BaseT hub with four connected computers

10BaseT and 100BaseT

The term *10BaseT* describes an Ethernet cabling system that uses a star bus topology. Unlike 10Base2 and 10Base5, 10BaseT uses UTP cabling rather than coax, but apart from this, many other basic characteristics remain the same—for example, the network operates at the same speed (10 megabits per second) and supports a maximum of 1,024 nodes.

Exam Tip

10BaseT is a classic example of a star bus topology network.

The name "10BaseT" doesn't quite follow the naming convention used for earlier Ethernet cabling systems. The *10* still refers to the speed: 10 megabits per second. *Base* still refers to the signaling type: baseband. The *T*, however, doesn't refer to a distance limitation but to the type of cable used: twisted pair. For the record, the maximum distance allowed between a node and a hub is actually 100 meters. Once you have come to grips with 10BaseT, it is not a quantum leap to understand the key selling point of 100baseT. Many modern Ethernet NICs automatically switch between 10- and 100-Mbps operation to match the hubs they're plugged into, and some modern hubs even support a mix of devices running at either speed.

Before we leave this section, you should know that there are two types of 100-megabit UTP Ethernet: 100BaseTX and 100BaseT4. 100BaseTX is by far the more popular version and runs over two pairs in a CAT 5 cable. 100BaseT4 is an earlier implementation that can run over CAT 3 cable, but it uses all four pairs; although this is not a problem for properly installed cabling; however, if anyone skimped in an older 10BaseT installation and wired two sockets into a single cable (called splitting the pairs), then 100BaseT4 is a nonstarter.

Gigabit Ethernet

Modern developments have cranked Ethernet up to the heady speed of 1,000 megabits per second while retaining compatibility with the CSMA/CD standard. Various others have now been ratified by the 802.3z Gigabit Ethernet Standardization project as follows:

- IEEE802.3ab.1000BaseT: Gigabit Ethernet over four pairs of CAT 5 UTP
- IEEE802.3z. 1000BaseX: Gigabit Ethernet over fiber (including 1000BaseSX and 1000BaseLX)

10/100/1000BaseT Summary

Here are the key features that distinguish 10/100/1000BaseT cabling:

- Speed of 10, 100, or 1,000 megabits per second according to standard
- Baseband signal type
- Distance of 100 meters from node to hub
- Two nodes per segment (node + hub port)

Objective 3.03 **Ring Topologies**

In a true ring topology, every computer system is connected together in a complete loop, but the loop itself is vulnerable to a single point of failure, and so two loops are often implemented in a fashion known as counter-rotating rings (see Figure 3-19). The idea is that if the primary ring suffers a cable failure, the two nodes on either side of the problem detect the fault and reroute the data signals to the secondary ring (see Figure 3-20). The data flow on the secondary ring proceeds logically in the opposite direction of the primary ring: hence, the counter-rotation.

FDDI

The fullest implementation of a true ring topology is a fiber standard called *Fiber Distributed Data Interface (FDDI)*, but it's not that common because it's expensive

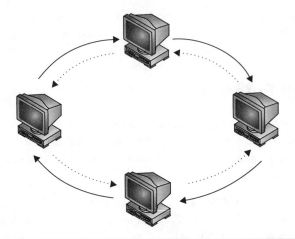

FIGURE 3-19 A ring topology network with counter-rotating rings

to install, especially if the network is quite large. So FDDI using a proper dual ring is installed only where the features of a robust fiber standard—security and distance—are required. A variant of the full FDDI standard is sometimes used to link systems together in computer rooms, but here the counter-rotating rings are

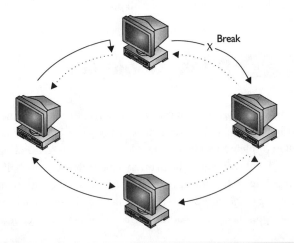

FIGURE 3-20 If the primary ring breaks, data is looped through the secondary ring.

actually built into the hubs and the computer systems connected via fiber patch leads. The only other fact that you need to know about FDDI is its speed: a very robust 100 megabits per second. We've slipped in the word "robust" because, unlike Ethernet's CSMA/CD system (which causes the whole setup to slow down as traffic increases), FDDI, like other ring-type topologies, uses a different method—called *token passing*—to get data onto the media. This, as we'll see later, yields much more solid and predictable performance.

Token Ring

If your network doesn't use an Ethernet-type kit, then it's probably based on Token Ring standards. Although Token Ring is a perfectly viable alternative to Ethernet—and, indeed, can offer greater speed and performance under load—its market share is much smaller, mainly because the kit is much more expensive.

Token Ring was originally a proprietary IBM technology, but the IEEE 802.5 committee now defines and maintains the standard. Just as there are minor differences between the original Xerox Ethernet standard and IEEE 802.3, the same situation exists between the original IBM standard for Token Ring and the IEEE 802.5 standard. These differences have little impact on the average network tech, and for all intents and purposes the terms *Token Ring* and *IEEE 802.5* refer to the same thing.

Exam Tip

Token Ring is defined by the IEEE 802.5 standard.

Although the IEEE 802.5 standard does support a true ring topology for a Token Ring network, where devices can be linked together in a ring, most practical implementations hide the logical ring inside a hub, technically referred to as a *multistation access unit (MAU)*; see Figure 3-21.

Local Lingo

multistation access unit (MAU or MSAU)   A Token Ring hub.

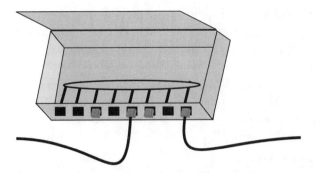

FIGURE 3-21 The logical ring is inside the MAU.

Individual nodes connect to the hub using either unshielded twisted-pair (UTP) or shielded twisted-pair (STP) cabling (see Figure 3-22). This arrangement gives us a configuration known as a *star-wired ring*. One benefit of this setup is that the last MAU doesn't have to be linked back to the first, although if this is done (it has to be supported by the MAUs being used), it will, in effect, offer the same level of fault tolerance as provided by a counter-rotating ring. Note that MAUs have special connectors—known as ring in (RI) and ring out (RO)—to link multiple units together. Up to 33 MAUs can combine to form a single logical ring. Building a network with more than 33 MAUs requires the use of bridges or routers; these devices are covered in Chapter 4.

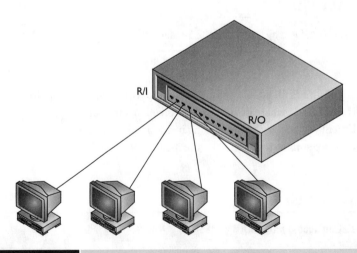

FIGURE 3-22 Token Ring nodes connect to the MAU.

Exam Tip
Token Ring networks can use a true ring topology. but most installations use MAUs in a configuration known as a star-wired ring.

Token Passing

Unlike Ethernet nodes, which broadcast their packets across a shared cable, Token Ring (and FDDI) nodes communicate directly with only two other machines: their upstream and downstream neighbors (see Figure 3-23). Access to the network is controlled by the technique token passing, instead of the CSMA/CD system used by Ethernet. Token Ring nodes can transmit data only when they receive a special packet called the token (see Figure 3-24). By preventing all collisions, token passing operates more efficiently than CSMA/CD, allowing Token Ring nodes full use of the network's bandwidth.

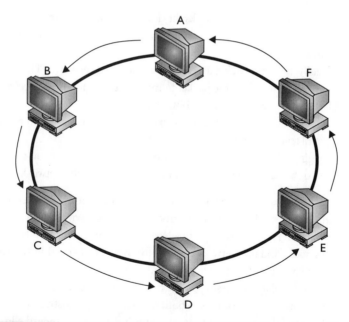

FIGURE 3-23   Node F is the upstream neighbor of node A; node B is the downstream neighbor of A.

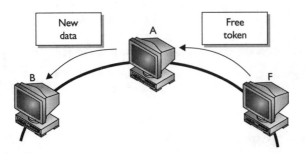

FIGURE 3-24   After receiving the free token, node A can send data around the network via its downstream neighbor, node B.

In a nutshell, token passing works like this:

1. A node receives a data packet containing the free token—it's that node's turn to use the network.
2. The node generates a packet addressed to its intended recipient and sends it to its downstream neighbor.
3. The downstream neighbor checks the destination MAC address to determine whether to process the data it contains or send the packet to its downstream neighbor.
4. Eventually, the data packet arrives at the intended recipient. The recipient reads the data, modifies the packet to indicate that it has been received, and sends it to its downstream neighbor.
5. The data packet makes its way back to the original sender, which registers a successful transmission.
6. The original sending machine generates a new token packet and sends it on its way to the next node to be given permission to use the network.

You might be wondering what happens if the token gets lost (for example, if the machine currently holding the token crashes or get switched off), or if the intended recipient is not there anymore. Well, don't worry—it's a bit beyond the scope of this book (and the Network+ exam) to cover such issues, but you can rest assured that all eventualities have been considered.

The amount of data processing power required on a Token Ring NIC to make the whole system work contributes to both the standard's robustness and the relatively high cost of the components. Because the Token Ring standard eliminates the randomness of network access associated with Ethernet and CSMA/CD, it is actually possible to determine which machine should have access to the network at a given moment—although it's not something that a network tech will have any inclination to do on a regular basis!

> ### Exam Tip
>
> Token Ring networks are called *deterministic* networks. Ethernet networks, with their random-access behavior, are called *probabilistic* networks.

Token Ring Speed

The original Token Ring network ran at 4 megabits per second, but this was later increased to 16 megabits per second. Modern MAUs allow 4- and 16-megabit devices to be mixed, but the network will run at 4 megabits per second.

> ### Exam Tip
>
> If you mix 4- and 16-megabit devices on some older MAUs, you will crash the network.

Token Ring Over STP

Originally, Token Ring networks used a heavily shielded version of twisted-pair cabling referred to as *Shielded Twisted Pair* (see Figure 3-25) and a special connector known as an *IBM Type 1* connector (see Figure 3-26). When using STP, a single Token Ring MAU can support up to 260 computers, and the STP cable connecting the computer to the hub may not be longer than 100 meters. STP cabling is an ideal choice for environments with high levels of electrical interference, but regular, corporate networks will use (cheaper) UTP cabling. Token Ring MAUs using UTP can support up to 72 nodes, and each node must be within 45 meters of the MAU.

Token Ring Versus Ethernet

The two mainstream network standards and topologies are often compared, and many polite, but heated, discussions have taken place over the merits of 4/16

FIGURE 3-25 Shielded Twisted Pair cabling

megabit Token Ring versus 10/100 Ethernet. Advocates of Token Ring argue that its token passing system uses available bandwidth more efficiently than Ethernet's random CSMA/CD process, and that it is more *scaleable*, meaning that it handles growth better. Ethernet advocates argue that their system is cheaper to install, and the faster basic speeds overcome the problems associated with CSMA/CD. In reality, Token Ring's expense is its major drawback, and while it will continue to exist in niche markets and in organizations with a large installed base of Token Ring equipment, Ethernet will retain its dominance in the marketplace for the foreseeable future.

Other Topologies

Having covered bus, star, and ring topologies, we've now considered the three main ways of stringing together network devices, but that's not the whole story. Numerous other ways and means of linking systems have been tried over the years

FIGURE 3-26 An IBM Type 1 connector

and are also evolving as technology improves. Although these topologies are not covered in as much detail as "the big three," don't skip over this section, as you might learn something to your (exam) advantage!

Objective 3.04   Wireless Networking

The IEEE 802.11b working group is responsible for Ethernet wireless networking standards, and most of the wireless networking kits now available from various sources will, thankfully, interconnect. It wasn't always this way, as some world-weary techs will tell you! The standard uses the 2.4-GHz microwave band designated for low-power, unlicensed use by the FCC in the US in 1985. The original 802.11 spec defined data speeds of 1 and 2 megabits per second, but the 1999 IEEE 802.11b spec also includes support for data rates of 5.5 and 11 megabits per second.

A simple wireless network consists of one or more cells that can support one or more nodes communicating with a base station. In technical parlance, 802.11 defines two pieces of equipment: a wireless station (say, a PC or notebook computer fitted with a wireless NIC) and an access point (AP), which connects the wireless devices to the main network.

Infrastructure Mode

In infrastructure mode, wireless devices connect to the main network through an access point (see Figure 3-27). The wireless part of the network can have more than one AP, in which case a number of cells will exist, creating a larger area of coverage. All of this coverage will appear to wireless devices as a single wireless section of network, with devices able to roam between cells without losing their network connections. The reception coverage of the APs must overlap to allow for a hand-over period as the user of the mobile device moves between cells.

Ad Hoc Mode

Ad hoc mode (also called peer-to-peer mode) allows wireless NICs to connect to each other directly, without using an AP (see Figure 3-28). The idea behind this mode is, for example, to allow a group of notebook computers to be set up in a conference room or other location without the need to install an access point or other network device.

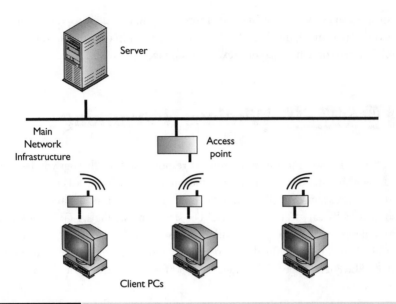

FIGURE 3-27   Wireless network infrastructure mode

CSMA/CA

No, that heading is not a typo! Wireless networks that conform to the IEEE 802.11b spec use a modified version of CSMA/CD to get their data onto the network. This is known as *Carrier Sense Multiple Access/Collision Avoidance (CSMA/CA)*, or the *Distributed Coordination Function (DCF)*. CSMA/CA is a slightly more complex

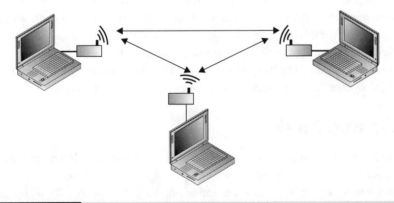

FIGURE 3-28   Wireless network ad hoc mode

procedure than CSMA/CD because the receiving device (AP or another wireless NIC) has to send an explicit packet acknowledgment (ACK) signal once it has received a data packet. If the original sender doesn't see an ACK signal, then it presumes that a data collision took place and will retransmit its data packet after a random period of time.

This explicit ACK mechanism does slow down network performance to a degree, but it helps cope with interference and other radio-related problems very effectively.

Wireless Network Coverage

Wireless network coverage varies according to the room layout, amount of metalwork (for example, filing cabinets) in the area, wall thickness and construction, and so on. It's not possible to give a definite answer, but best-case figures provided by various equipment manufacturers quote typical distances of up to 150 meters indoors and 500 meters outdoors at a data rate of 1 megabit per second. If you try to stretch things too far, the wireless system steps down the speed to compensate for the weaker signal.

Security

IEEE 802.11b includes two basic security mechanisms. Direct Sequence Spread Spectrum (DSSS) breaks the available signal bandwidth into 14 overlapping 22-MHz channels and spreads the transmitted signal among the channels, which makes it very difficult for an unsynchronized third party to keep track of the signal. The second security mechanism is a packet encryption scheme called *Wired Equivalent Privacy (WEP)*. In general, intercepting the signal from a wireless device is extremely difficult, but recent concerns have focused on the ease with which third parties can connect to an AP, join a network, surf the net for free, or access other computers that aren't as tightly locked down as they should be.

Objective 3.05

Distributed Star Topology—ARCNet

The distributed star topology was championed by an older networking standard called ARCNet (or Attached Resource Computer Network). Although ARCNet predates the IEEE standards, it resembles IEEE 802.4, which defines a token passing, bus-based network. In fact, ARCNet could be run over a bus-based or star-based topology at a blazing 2.5 megabits per second (a later version called ARCNet Plus ran at 20 megabits per second) and was very popular from its launch in 1977 to late 1980s, mainly because it supported a maximum distance of 2000 feet (610 meters) from node to hub, and it was very easy to extend an existing installation. ARCNet supported coax and (later) UTP and fiber media, but it was really killed off by the mass adoption of Ethernet and UTP wiring systems, which also allowed relatively easy expansion, and, of course, by faster networking standards.

Objective 3.06   Mesh Topology

The mesh topology isn't used to connect computing devices together, but it *is* used to connect networks together (see Figure 3-29). In essence, any series of interlinked networks where there is more than one possible data path between network locations can be considered to be using a mesh topology.

Exam Tip

The best example of a mesh topology is the Internet.

Because mesh topologies support multiple paths between networks, the level of fault tolerance improves as the number of paths increases.

●=LAN

FIGURE 3-29   Mesh topology

CHECKPOINT

✔ **Objective 3.01: The Bus Topology and Ethernet** Ethernet is a very common networking standard and was first developed for use with a bus topology, where all computing devices are interconnected via a single run of coaxial cable, known as a segment. Although bus-based networks are relatively simple to install, the main drawback to these types of networks is that they have a single point of failure—one break will stop the entire segment from working. The ends of the bus must also be terminated properly for correct operation. Ethernet networks use a system called Carrier Sense, Multiple Access/Collision Detection (CSMA/CD) to determine which computer should use the shared cable at a given moment. The IEEE 802.3 standard defines how Ethernet operates.

✔ **Objective 3.02: The Star Bus Topology** This topology overcomes some of the limitations of the bus topology by placing a logical bus within a hub and allowing multiple hubs to be interconnected to form a larger network. The hubs isolate cable problems to individual ports and devices so that only the device attached to a faulty cable is stopped from using the network. Classic examples of this topology include the 10BaseT and 100BaseT standards.

✔ **Objective 3.03: Ring Topologies** True ring topologies, such as a full implementation of a fiber standard known as FDDI, are expensive to install because they require a large amount of interconnection between all devices on the network, but a modified version, known as a star-wired ring, is used for Token Ring networks. The star-wired ring topology also uses hub-type units to connect devices to the network; the correct term for these hubs is Multi Station Access Units (MAUs or MSAUs). Token Ring offers predictable (deterministic) network performance by using a system known as token passing to determine which computer can use the network at a given moment. The IEEE 802.5 standard defines how Token Ring operates.

✔ **Objective 3.04: Wireless Networking** Wireless networking is now firmly defined by the IEEE 802.11b standard. Prior to this standard, there were a number of incompatible products on the market. The basic principle of operation is called infrastructure mode, and it allows one or more access points (APs) to be installed and accessed by the wireless device NICs. Direct NIC-to-NIC communication (so-called ad hoc mode) is also possible. Wireless networking solves the problem of providing network connectivity where physical cabling is not possible or not wanted, but the actual distances that can be achieved vary according to local conditions. IEEE 802.11b networks use a system called Carrier Sense, Multiple Access/ Collision Avoidance (CSMA/CA) to determine which computer can use the network at a given moment.

✔ **Objective 3.05: Distributed Star Topology—ARCNet**   ARCNet is an older networking standard that was once very popular but not so common nowadays. ARCNet used a token-passing system over coaxial cable and ran at 2.5 megabits per second. Now superceded by other systems, ARCNet's popularity was partly due to the long distances it supported. ARCNet approximates the IEEE 802.4 networking standard.

✔ **Objective 3.06: Mesh Topology**   The mesh topology is commonly used to interconnect networks, not just devices on individual networks. By providing multiple pathways between networks, the mesh topology provides fault tolerance in the event of problems on one or more pathways and is the topology used by the Internet.

REVIEW QUESTIONS

1. Which of the following network types uses a bus topology?

   A. IEEE 802.5
   B. IEEE 802.3
   C. IEEE 802.4
   D. FDDI

2. What name is given to the system used by Ethernet networks to determine which device can have access to the media?

   A. Token passing
   B. Collision Domain Management (CDM)
   C. CSMA/CA
   D. CDMA/CD

3. You have been asked to extend an existing 10BaseT network to add 10 machines to the existing 25 on the network. The required objective is to

ensure that the new machines connect successfully to the network. One optional objective is for all of the new machines to operate at a faster speed across the network to a new server (which is also one of the new machines). Your proposed solution is to install all new machines on a 10/100 hub daisy-chained to the existing hub. What will this achieve?

A. This meets the required and optional objectives.

B. This meets only the required objective and not the optional objective.

C. This meets the optional objective only.

D. This does not meet the required or optional objective.

4. Removing a terminator from a 10BaseT network

A. Will cause the entire network to fail

B. Enables the network to expand

C. Is not possible because 10BaseT networks don't use terminators

D. Will improve network performance

5. Which of the following network types can use a ring topology? (Select two answers.)

A. IEEE 802.5

B. IEEE 802.3

C. IEEE 802.4

D. FDDI

6. Which of the following connector types is similar to a MIDI/joystick connector?

A. AUI

B. BNC

C. FDDI

D. Coax

7. What network topology is most fault tolerant?

A. Bus

B. Ring

C. Star

D. Mesh

8. Which of the following is true of Token Ring networks?

   A. Collisions between packets slow down the network.

   B. Data packets are broadcast to all nodes using tokens.

   C. Data packets are transmitted in counter-rotating directions.

   D. Collisions do not happen.

9. Which of the following represents a wireless network standard?

   A. 10BaseT

   B. 10BaseW

   C. IEEE 802.5

   D. IEEE 802.11

10. Which of the following is *not* a feature of a network based on the 10BaseT standard?

   A. Uses screened cable.

   B. Maximum segment distance is 1,000 meters.

   C. Multiple token packets are supported.

   D. All of the above.

REVIEW ANSWERS

1. **B** Of the possible answers, only IEEE 802.3 represents a bus standard.

2. **D** Ethernet uses CSMA/CD, token passing is used on FDDI and Token Ring networks, CDM is fictional, and CSMA/CA is used on wireless and AppleTalk networks only.

3. **A** Installing a 10/100 hub will provide the expansion needed and also allow all the new machines to operate at 100 megabits per second.

4. **C** Sure enough, it's a "trick" question—10BaseT networks don't use terminators.

5. **A** **D** Both Token Ring (802.5) and FDDI networks can be configured as true rings. IEEE 802.3 is a bus topology standard, and 802.4 (ARCNet) is a distributed star.

6. **A** AUI ports are dangerously similar to the MIDI/joystick connector.

7. **D** The mesh topology is the only one to allow multiple pathways between networks.

8. **D** There should be no collisions on a fully working Token Ring network.

9. **D** 802.11 is a wireless network standard.

10. **D** All of the above.

Network Hardware

	NEWBIE	SOME EXPERIENCE	EXPERT
ETA	4 hours	2 hours	1 hour

So far, this book has covered the basics of networking and the components that make up the network infrastructure (all that media and connectors stuff—you were paying attention, weren't you?). I've also mentioned some hardware up to this point. Now it's time to go into greater detail on those items and some of the other gear that links the parts of your network together, or extends your network to another site.

As you read through this chapter, you'll notice yet again that I often reference the topics I cover to the OSI 7-layer model. The Network+ exam is quite keen on this, so make sure you store this information away for future use.

Objective 4.01   Network Interface Cards

Network Interface Cards, or NICs, provide a piece of equipment with the ability to send and receive data across a network. They provide an interface between the equipment's data bus and the network medium, whether it's copper (coax or UTP), wireless, fiber, or what have you. Quite a few modern computer systems (especially notebook computers) have a built-in NIC; even though it's probably made from a few components on the main circuit board, we still refer to it as a NIC. Many items, such as printers and other systems that might need to be shared directly via a network connection—for example, a stack of CD-ROM drives—also now come with built-in NICs or the ability for NICs to be installed.

Exam Tip

Network Interface Cards are Data Link layer (layer 2) devices with reference to the OSI seven-layer model.

Choosing a NIC

The first issue I'll tackle in this chapter is choosing the right type of NIC for the job at hand, which presumably is to get a PC onto a network. Requirement number one is that the NIC must be compatible with at least one of the expansion buses or ports inside the host equipment.

If you're familiar with PC technology, you might already understand terms such as *ISA* or *PCI expansion bus*; these items are really the domain of the CompTIA A+ exam, so they won't figure in our plans for N+ domination. It's worth remembering, though, that in the real world if you turn up on site with a PCI Ethernet NIC and the customer's PC only has a spare ISA slot, you'll be making another round trip real soon to get a part that fits! Don't forget that there are also alternatives to the classic plug-me-in-the-PC network card; for example, notebook PCs have expansion connectors that conform to the various "credit card module" expansion standards (PC Card, CardBus, and PCMCIA) and external, plug-in USB (Universal Serial Bus) NICs are also available. Finally, for you youngsters out there, once upon a time the only way to get some notebook PCs onto a network was by using an adapter that plugged into the parallel printer port.

After this, what do you need to know? Well, how many mainstream network technologies do you know? That's right: Ethernet and Token Ring. So, your NIC also has to be right for the network type being used. No one has yet produced a dual- or multitechnology card that will configure itself to whatever standard is being used. Also, don't forget that there are other networking standards, too. Maybe your customer has an old ARCNet network; no good fitting an Ethernet card then!

All done? Hmm—not quite! How many *speeds* of each networking standard do you know? Great, you're way ahead of me here! Ethernet comes in three main flavors: 10, 100, and 1,000 megabits per second; and Token Ring comes in two: 4 and 16 megabits per second. It is quite likely that your NIC has to match the rest of the network, but even if you know that the networking equipment in use will allow a mixture of speeds, you should probably "go for the best" if it's supported.

Some modern NICs will operate at various speeds—for example, 1,000/100/10 or 10/100 Ethernet NICs or 4/16 Mbps Token Ring NICs. These components autosense how they should set themselves up, but be prepared for situations where the autosense somehow manages to do the opposite of what you want, in which case you'll need to use the software supplied with the NIC. You can also use the Device Manager or Network settings under Windows, if the card is fully Plug-and-Play compatible, to set the speed you want. Finally, don't forget that there are two standards for 100-megabit Ethernet networking: 100BaseTX and 100baseT4; your NIC must support the right standard, or it'll be very quiet on that PC.

Okay, the card fits your PC, it's the right type and speed. You're now at that Lieutenant-Columbo-reaching-for-the-door-handle moment: you know, when he stops and says, "There's just one more thing…"

Media! Yes, it's a good idea if the NIC can interface with the network media—or put simply, if it can plug in. Your head should already be full of terms such as "BNC," "RJ-45," "AUI," and so on, so don't forget that the NIC you're installing must have a socket or connector that matches the ones being used by the network media.

Sometimes this requirement is straightforward. For example, if you're working with a coax-based Ethernet network, you know you'll need either a BNC (Thin

Ethernet) or AUI (Thicknet) connector. If the network media is UTP, though, you're dealing with RJ-45. Token Ring networks may also be UTP-based (RJ-45 connectors), but the older style that used STP media requires a nine-pin female DB connector (a so-called DB-9F connector). Oh, and did I mention fiber? How many connector types do you remember for fiber? I can think of three. Sorry, no clues this time; go back and check Chapter 2 if you're not sure.

Many network cards have a combination of connector types to suit all possible media options. These so-called "combo" cards will often autodetect the interface being used, but some older ones need to be set via software or by adjustable metal shorting links, called shunts or straps, on the card itself (see Figure 4-1).

To summarize, when choosing a NIC, you must ensure that it meets specific criteria to work properly with your equipment and network. These criteria are as follows:

- The NIC must have the right interface for your PC (or whatever it is you're going to network): bus type or expansion port type (USB, PC Card, CardBus, PCMCIA, and so forth).
- The NIC must support the right networking technology (Ethernet, Token Ring, and so forth).
- The NIC must operate at the right speed (10 or 100 megabits per second for Ethernet and 4 or 16 megabits per second for Token Ring, for example).
- The NIC must be compatible with the media connector (BNC, RJ-45, AUI, fiber, and so forth).

If all this sounds pretty obvious, then great—you're bound to get some points on the exam. So what's the catch? Well, look out for questions that mix and match

FIGURE 4-1   An Ethernet combo NIC

all these issues to give plausible, possible answers that don't actually represent a valid combination. For example, there's no such thing as a BNC Ethernet NIC that supports 100 Mbps over coax.

Additional NIC Functionality

We're nearly done with NICs, but we still need to cover a few other features before we can move on.

Link LEDs

Most NICs have one or more diagnostic LEDs to give a quick visual indicator of the state of the network link. Typically, there will be a LINK LED that confirms that the NIC senses that it is physically connected to usable media, and an ACT (for *activity*) LED that blinks every time the NIC detects some data being sent or received (see Figure 4-2). Sometimes one LED serves both purposes. A quick look at these LEDs *before* diving into more complex troubleshooting procedures can sometimes pay dividends. How many times have you reconfigured Windows networking only to discover that the problem is due to a loose or disconnected cable?

Full Duplex

NICs using traditional (coax-based) Ethernet can only *either* send or receive data at any time. This is known as *half-duplex* operation, and is similar to the way in which CB radio operates: You can talk or listen, but you can't do both at the same

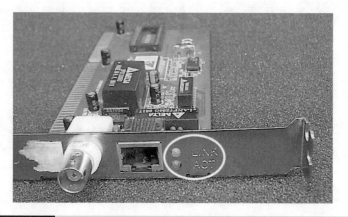

FIGURE 4-2   A 10Base2/10BaseT Ethernet NIC with LINK and ACT LEDs

time. Ethernet over fiber or UTP (10, 100, and Gigabit), however, supports *full-duplex* operation, meaning a NIC can be transmitting and receiving at the same time. If your NIC and hub both support full-duplex operation, you might want to enable this feature to give the PC-to-network connection a performance boost (see Figure 4-3). If you enable full-duplex operation at the NIC and it's *not* supported by the hub, things may go a bit quiet. Most hubs that support full-duplex operation autodetect that it has been enabled at the NIC, and so don't need to be manually configured.

Exam Tip
Full-duplex Ethernet works on UTP and fiber only, not coax.

MAC Address

Every network card has a built-in, unique ID, known as its Media Access Control (MAC) address. This address is fundamental to the operation of all mainstream networking technologies, as it is the one address that can uniquely identify a specific card—and thus a specific computer (or other device)—on the network. As you'll see in Chapter 6, there are other addressing schemes that are put in place when you're setting up a practical network, but these addressing schemes are *not*

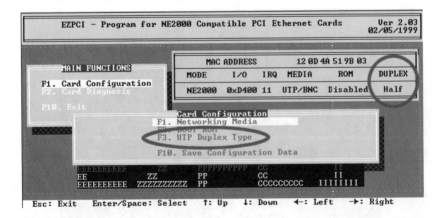

FIGURE 4-3   Configuring a network card to full duplex using its setup program

the ones used to pump data around a network; that's the job of the MAC address. In general, it is not essential to worry about the MAC address of your NIC during installation and setup, because the software parts of your setup that *do* need to know can easily find it out by asking the NIC. It is, however, worth knowing that the MAC address exists because some configuration and diagnostic tools will display it, and that it can also be used for network security. Network operating systems such as Microsoft Windows NT and Novell NetWare allow you to restrict the locations from which a user can log in by specifying the MAC addresses of the relevant workstations.

Travel Advisory

If you change the NIC inside a PC, you also change the PC's MAC address. Don't restrict a critical network account, such as Administrator, to one machine! If the NIC fails and has to be replaced, this account may not be able to log in and administer the network anymore.

In their raw form, MAC addresses are 48-bit binary numbers, such as the following:

000000001110000010011000000000010000100100001110

To make these numbers easier to read and document, they are usually written in hexadecimal (base 16) format. This means that the above address can also be written as

00 E0 98 01 09 0E

Being 48 bits long allows for a possible 2^{48} (281,474,976,710,656) MAC addresses—that should keep us going for a while!

Because the pool of possible MAC addresses is so large, the IEEE has been tasked with ensuring that no two network interface cards ever share the same MAC address. To achieve this, NIC manufacturers are assigned one or more *start* addresses—the top 24 bits of the MAC address, which the IEEE calls the *Organizationally Unique Identifier (OUI)*—and the manufacturer then uses the remaining 24 bits to give each card it produces a truly unique address. For example, the MAC address of the NIC inside the computer used to write this paragraph

Travel Assistance

You can look up OUIs at the IEEE web site at http://standards. ieee.org/regauth/oui/index.shtml.

is 00 D0 59 0E 0B C8, the top 24 bits therefore being 00 D0 59 (each hexadecimal pair of digits represents 8 bits).

Using the IEEE web page, I can find out that this NIC was manufactured by Ambit Microsystems Corp (actually, the NIC is built into an Acer notebook PC, and a further Web search reveals that Ambit is part of the Acer InfoSystems Group of companies).

How can you find out the MAC address of your network card? Well, if you're running Windows 2000, there's a command-line utility called IPCONFIG (see Figure 4-4) that displays this information. The same command works under NT. In either case, to see the MAC address, use the command IPCONFIG /ALL. On Windows 9x, you can also run the WINIPCFG program, as shown in Figure 4-5. Note that these commands may only be available if the computer has the TCP/IP networking protocol installed (more about this later). The setup program supplied with many NICs will also probably show the MAC address of the card, and many manufacturers also place a MAC address label on the NIC, as shown in Figure 4-6.

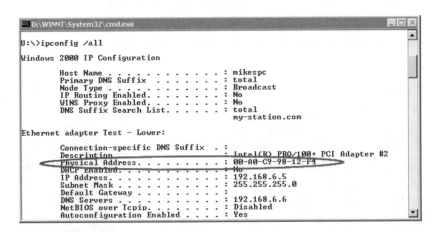

FIGURE 4-4   IPCONFIG showing the MAC address of the NIC

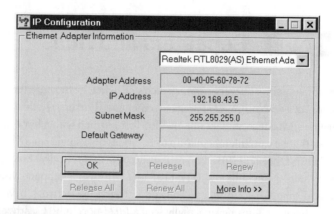

FIGURE 4-5   WINIPCFG also showing the MAC address

Exam Tip

MAC stands for Media Access Control. A MAC address is a unique identifier for each machine (NIC) on a network.

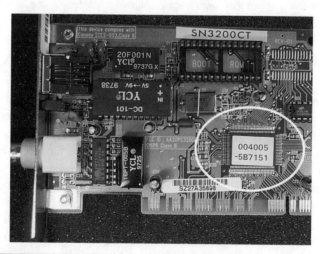

FIGURE 4-6   Label on a NIC showing its MAC address

Objective 4.02 Repeaters and Hubs

There comes a time in every network tech's life when he or she actually wants to connect a few computer systems together and (horrors!) build a network. Let's imagine such a tech, and let's name him Tom. Armed with a few basic facts, Tom knows that he can link together up to 30 nodes on a single run of up to 185 meters of Thin Ethernet (10Base2), or that he can (theoretically) link together 1,024 computers using hubs and UTP (10BaseT). But what happens when Tom needs to add that 31st computer to the coax, stretch the network beyond 185 meters, or—hang on—he's never actually seen a *1,024*-port hub?! Clearly, our tech needs some more insight.

Repeaters

If you want to stretch your coax-based Ethernet network beyond the basic specs, you will need a repeater.

Local Lingo

repeater   Any device that takes all of the signals it receives on one Ethernet port and passes out a copy on all its other ports (and does pretty much nothing else).

Although the electrical signals handled by a repeater represent data bits that ultimately form packets of data, the repeater doesn't know this. A repeater simply takes the incoming electrical signals, corrects any voltage drops, and then retransmits the cleaned signals. In this respect, the repeater does *not* function as an amplifier, although this term is often used incorrectly to describe a repeater. Amplifiers boost signals, flaws and all, like a copy machine making a copy of a bad original.

A repeater increases the maximum possible distance between machines by linking together two or more segments. Each segment retains its own distance limitation. If a repeater connects two 10Base2 segments, for example, the maximum distance that can separate two machines on different segments is 370 meters (2×185 meters, see Figure 4-7). Two 10Base5 segments connected by a repeater can cover 1,000 meters (2×500 meters).

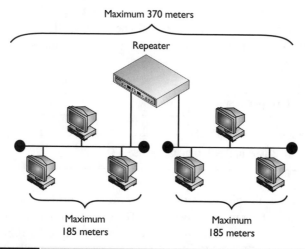

FIGURE 4-7 Two 10Base2 segments joined by a repeater

Repeaters also increase the number of machines that can connect to the network. If a repeater connects two 10Base2 segments, the network can have 60 computers attached to it (2 segments × 30 nodes per segment, see Figure 4-8).

Repeaters also add a degree of *fault tolerance* to a network: if one of the segments breaks, only that segment will fail. Computers on the remaining segment

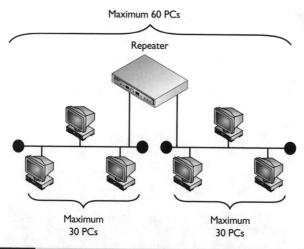

FIGURE 4-8 As well as increasing overall network distance, a repeater allows you to add more machines.

will continue to function, unaffected when communicating within their own segment. The segment with the cable break fails because of reflections, but the segment on the far side of the repeater remains properly terminated and functions normally.

Local Lingo

Fault tolerance   The ability of a system to continue functioning even after some part of the system has failed.

Repeaters can also give network designers the flexibility to combine different cabling types on the same network. Both 10Base5 and 10Base2 networks use exactly the same packet structure, so a repeater can connect a 10Base5 and a 10Base2 segment without difficulty; many repeaters come with both AUI and BNC connectors for that purpose (see Figure 4-9).

Exam Tip

Many repeaters have only two ports, but they can have more (so-called multiport repeaters).

Repeater Summary   To summarize, repeaters offer four key benefits:

- They extend the distance that a network can cover.
- They increase the number of machines that can connect to the network.
- They provide a measure of fault tolerance, limiting the impact of breaks in the cable to the segment on which the break occurs.

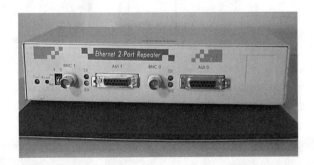

FIGURE 4-9   An Ethernet repeater with AUI and BNC ports

- They can link different types of (Ethernet) cabling segments together.

Repeaters do not help reduce or manage traffic on networks that experience too much traffic, but they remain important tools for network technicians and architects.

Hubs

Do UTP-based Ethernet networks use repeaters? Well, sort of, but they're called *hubs* (see Figure 4-10). In other respects, there's not a great deal of difference between a multiport repeater and a hub. For example, they're both Physical layer devices, and you can deduce from this that both repeaters and hubs don't do much except pass electrical signals from one port to another. When it comes to 10BaseT networking, though, hubs are essential parts of the topology, and are not there just to extend the size of the network beyond some basic limits.

A multiport hub allows a specific number of devices to connect to the network (one per port) and often, but not always, includes a separate port to allow hubs to be linked together to grow the network. Some hubs also include connectors for different media types—BNC, AUI, or fiber—but they cannot interface between networks that are based on different technologies (for example, Ethernet to Token Ring). This would require capabilities beyond the scope of a simple Physical layer device.

Exam Tip

Repeaters and hubs are layer 1 (Physical layer) devices because they only work with electrical signals and don't understand more complex structures, such as data packets and network addresses.

FIGURE 4-10   UTP (10BaseT) hub, patch cable, and NIC. Note that this hub also has a BNC connector.

Repeater and Hub Diagnostic Indicators

Both device types often include a number of status LEDs. A repeater may have an LED for each port (network segment) to indicate whether the attached segment is terminated properly. If the repeater detects a faulty segment, in addition to turning on the LED it might (if it's part of the repeater's spec) isolate, or *partition*, the faulty segment in order to stop its signal reflections from affecting the rest of the network. Remember that repeaters pass everything—even reflections.

Here's a wonderful term: *jabber protection*. If a faulty Ethernet NIC starts to send out an endless stream of unintelligible data, it is said to be *jabbering*. Jabbering is sort of similar to deliberately generated reflections, and will stop every other device from using the network. Many hubs and repeaters support jabber protection and will turn off the affected port until the problem is corrected. In the case of a repeater, this could possibly isolate all of the machines on the affected coax segment from the rest of the network, but on a hub this will usually only affect the one machine on the one port.

The last indicator that's often seen on a repeater or hub is the *collision LED*; this will generally light up every time the number of collisions on a segment exceeds a specific threshold. Don't forget that collisions are fundamental to Ethernet's mode of operation (remember CSMA/CD?), so it is not necessarily a problem if the collision LED comes on. It's best to read the instructions that came with the repeater or hub to see what this LED is trying to tell you. In other respects, you'll probably get the feeling that excess collisions are a likely problem, because most of the network users will be on the phone every five minutes complaining that the network's very slow!

Hub Summary

- Hubs are found in UTP-based Ethernet environments and are similar in general function to multiport repeaters.
- Unlike a repeater, a hub can have only one device per port—either a NIC or another hub.
- Most hubs can detect problems on their ports (such as jabbering) and will isolate problem ports from the rest of the network.

You've Gone Too Far: The 5-4-3 Rule

Although it might seem feasible to create very large networks just by using many repeaters or hubs, in practice there are some technical limitations that prevent the ability to sprawl without careful planning. The main problem is that repeaters pass all signals to all their ports. This means that the network, however large, appears as a single entity as far as all data traffic is concerned; in technical terms, the network has a single *collision domain*.

For Ethernet networks to function properly, each node must detect when its own transmissions collide with those of any other node (remember CSMA/CD, specifically the *CD* bit: collision detection). Ethernet nodes cease checking for collisions once they send the last byte of each data packet. If the network is large enough that the last byte leaves the sending node before the first byte reaches every other node on the network, undetected collisions can occur. If the sending node fails to detect a collision, it won't know that it has to resend the packet, so the packet is lost.

Exam Tip

The most common reason for a machine to fail to detect a collision is that the network is too large.

The 5-4-3 rule avoids the need for complex math to work out whether a real-life Ethernet network is physically too large. The rule states that in a collision domain, no two nodes may be separated by more than

- Five repeaters
- Four segments
- Three populated segments

A *populated segment* is an Ethernet segment with at least one machine directly connected to it, either a segment of coax or a UTP connection to a hub. Each hub also counts as a repeater. Figure 4-11 shows an example of a network with the maximum numbers of elements.

To see whether a network complies with the 5-4-3 rule, trace the worst-case path between two machines—that is, the path between the two machines that will yield the highest number of segments, repeaters/hubs, and populated segments. Figure 4-12 shows a network with five segments, four repeaters, and three populated segments. The path between machines A and C represents the worst-case path because the packets must pass through all of the segments and repeaters on the network. The paths between A and B or B and C are irrelevant for calculating compliance with the 5-4-3 rule, because a longer path exists between two other

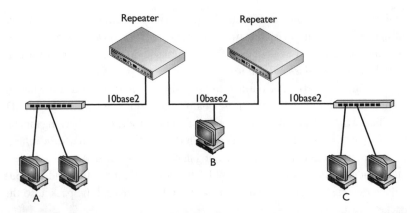

FIGURE 4-11   A network with five segments, four repeaters (includes 2 hubs), and three populated segments (A, B, and C).

machines. The path between machine A and machine C uses all five segments, all four repeaters, and all three populated segments. It is possible for a network with more than five total segments to comply with the 5-4-3 rule, as long as the worst-case path includes no more than five segments.

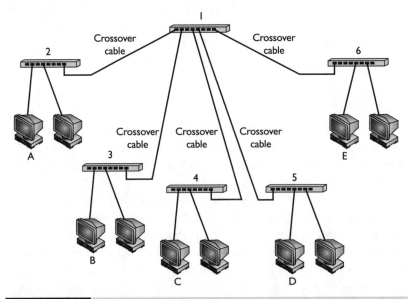

FIGURE 4-12   A network with six segments that still complies with the 5-4-3 rule

Linking Hubs Together: Daisy Chaining

Extending a hub-based network—within the scope of the 5-4-3 rule, of course!—can be achieved by plugging a patch cable between a pair of ports on the hubs, but this might not actually work. Hub ports expect to be connected to NICs—not to other hubs—so this can lead to an electrical misconnection between the two devices. This problem is easily fixed, however, by using a patch lead that has been made up to cross over the misconnecting signals to correct the problem. It's even easier if the hub has a special *crossover* port that does this for you; sometimes one of the ports even has a switch that enables it to act as a standard NIC connection or as a crossover port without the need for a crossover patch cable. Look for a port marked "MDI-X" or a switch marked "MDI/MDI-X".

Stackable Hubs

Stackable hubs are hubs with a special proprietary connection that enables them to combine and function as a single device (in effect, they are not seen as daisy chained). For the purposes of the 5-4-3 rule, all of the hubs in a stack are a single segment, repeater, and populated segment. There will still be a limit to the number of hubs that can be stacked, but this is usually (not always) more than the four allowed in a daisy chain. For example, the classic IBM 8237 Ethernet hub allows a stack of 10, creating a 170-port unit.

Switching Hubs: Hubs with Attitude

The curious (sorry, *probabilistic*) nature of Ethernet, with its CSMA/CD technology, means that, depending on the specific demands placed on the network's bandwidth, the number of machines that can peacefully coexist in a single Ethernet collision domain while still giving acceptable performance can vary from over 100 to as few as 2.

Over the last few years, a new type of hub has become very fashionable: the so-called switching hub or *switch*. Switching hubs have more intelligence than your average kind of hub, and they *do* analyze the traffic passing through each port in order to decide where it actually needs to go. By passing data traffic only between a specific pair of ports, a switch isolates this traffic into its own collision domain, significantly improving overall performance. Network-wise, switches are often used to link sections of a building together and then feed everything into the server group. A classic installation is every floor in a building connected to its own 10-Mbps port on a switched hub, with the servers connected into the switch via its 100-Mbps port.

Switches have to analyze the data traffic and make decisions about what to do with it very rapidly. This makes them quite expensive, certainly compared to regular hubs, due to the processing power involved. Switches can process the data packets in two ways:

- **Store-and-forward** switches *store* an entire data packet in memory while they analyze it, check its addressing, and check it for errors. Once the switch is happy with the data packet, it *forwards* the data packet to the appropriate port. If, however, the data packet doesn't look right—for example, if it seems to have been corrupted somehow—it will be discarded.
- **Cut-through** switches start to forward data packets as soon as their destination addresses have been analyzed. The remainder of the packet follows without any analysis. This approach improves performance at the expense of not stopping bad packets, which can lead to problems under some circumstances.

Some switches only support one or the other mode of operation, while others can be configured according to the network manager's wishes. Some modern switches can even be configured to perform cut-through switching on a per-port basis until a set error threshold is reached, whereupon they automatically change to store-and-forward mode. When the error rate falls below the threshold, the port automatically changes back to cut-through mode.

Exam Tip

Switches operate at layer 2 of the OSI model, also known as the Data Link layer, because they understand and can analyze data packets and network addresses.

Objective 4.03   **Bridges and Routers**

Before switches arrived in the early 1990s to save the day (and well before their prices tumbled in the mid-90s to actually make them affordable!), two other devices were already available to help manage bandwidth: bridges and routers. At the simplest level, both of these devices can also manage (filter) traffic between sections of a network in order to make the best use of available bandwidth, but they can also do other things.

Bridges

Bridges behave in a similar way to switches: they filter and forward traffic between two or more segments of a network based on the MAC addresses contained in the data packets. To *filter* traffic means to stop it from crossing from one network segment to the next; to *forward* traffic means to pass traffic originating on one side of the bridge to the other. Figure 4-13 shows two Ethernet collision domains connected by a bridge. The bridge is represented as a simple box because the physical appearance of a bridge can vary a great deal. The bridge can be a stand-alone device that looks similar to an Ethernet repeater or hub, or it might be a PC with two NICs running special bridging software. The bridge might even be built into a multi-function device that provides other functions in addition to acting as a bridge.

How Bridges Function

Ethernet bridges behave just like repeaters when first switched on: they forward all data packets on the basis that they haven't got a clue whether they should or not. After a short while, however, the bridge starts to build up a list of the active MAC addresses on either side of its electronics. With a complete table listing each machine's MAC address and the side of the bridge on which it sits, the bridge can look at every incoming packet and decide whether or not to forward or filter it.

Exam Tip	
Bridges operate at layer 2 of the OSI model, also known as the Data Link layer.	

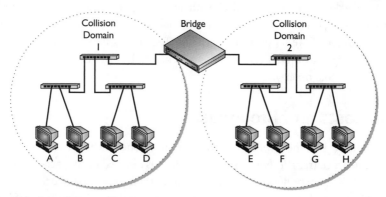

FIGURE 4-13 Two Ethernet collision domains connected by bridge

Bridges provide a performance benefit by forwarding or filtering data as required. Bridges also do exactly what a repeater can do: extend the network over another segment (another 185 meters and/or another 30 nodes). Obviously, though, if that's all you want to do, a bridge is an expensive way of doing it!

One key difference between a bridge and a repeater is the fact that you can have five segments, four repeaters, and three populated segments of machines *on either side of the bridge*. This is because forwarded packets are seen to originate from the bridge—not the original sender—and the bridge will retransmit a forwarded data packet if it detects a collision.

Adding a bridge to a network does not require any major reconfiguration; simply split the network into two segments and rejoin them using the bridge. The individual network segments still behave and operate as one single network. The invisible nature of bridges makes them the easiest way to break an Ethernet network into multiple collision domains.

Exam Tip

Bridges also exist for other technologies, such as Token Ring, but they cannot connect an Ethernet network to a Token Ring network because of differences in the structure of the packets—something bridges cannot change.

Transparent Bridging

The type of bridging described here is *transparent bridging*. Some documentation, especially documentation that deals with networking theory, may refer to *translational bridges*, which *can* translate between different packet formats. Translational bridges rarely if ever appear in Ethernet or Token Ring networks. If you see the term "bridge," assume it refers to the transparent bridge discussed here unless specifically told otherwise.

Unicasts and Broadcasts

Most network traffic is *unicast* traffic—sent from one machine to another—but some network traffic is *broadcast* traffic, which is directed to all machines on the network. Because bridges identify that broadcast traffic is not destined for a specific machine, they play it safe and forward all broadcast traffic; this increases traffic on both sides of the bridge, but allows all functions that rely on broadcasts to work correctly. For example, you now know that MAC addresses are ultimately used to send data packets from one machine to another, but many PC network setups require your machines to be given unique *computer names* and perhaps a dot-laden *IP address* (addresses like 192.168.1.10—don't worry if you haven't seen this sort of thing before, as there's lots more about IP addresses later).

Broadcast traffic is used for many purposes, one of which is to identify the relationship between a MAC address and the addressing scheme used by a specific network protocol. For example, if your computer wants to send a data packet to a computer known as SERVER1, it first broadcasts a request for SERVER1 to return its actual MAC address. Every machine on the network must examine that broadcast and determine whether or not its name and MAC address are the ones being sought. Most machines will ignore the broadcast, but the machine named SERVER1 will respond to your computer with a unicast packet confirming its MAC address.

Loops and Spanning Trees

If you like the sound of bridges so far, here's where I reveal their dark secret: they don't like loops! Figure 4-14 shows a network with multiple bridges that create a bridging loop. When machine A transmits a packet, bridges 2 and 3 will both forward the packet to bridge 1, making it appear to bridge 1 that machine A lies on both sides of bridge 1. This confuses many bridges and networked PCs, causing all sorts of weird error messages. In reality, *some* bridges don't actually mind loops (I confess I may have overplayed the dark secret bit) because they support an IEEE protocol called 802.1d—also known as the *Spanning Tree Algorithm (STA)*—that detects loops and blocks traffic that would otherwise circle indefinitely. The STA also allows blocked sections of a loop to unblock in the event that the other way around stops working, thus providing a rudimentary form of fault tolerance.

> **Exam Tip**
>
> The Network+ exam does not cover the Spanning Tree Algorithm; the term is mentioned here only for completeness.

Bridge Summary

- Bridges filter or forward traffic based on the MAC addresses contained in each data packet.

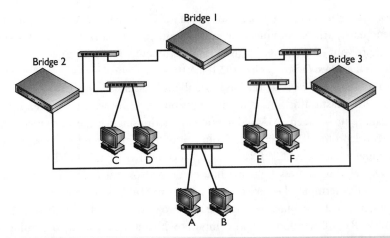

FIGURE 4-14 　Bridges connected in a loop—only permitted if the bridges support the Spanning Tree Algorithm (IEEE 802.1d)

- Bridges always forward broadcast packets.
- Bridges operate at the Data Link layer, layer 2 of the OSI model.
- A bridge can only connect two network segments if they use the same type of data packets (for example, Ethernet to Ethernet, Token Ring to Token Ring).
- Some bridges cannot be used to provide multiple routes between machines.

Routers

Routers provide a more flexible and robust alternative to bridges under many circumstances. They can do everything that a repeater can to extend a network; they can filter and forward traffic just like a bridge; they support multiple routes between networks; *and* the networks connected by the routers can be different types of networks (for example, Ethernet and Token Ring). What more can I say—go buy one today!

Routers and routing technology hold together the Internet, providing multiple pathways between the hundreds of networks that make up the whole system (see Figure 4-15). Most routers, however, see much more humble service doing the same kind of thing as bridges, linking networks or sites together to form a wide area network (WAN). One very important difference is that the two sides of a router are considered to be separate *networks*. If you step back through this chapter,

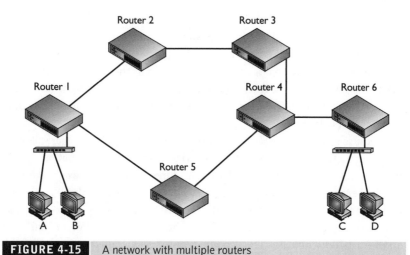

FIGURE 4-15   A network with multiple routers

you'll note I was very careful to refer to the two *segments* on either side of a bridge or repeater—not two *networks*. What's the difference? Well, it affects how the networks are set up, and it means that you have to pay more attention to the addresses given to the machines on the network. If you get things wrong, parts of one or more interconnected networks won't work. You'll learn more about this in Chapter 5.

Exam Tip

Because routers can change the nature of data packets (for example, convert them from Ethernet ones to Token Ring ones or vice versa), and because routers can make decisions about the path a data packet takes between networks, they are said to operate at layer 3 of the OSI model, also known as the Network layer.

How Routers Function

Unlike bridges, routers discard all broadcast traffic by default. This is because routed networks tend to consist of two or more local area networks (LANs) connected to form a Wide Area Network (WAN), and often the interconnections between the LANs have a limited bandwidth, perhaps down to 56 Kbps. If all the broadcast traffic from each LAN were forwarded over those slower WAN links, the internetwork links would quickly bog down. In addition, in very large WANs (such as the Internet), most broadcast traffic is irrelevant to most machines outside the local LAN and so does not need to be seen by them. Imagine how many machines there are on the Internet at any instant, and then imagine how much slower everything would be if every machine saw every other machine's broadcast packets (see Figure 4-16)!

Because routers discard broadcast packets, they cannot learn where all of the machines on the network are by listening to their traffic the way that bridges do. Instead, they rely on an additional level of addressing called *network addressing* (remember we said that routers operate at the Network layer of the OSI model—well, here's one tie-in). A network address tells the router two pieces of information: the specific machine to which a packet should be delivered, and the network on which that machine lies. The IP addresses used on the Internet are examples of network addresses (see Chapter 5 for a discussion of IP addressing).

Given the destination network address, a properly configured router can determine the best route to the destination machine. In Figure 4-17, router 1 needs to deliver a packet from machine A to machine D. Assuming that all of the links between the routers operate at the same speed, the most efficient route for the packet should be router 1 to 5 to 4 to 6. That route requires four hops. A *hop* is the process of passing through a router en route to the final destination.

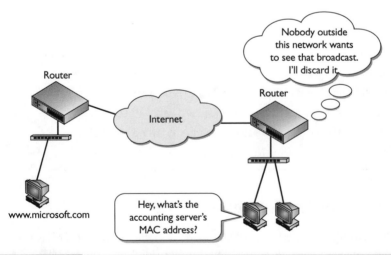

FIGURE 4-16   Routers block broadcast packets to avoid flooding all other interconnected networks with irrelevant data.

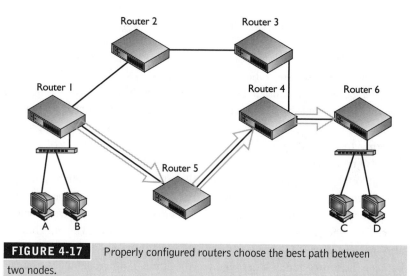

FIGURE 4-17 Properly configured routers choose the best path between two nodes.

Alternative routes exist, but the router ignores them because they require more hops. In the event of a break in the link between routers 1 and 5, router 1 should automatically calculate the next best route (if one exists) and redirect traffic to the alternative route: router 1 to 2 to 3 to 4 to 6 (see Figure 4-18).

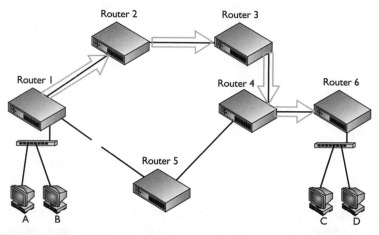

FIGURE 4-18 In the event of a break in the cable, properly configured routers automatically switch to an alternate route if one is available.

Routed networks require significantly more planning and configuration than bridged networks. In a bridged network, the bridge does all the work, building up a table of MAC addresses found on each of its network interfaces. In a routed network, each node must know the network address of its local router. Although this can often be assigned automatically, it might actually be necessary for a network tech to key in this information on every machine on the network (and if there's a configuration change…!). The routers also need to know about all the possible networks to which they might route data packets, and this may also involve a degree of manual setup.

Although this might sound too complex to be worthwhile, the benefits of a routed network include fault tolerance and a high degree of control over how data gets around a WAN. For example, routers can be configured to favor faster routes over slower ones, or vice versa if the fast routes are getting bogged down. They can also make routing decisions based on how many intermediate networks exist between the source and destination ones (the number of *hops*) and how much it costs to use a particular route.

Routers and Wide Area Network Links

On a LAN, a router may not look much more exciting than a module with two network ports—in fact, the simplest form of router is two NICs in a server, with the server itself managing the routing. This would work on a small-to-medium network, but would place too much of a burden on a big, corporate server, and so the two-card trick—creating a so-called multihomed server—is not always the best approach. On a WAN, a router may be as simple as a modem connected to a server and an analog telephone line; this is workable but obviously very slow, maybe 56 Kbps. Other services, such as a *leased line*, may be more practical if speed is important—there's more about wide area networking and connectivity in Chapters 7 and 8.

Router Summary

- Routers filter and forward traffic based on network addresses (such as IP addresses), not based on MAC addresses.
- A router can choose among multiple paths between two nodes.
- Routers operate at layer 3 of the OSI model, known as the Network layer.
- A router can link two networks in-house or via communications circuits between sites to create a wide area network.

Objective 4.04 **Gateways**

You might have noticed that I've been slowly working my way up through the OSI layers—from hubs and repeaters at the Physical layer (layer 1), through bridges (layer 2), to routers (layer 3). So guess what's next? Yes! Gateways at layer … well, hang on a moment.

I've stopped for breath because in the networking world, the term "gateway" has two meanings. Yes, it can mean a device or system that operates at the higher OSI layers, but if our conversation is totally focused on the world of networking using the TCP/IP suite of protocols, then the term "gateway" is often used interchangeably with the term "router." So, in TCP/IP terms, a router is a gateway. Confused? Well, don't worry too much—the context in which the term is used will make it clear what's meant, and that goes for the Network+ exams, too!

> **Exam Tip**
>
> Routers in TCP/IP-based networks are often referred to as gateways.

Now that I've got that out of my system, let's look at the other definition of a gateway.

A *gateway* is a device or system that allows two dissimilar networking or application environments to exchange information.

The principle of operation is that a gateway not only passes information between different systems, but can also change (*edit*, if you like) the information to make it acceptable to the other system. You've probably used this type of gateway without even knowing it. For example, a mail gateway on your site might allow your PC-based e-mail system to transfer messages to and from a mail application based on an IBM mainframe, where the character set and text format is different; the gateway translates the PC text into IBM format and vice versa without you having to lift a finger. As another example, you might be running Microsoft's *Gateway Services for NetWare* on one of your NT servers. This allows users on the network to access file and print resources on a server running Novell NetWare via the NT server (the NetWare resources appear as if they were based on the NT server); the gateway software translates the Microsoft client requests into ones that the NetWare server can understand and vice versa.

OK, so back to the OSI model—where does this definition of a gateway sit? Well, stand by for heated debates between groups of network techs. Some say that gateways operate at every level of the OSI model, while others say that they operate at layers 4–7 (Transport, Session, Presentation, and Application), because this is where data actually gets generated, processed, and generally managed. For the purposes of the Network+ exam, I'd go with the 4–7 brigade, and also point out that the exam is really more interested in finding out what you know about the lower layers. Don't expect too many probing questions based on the top end of the OSI model.

Exam Tip

Gateways act as translators between different operating system and application environments, and are said to operate at the higher OSI layers (4–7).

CHECKPOINT

✔ **Objective 4.01: Network Interface Cards** A Network Interface Card gets you on the network, but it must be the right fit for your computer system, or whatever you're plugging it into. You must also make sure that it has the right connectors for the network media, and that it supports the right network standard and speeds—for example, 10/100 Ethernet or 4/16 Token Ring. Many NICs include diagnostic LEDs that help with basic fault-finding, so don't forget to check them. One very important task performed by a NIC is to give your computer system a unique address in the network; this is known as the Media Access Control (MAC) address. This address is unique on every NIC produced, but the top 24 bits of the MAC address can be used to identify the NIC (or NIC component) manufacturer.

✔ **Objective 4.02: Repeaters and Hubs** Repeaters provide a simple way to extend a bus-based network over the basic 185 meter (Thinnet) or 500 meter (Thicknet), 30/100 device (Thin/Thick) segment maximums. Hubs behave like multiport repeaters to connect machines to a star-bus network.

Both devices have no specific understanding of the data they are passing between ports, and so do not provide any form of traffic management. Repeaters and hubs also have diagnostic LEDs, and may be able to isolate faulty segments or devices if they detect problems such as a broken cable or jabbering NIC. There is a limit to the number of repeaters or hubs that you can link together (the 5-4-3 rule), but this can be overcome by using stackable hubs. A more sophisticated hub—known as a switching hub—can intelligently pass traffic between selected ports to reduce data collisions and thus improve throughput.

✔ **Objective 4.03: Bridges and Routers**   Bridges can link sections of a network together, just like a repeater, but they also build up an internal MAC address table identifying the computer systems on either side of their interfaces so they can determine whether a data packet does actually need to pass across the bridge; this helps with traffic management, and so improves overall network performance. Bridges pass broadcast network traffic to ensure that computer systems on the network can identify the MAC addresses of other machines with which they want to communicate. Routers can do all the things that bridges can do, but they also support multiple paths between networks and can link together dissimilar network types, such as Ethernet and Token Ring. Routers are often used for wide area networking, providing interconnectivity between networked sites. Routers do not pass broadcast traffic; instead, they manage the identification of machine locations themselves, using network addresses that contain both a machine's address and the network on which it is located.

✔ **Objective 4.04: Gateways**   In TCP/IP terms, *gateway* is another term for a router. In general networking language, however, a gateway is a device or program that can pass information between different operating environments or applications, changing (translating) the data being processed if necessary. A classic example of this type of gateway is an application that can take formatted messages from one e-mail environment and pass them on to another—for example, between a PC-based mail system and a mainframe computer.

REVIEW QUESTIONS

1. A user complains that his PC has just stopped letting him log into the network, although he can log in successfully from another system. You have checked the PC's network setup and it seems fine, and the NIC also passes its diagnostics. What should you do next?

    A. Replace the NIC.

    B. Replace the BNC T-piece.

    C. Check the MAC address of the NIC.

    D. Check the LINK LED on the NIC.

2. Your corporate, 10BaseT network is running slowly and you have been tasked with improving overall performance. Which of the following options provides the most practical, lowest-cost solution?

    A. Install a router.

    B. Install a switch.

    C. Upgrade to 100BaseT hubs and NICs.

    D. Install a fiber backbone.

3. Which of the following will improve performance on a 10Base2 network?

    A. Installing a switch

    B. Setting the NICs to full duplex

    C. Reconfiguring to use AUI ports

    D. None of the above

4. Which address type is built into every NIC made?

    A. A unique MAC address

    B. A common Ethernet network address

    C. A TCP/IP address

    D. None of the above

5. What is the maximum possible end-to-end network distance on a 10Base2 network?

    A. 185m

    B. 200m

    C. 500m

    D. 925m

6. At which layer of the OSI 7-layer model does a bridge operate?

    A. 2

    B. 3

    C. 4

    D. 5

7. At which layer(s) of the OSI 7-layer model does a mail gateway operate? (Select all that apply.)

    A. 3
    B. 4
    C. 1
    D. 2

8. Which is the most cost-effective and simple way to link two hubs?

    A. A fiber duplex cable
    B. A switch
    C. A crossover patch cable
    D. A full duplex cable

9. Which of the following statements is true?

    A. Bridges pass broadcast traffic.
    B. Bridges block unicast traffic.
    C. Routers pass broadcast traffic.
    D. Routers block network packets.

10. Which of the following correctly represents the 5-4-3 rule?

    A. Five hubs, four segments, three populated segments
    B. Five segments, four repeaters, three populated segments
    C. Five populated segments, four repeaters, three crossover cables
    D. Five hubs, four populated segments, three routers

REVIEW ANSWERS

1. **D** Check the LINK LED. The card diagnostics may not tell you whether there's a good connection to the network.

2. **B** Installing a switch is the best solution. A router won't improve network speed overall, and fiber would be very expensive.

3. **D** Switches are for hub-based networks, and 10Base2 is coax. Similarly, full-duplex mode is only supported by hub-based networks. AUI ports aren't used on 10Base2 networks (they're used on 10Base5), and wouldn't offer any performance increase anyway.

4. **A** Every NIC has a unique MAC address.

5. **D** The maximum end-to-end distance, according to the 5-4-3 rule, would be five segments of 185 meters each, for a total of 925 meters.

6. **A** Bridges operate at the Data Link layer (layer 2).

7. **B** Gateways operate at layers 4–7, but only answer B (layer 4) is in this range.

8. **C** Linking two hubs requires a crossover patch cable.

9. **A** Bridges pass broadcast traffic; all other statements are false.

10. **B** The 5-4-3 rule states that the maximum end-to-end distance on a bus-based network can be five coax segments connected together by four repeaters, with only three populated segments.

Protocols and Protocol Suites

	NEWBIE	SOME EXPERIENCE	EXPERT
ETA	2 hours	1 hour	30 minutes

Standards, standards everywhere! There's an old joke that a giraffe is actually a horse designed by committee, and that animal we call networking has also had its share of committees and standards over the years. Actually, it has fared quite well, though you might not think so when you're knee-deep in service packs and your main server's a quaking mass of nonbooting metal. The standards and protocols that underpin the main networking protocols are actually very well put together, which is quite important considering the vital role most business networks play in keeping the whole operation running.

Overview of Protocols and Protocol Suites

Even without thinking about it, as soon as you press a key on your keyboard or click your mouse button, you are using protocols and standards. Let's take a key press as an example. First, the keyboard controller chip in your PC senses that you have pressed a key and works out which one. Next, the keyboard controller turns this information into a *scan code*, a piece of data that represents the key you pressed, and stores it in a small block of memory called a *buffer*. The PC's operating system then checks the keyboard buffer for data, sees that something is in there, and reads it. Finally, the data is passed back to the application currently waiting for input, where the keyboard data is analyzed and acted upon—maybe adding a character to a document or completing a password entry sequence. All the way through this process, things must happen just so, or it won't work properly; in other words, there are *protocols* involved. To handle input from the keyboard, for instance, several protocols and standards are in place to eliminate potential problems:

- If every manufacturer used a different set of scan codes for its keyboards, then the operating system would have to cater to every possibility. Just imagine: Windows 2000 for Compaq keyboards, Windows 2000 for Dell keyboards, Windows 2000 for that-budget-keyboard-you-bought-at-the-local-store-for-not-much-more-than-the-cost-of-a-fast-food-burger-please-please-please-let-it-be-supported—it would be a nightmare! With a few minor exceptions, all modern keyboards use the same scan codes to represent the keys.
- What would happen if the operating system read the keyboard buffer data just as the keyboard controller was updating it? Would the data be valid? How do we know when it's valid?

- How does the operating system pass data to a specific application? Wouldn't it be sensible if the hand-over sequence was standardized so that it was the same in every case? Of course it would be, and in fact it is.

Phew! And that's just for a keyboard!

Protocol Categories

We can break down networking protocols into several broad categories:

- Protocols that state how and when data can be placed on the network media and what that media can be.
- Protocols that identify the format of data structures, such as packets.
- Protocols that help identify individual computers and systems and how to get data between them.
- Protocols that handle errors in transmission and manage the flow of data across a network.
- Protocols that help establish initial communication between systems that want to exchange information.
- Protocols that give meaning to specific data sequences.
- Protocols that allow general applications to work with the networking environment.

Hey, have you spotted something? No? How many categories are in this list? Seven. Hmm…. Now where has that number come up before?

Yes, you've got it! We've broadly mapped our protocol categories to the OSI seven-layer model, and that's no coincidence because that's where you'll find all the protocols you need to know for the Network+ exam.

Protocol Suites

Networking is not simply a case of randomly picking one protocol from each layer and, presto, you have a working system; the reality is that protocols work together in families, or *suites*. So even though there may be several protocols listed for a layer of the OSI model, your network will use and support only one or some of them (see Figure 5-1). We've already discussed the three most popular protocol families that you're likely to encounter in the real world and on the Network+ exam: NetBEUI, IPX/SPX, and TCP/IP. To see the point here, consider this: within the TCP/IP protocol suite, IP is the protocol responsible for device addressing. The

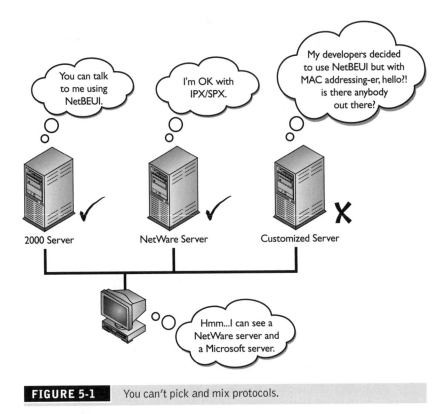

FIGURE 5-1   You can't pick and mix protocols.

IPX/SPX network standard (the IPX protocol) uses another way of managing addresses, but there's no such thing as the TCP/IPX protocol suite. It's theoretically possible, but don't even *think* about it, because your network would be the only one in the world using it. Try asking Microsoft to write a Windows 2000 protocol driver for *that*!

The most complex (and popular) protocol suite you need to know about for the Network+ exam is TCP/IP, but TCP/IP is *such* an important part of the exam (and real-life networking, too) that it has its own chapter (Chapter 6, right after this one). As you'll see, there's much more in the suite than just TCP and IP; the same is true for IPX/SPX and, to a lesser extent, NetBEUI, too. In an ideal world, you'd have only one networking protocol suite to learn about—TCP/IP may well get there one day—but for now, you also need to know the ins and outs of IPX/SPX and NetBEUI as well.

Role and Function of NetBEUI

Objective 5.02

NetBEUI provides a fast, simple set of network protocols, mainly for use with smaller LANs. This protocol suite is most closely associated with IBM and Microsoft networking environments such as IBM LAN Manager (a bit long in the tooth now), OS/2, and Windows NT. All of Microsoft's general desktop environments (Windows NT, 9x, 2000, ME, XP) can use NetBEUI for small peer-to-peer networks (see Figures 5-2 and 5-3); some third-party products, such as Artisoft's LANtastic, also support it. The NetBEUI protocol suite consists of two main protocols: NetBIOS and NetBEUI (see Figure 5-4). When you install NetBEUI for a Microsoft product, you are actually installing both protocols.

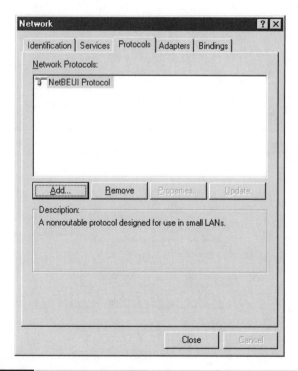

FIGURE 5-2   NetBEUI in a Windows NT environment

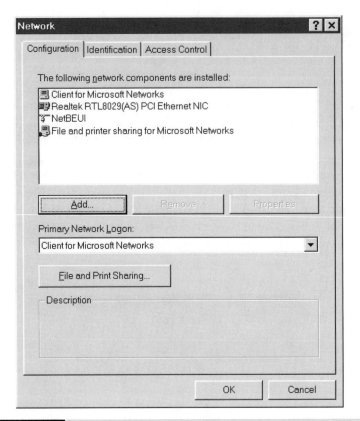

FIGURE 5-3   A peer-to-peer computer running Windows 9x using NetBEUI

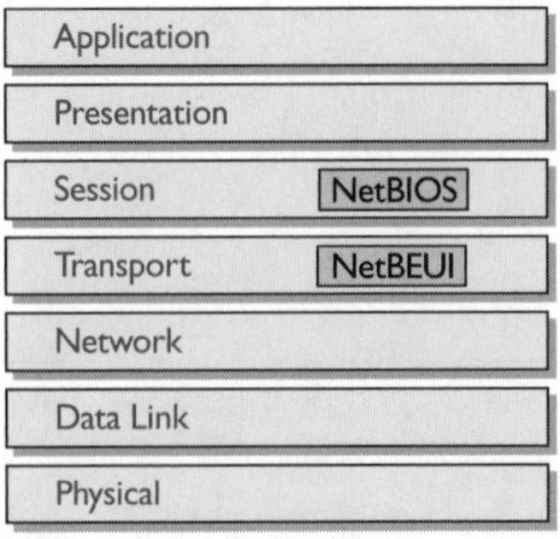

FIGURE 5-4   NetBIOS and NetBEUI in the OSI model

NetBIOS

NetBIOS handles the Session layer functions for NetBEUI networks and, as you now know, this means that it manages the connections between machines: setting things up for data transmission and closing the connections afterward. One of the prerequisites for this task is knowing who you're talking to; NetBIOS manages connections based on the names of the computers involved. Figure 5-5 shows a typical NetBIOS name.

Exam Tip

NetBIOS is a Session layer protocol.

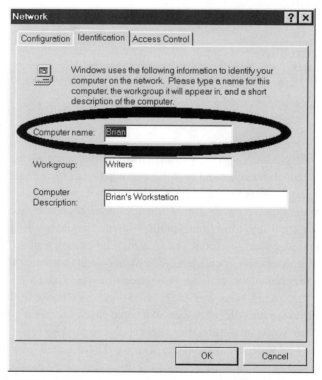

FIGURE 5-5   The NetBIOS computer name in Windows 98 is set up using the Network control applet on the control panel.

NetBIOS is actually well supported by other general networking protocols, too, and it often handles the Session layer in other protocol suites as well (see the discussions of IPX/SPX and TCP/IP later in this chapter and in Chapter 6, respectively). This is why all networkable versions of Windows require each computer attached to the network to have a unique computer name, even if your main protocol suite is TCP/IP or IPX/SPX.

NetBIOS Names

NetBIOS names can be up to 15 characters long and must be unique; otherwise, it would be impossible to identify specific machines. If there were duplications, it would be like several houses in your neighborhood having the same telephone number: messages (data) wouldn't get through to the right location. If duplicate addresses are set up on your network, the affected machines will detect this and display an error message.

Exam Tip

NetBEUI (through the NetBIOS protocol) identifies individual computers by their computer names.

Although NetBIOS is great for small networks, it does not scale well for larger ones. The main drawback is that NetBIOS uses a *flat name space* model, meaning that every machine has a single name to identify it, but no way to identify a location. Each machine has a *node* address, but no *network* address. If this type of flat model were applied to the national phone system, it would be like having telephone numbers but no area codes. You *could* make a workable system (boy, would all the phone numbers be long!), but because you couldn't automatically position a specific telephone to a particular area, every time you dialed a number—for example, your friend Jo on 23664322214045—every exchange in the country would have to see your dialing request so it could check whether it's responsible for the phone you want to ring. If you now apply this analogy to a (theoretical) NetBEUI-based wide area network (WAN), you'd have a situation where *every* request by one computer to communicate with another would have to be broadcast to *every* other interconnected network, in effect swamping the network and pretty much grinding everything to a halt. There would be no time for data on *this* network!

OK—are you sold on this? NetBEUI is for small LANs only. In fact, routers block NetBEUI for the reasons just mentioned. You can, however, still split a large LAN into smaller sections using bridges, because these *do* forward NetBEUI data packets. Repeaters are also still usable because they forward everything—remember, they don't know anything about protocols and packets, just electrical signals.

> **Exam Tip**
>
> NetBEUI is a nonroutable protocol.

On your small LAN, though, once NetBIOS establishes a connection, it passes the packet down to the NetBEUI protocol, which operates at the transport layer.

The NetBEUI Protocol

NetBEUI (as an individual protocol, not the name of the suite—you'll have to get used to this double-meaning stuff because it happens a lot!) does what all good Transport layer protocols do: it breaks larger chunks of data into smaller pieces on the sending machine (performs fragmentation) and reassembles them on the receiving end (performs defragmentation). See Figure 5-6.

Because NetBEUI is a nonroutable protocol, there's no need for the Network layer (where routing activities take place) to do anything, so there's no Network layer protocol in the NetBEUI protocol suite. If a router receives a NetBEUI packet, it simply discards it (Figure 5-7). Everything gets passed directly to the

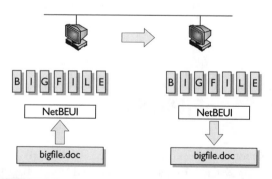

FIGURE 5-6 NetBEUI breaks a file into smaller pieces for transmission and reassembles the pieces on the receiving end.

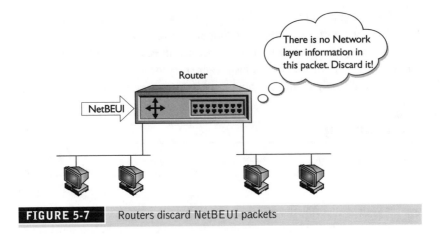

FIGURE 5-7 Routers discard NetBEUI packets

Data Link layer, where it's all packaged up ready to whiz around the network to the destination machine.

NetBEUI Summary

If your needs are simple and LAN-like, NetBEUI might be the protocol for you. Here's a summary of its key features:

- Fast, Transport layer protocol suitable for small networks (LANs)
- Nonroutable and so not suitable for WANs
- Uses the NetBIOS protocol at the Session layer to identify and manage computer names and connections
- Traditionally associated with IBM- and Microsoft-oriented networking environments

Objective 5.03

Role and Function of IPX/SPX

The IPX/SPX protocol suite is firmly associated with the NetWare series of network operating systems from a company called Novell. Based on an older Xerox protocol called XNS, IPX/SPX provides a more scaleable solution for networks than NetBEUI (NetWare servers don't support NetBEUI anyway). From the late 1980s to the mid-1990s (we *could* call these the golden days of NetWare, but we won't because that's too corny), NetWare was *the* network operating system to use, with a claimed market share in the 70 to 80 percent range. NetWare is still going strong today, but the likes of Windows NT have seriously eroded its dominant market position. Nevertheless, a large base of client-server networks still use NetWare as their main server software platform. Even Microsoft supports IPX/SPX through its own version of the protocol, NWLink, allowing Windows-based clients to access NetWare resources as well as Microsoft-based servers (you could also use true IPX/SPX by installing a Novell-supplied client kit). Modern versions of NetWare also fully support the TCP/IP protocol.

The IPX/SPX Protocol Suite

IPX/SPX represents a much more sophisticated protocol suite compared to NetBEUI, and it operates at layers 3 through 7 of the OSI model, which immediately tells us that it is a routable protocol (because it uses layer 3, the Network layer).

Figure 5-8 shows some of these protocols in relation to the OSI model. At the Network layers, the Internetwork Packet eXchange (IPX) protocol handles the routing of data packets between networks. At the Transport layer, Sequenced Packet eXchange (SPX) handles the process of breaking data into smaller chunks on the sending machine and reassembling the data on the receiving machine. The Service Advertising Protocol (SAP) handles the Session layer by regularly broadcasting the availability of servers, print servers, and other services across the network, and the NetWare Core Protocol (NCP) handles a variety of Presentation and Application layer issues.

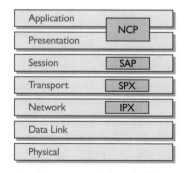

FIGURE 5-8   IPX/SPX includes protocols operating at OSI layers 3 through 7.

Exam Tip

The Network+ exam does not require knowledge of the individual protocols that make up the IPX/SPX suite.

IPX/SPX Addressing

IPX/SPX uses the MAC address built into the Network Interface Card (NIC) to uniquely identify a computer on the network, and so, unlike NetBEUI, which requires someone to assign each computer a name, IPX/SPX node addressing requires no manual setup. Because IPX/SPX is routable, however, every client needs a network address, which is entered as part of a server's configuration. The important point to remember here is that every server on the same network must be configured with the *same* network address. Think of our earlier phone analogy: your telephone and that of your neighbor will have the *same* area code (unless your two houses straddle phone districts, but let's assume they don't).

Exam Tip

IPX/SPX uses MAC addresses to identify computers.

NetWare Packet Formats

NetWare has evolved over time, and one of these evolutionary stages brought NetWare's packet (frame) format into alignment with the rest of the industry. Early versions of the NetWare operating system use a slightly nonstandard packet format that Novell, somewhat confusingly, called Ethernet_802.3. Later versions of NetWare fell in line with the rest of the world and used, by default, a packet format that Novell called Ethernet_802.2. To cap it all, NetWare also supports two other frame types called Ethernet_II (used with TCP/IP) and Ethernet_SNAP. The upshot of this is that every machine on a NetWare-based network must use a common frame format (usually now Ethernet_802.2) to be able to communicate. This may require the network techs to check the configuration of existing servers carefully when adding a new server to ensure that the required frame type(s) are supported. Windows 9*x* and Windows NT/2000 systems simplify the process by

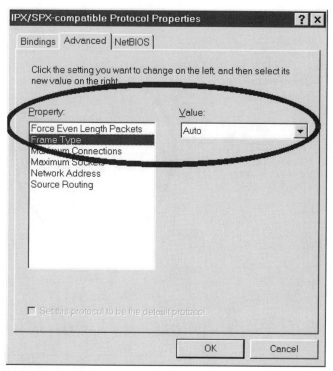

FIGURE 5-9   Microsoft's NWLink default setup autodetects IPX/SPX frame types.

automatically detecting IPX traffic by default and configuring each machine to use whichever frame type is detected on the network first (see Figure 5-9). Under some circumstances, however, a specific frame type may need to be set using the Network control panel applet, shown in Figure 5-10.

Wide Area Networking with IPX/SPX

Although IPX/SPX is a routable protocol, it does not scale well for large WANs. The main problems are associated with the way that servers and other network services broadcast their availability and the way that routers and servers intercommunicate routing information, although there is a fix for the latter.

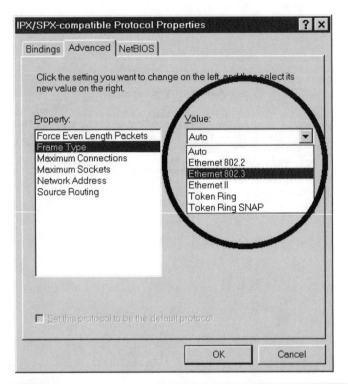

FIGURE 5-10   Microsoft's NWLink setup can also have the frame type set manually.

SAP Traffic

On a NetWare network or WAN, servers and other network services broadcast their availability using the SAP protocol every 60 seconds. While this configuration works well on small- and medium-sized networks, as a network grows to include hundreds of servers and thousands of clients, the SAP traffic increases to a point where it begins to use a significant part of the available network bandwidth, slowing down the network.

RIP Traffic

Novell's Routing Information Protocol (RIP) is used by NetWare servers to broadcast information about available routes on WANs, and this can lead to further congestion. More recent versions of NetWare use a different protocol called NetWare Link Services Protocol (NLSP) that broadcasts only *changes* to routing information as they occur. Like SAP, RIP broadcasts everything, every 60 seconds, even if the information hasn't changed since the last broadcast, as with SAP, it can consume serious quantities of bandwidth, significantly slowing down the network (Figure 5-11).

IPX/SPX Summary

Here's the bottom line on NetWare:

- Routable protocol
- Supported by Microsoft using the Microsoft NWLink equivalent protocol
- Uses MAC addressing to identify nodes on the network
- Supports different packet (frame) types

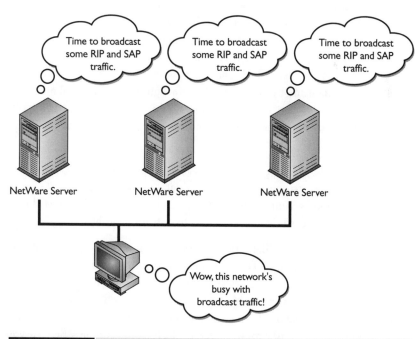

FIGURE 5-11   SAP and RIP traffic can eat into network bandwidth.

- Uses SAP broadcasts to advertise network services, often slowing down very large networks
- Uses RIP to broadcast routing information, although later NetWare server products can also use NLSP
- Does not support NetBEUI , although modern NetWare servers do support TCP/IP

Objective 5.04
Connection-Oriented vs. Connectionless Protocols

Transport layer protocols, such as SPX, are classified as *connection-oriented*, or *reliable*, protocols. This is a strange classification, because surely you'd expect every protocol to work reliably—wouldn't you? The trick here is not to think of the word *reliable* as having anything to do with reliability or success; in the networking world, a reliable protocol is simply one that verifies whether *each and every* packet it sends actually makes it to its destination, and that all packets arrive in the right order. Reliable protocols also check whether the destination device is actually present before sending it any data; they are said to establish a circuit between the sending and receiving device prior to data transmission.

On the other hand, so-called *connectionless*, or *unreliable*, protocols expect some other mechanism or protocol (usually at a higher level in the OSI model) to sense when things have gone wrong and then to do something about it. The difference in the two approaches can be summed up (a bit crudely, but it will do) thus:

- Connection-oriented (reliable) protocols are pessimistic and paranoid and check everything before and after data transmission.
- Connectionless (unreliable) protocols assume that everything's working fine and expect something elsewhere to notice any problems.

Because of the smaller data transmission management overhead, connectionless protocols tend to be faster than connection-oriented ones and so are preferable in some circumstances, especially where the underlying network can be considered stable, such as on a LAN. Connectionless protocols are also used where there's no guarantee that the data recipient is actually present on the network; for example, all broadcast traffic must, by definition, be connectionless, because you don't know exactly who's going to receive it.

Exam Tip

SPX is a connection-oriented (reliable) protocol. IPX is connectionless (unreliable). NetBEUI can provide both connection-oriented and connectionless packet delivery services. Later chapters contain further examples you should remember.

Objective 5.05 — Core Network Operating System Protocols

The protocols covered so far in this chapter have to do with getting data around a network, but when a packet is received by a machine, it has to know what to do with it. Is it part of a file, a login request, or an instruction for the server to do something? This short section outlines three protocols that are responsible for deciding what to do with the contents of a packet. Because these protocols ultimately interface with the network operating system in question—in fact, they are generally part of the network operating system—they are said to operate at the Application, Presentation, and Session layers of the OSI model (layers 7 down through 5).

Microsoft Networking: Server Message Blocks

All of the functionality of a Microsoft server is defined by a set of protocols (procedures) known collectively as Server Message Blocks (SMBs). If a client wants to log onto an NT server, for example, the client sends a data packet formatted with the appropriate SMB data to attempt a login; this reaches the server and travels up through the OSI layers until the data itself hits the core operating system, where it is decoded and understood.

Novell Networking: NetWare Core Protocol

The NetWare Core Protocol defines the functionality of a NetWare server in a way similar to what SMB does for a Microsoft-type server: an NCP request (packet) from a client machine is interpreted by the NetWare NOS and causes a specific action to take place.

UNIX and SAMBA

UNIX (in various flavors) has been around for a long time, traditionally providing a high-performance, centralized data processing environment that people can access using a screen and keyboard terminal. This is still the case today; UNIX is very much alive and kicking both for data processing purposes and for the running of Internet-based services, such as web sites. In 1992, Andrew Tridgell published the code for an installable UNIX environment that would make the system look and behave like a Microsoft-type server, in effect implementing the SMB protocol on the UNIX system. The result was an open-source product called SAMBA. Once SAMBA is installed and configured (a very simple task), Microsoft clients see shared disk space and printers on a UNIX system in exactly the same way that they would if they were accessing a true Microsoft server (Figure 5-12). Before

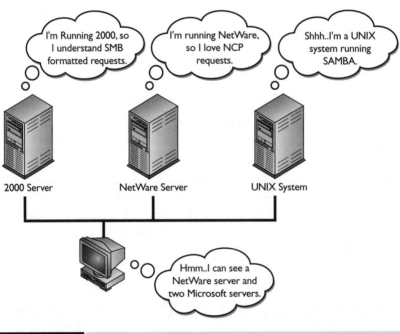

FIGURE 5-12   SAMBA makes a UNIX server look like a Microsoft server to its clients.

SAMBA, it was possible to share files between UNIX systems and other platforms using various file transfer programs and disk tools, but SAMBA makes things very tidy.

> ### Exam Tip
>
> The *Common Internet File System* (CIFS) is a backward-compatible develop-ment of SMB, published as a public-domain standard. CIFS is defined by Microsoft as "a standard remote file system access protocol for use over the Internet," and many publications and technicians now treat SMB and CIFS as the same thing.

CHECKPOINT

✔ **Objective 5.01: Overview of Protocols and Protocol Suites**   Protocols define how everything works, at various levels, on a network, from the for-mat that a packet of data must have to how machines are uniquely addressed. There is no single protocol that covers every aspect of network-ing; instead, families, or suites, of protocols work hand in hand to make things happen. Over the years, three protocol suites have emerged as indus-try standards: NetBEUI, IPX/SPX, and TCP/IP, with the latter being the most popular.

✔ **Objective 5.02: Role and Function of NetBEUI**   NetBEUI is a small, fast networking protocol suite suitable for small networks. Because it's a non-routable protocol, it is not suitable for wide area networks. Within the NetBEUI protocol suite, NetBEUI itself is the Transport layer protocol responsible for packet fragmentation and defragmentation, and NetBIOS provides the addressing functionality, using computer names. Historically, NetBEUI has been associated with Microsoft and IBM networking products.

✔ **Objective 5.03: Role and Function of IPX/SPX**   IPX/SPX was developed by Novell for its NetWare range of network operating systems. This proto-col uses MAC addresses to identify computers on a network and, since a unique MAC address is built into every NIC, this means that there's no need to set addresses manually. Although IPX/SPX is a routable protocol, it does not scale well for big WANs because its SAP (Service Advertising Protocol) and RIP (Routing Information Protocol) traffic can consume significant network bandwidth. Later versions of NetWare can use the NetWare Link Services Protocol (NLSP) to reduce the amount of RIP traffic on the network. Partly because of NetWare's popularity, Microsoft implemented its own, compatible version of IPX/SPX, called NWLink.

✔ **Objective 5.04:** Connection-Oriented vs. Connectionless Protocols Connection-oriented protocols, such as SPX, check every data packet for successful transmission and also establish a network connection to the recipient before actually sending any data. By contrast, connectionless protocols just send data packets without any before or after checking. This makes them faster, but not suitable for applications that need to be sure of complete data transmission integrity at all times. In general, however, most client-to-server network traffic uses a connectionless protocol. NetBEUI is capable of both connection-oriented and connectionless operation.

✔ **Objective 5.05:** Core Network Operating System Protocols   Up to this point, our discussions have focused on protocols for getting data across a network to its destination. This section refers to the protocols or standards that lie at the heart of a network operating system and define how specific data patterns can be sent to a server to make certain things happen. In the Microsoft world, the functionality of a server is defined by a set of protocols known collectively as Server Message Blocks (SMBs). In the NetWare world, server functionality is defined in a similar way by the NetWare Core Protocol. Finally, we discussed SAMBA, an application that allows UNIX-based systems to understand SMBs and to look and behave on a network like a Microsoft server.

REVIEW QUESTIONS

1. You have been asked to network three computers in a small office. The main objective is to share a printer and some disk space. A secondary objective is to allow for future wide area networking. Your chosen solution uses the NetBEUI protocol. This solution:

   A. Meets both objectives
   B. Meets the main objective only

    C. Meets the secondary objective only

    D. Doesn't meet either objective

2. At which layer of the OSI model does the NetBEUI protocol operate? (Select one answer.)

    A. Application

    B. Session

    C. Transport

    D. Network

3. Your office has three NetWare servers installed and one NT server. Which of the following protocols would *not* allow you to communicate with all the servers? (Select one answer.)

    A. TCP/IP.

    B. NetBEUI.

    C. NWLink.

    D. They would all be suitable.

4. Which of the following statements about the IPX/SPX protocol is true?

    A. IPX/SPX supports computer name addressing.

    B. IPX/SPX is not a routable protocol.

    C. SPX handles machine addressing.

    D. IPX/SPX uses MAC addressing.

5. You have just added a client computer to a NetWare server-based network, and the machine cannot access any of the servers. You have checked the cabling, NIC, and driver setup. What should you check next? (Select one answer.)

    A. The computer name

    B. The power supply

    C. The frame type

    D. The server's NCP address

6. Which of the following is a connectionless-only protocol? (Select one answer.)

    A. SPX.

    B. IPX.

    C. NetBEUI.

    D. They are all connectionless.

7. You have been asked to add a NetWare server to your existing network of Microsoft systems. Which of the following protocols could you add to your client PCs to allow access to the NetWare server? (Select two answers.)

   A. NCP
   B. IPX/SPX
   C. NetBEUI
   D. NWLink

8. Which of the following devices will forward NetBEUI data packets? (Select all that apply.)

   A. Repeaters
   B. Routers
   C. Hubs
   D. Bridges

9. You have been asked to install a UNIX-based system on your Microsoft network. The primary objective is to allow data to be transferred to the UNIX system from the Microsoft servers. A secondary objective is to allow all users easy access to the UNIX printers. You decide to install NWLink on the NT servers. This solution meets:

   A. Neither of the objectives
   B. The primary objective only
   C. The secondary objective only
   D. Both objectives

10. Which of the following is a Session layer protocol? (Select one answer.)

    A. NetBIOS
    B. NetBEUI
    C. NCP
    D. SMB

REVIEW ANSWERS

1. **B** NetBEUI will certainly meet the main objective and let you share resources, but it won't meet the secondary objective. This is because NetBEUI is a nonroutable protocol and so not suitable for wide area networking.

   2.   **C**   NetBEUI is a Transport layer protocol.

   3.   **B**   NetWare does not support the NetBEUI protocol.

   4.   **D**   NetWare uses MAC addressing to identify computers on the network.

   5.   **C**   Always make sure that clients on a NetWare network are using the right frame type. Autodetect works under most circumstances, but you may need to set the frame type manually.

   6.   **B**   IPX is the only completely connectionless protocol on the list.

   7.   **B** **D**   You could use IPX/SPX (B) using a NetWare client kit, or NWLink (D) using Microsoft's client.

   8.   **A** **C** **D**   NetBEUI is nonroutable, so that eliminates routers (B), but all of the other devices listed will forward NetBEUI data packets.

   9.   **A**   NWLink is not a protocol generally associated with UNIX, so installing it on all the NT servers is unlikely to provide any connectivity.

  10.   **A**   NetBIOS is a Session layer protocol.

TCP/IP

	NEWBIE	SOME EXPERIENCE	EXPERT
ETA	6 hours	3 hours	2 hours

If you've been "out of the country" (well, off the planet, maybe!) for the last ten or so years and haven't heard of the TCP/IP protocol suite, the fact that we've given it its own chapter should be a clue that it's an important topic! All major operating systems, including UNIX, Windows 95/98/ME, Windows NT, Windows 2000, and Novell NetWare, support TCP/IP—in fact, UNIX has used TCP/IP since the protocol was first announced in the early 1970s. We were joking about committees at the start of Chapter 5—as you'll see later, TCP/IP is the biggest "committee job" going!

TCP/IP was first proposed as part of a U.S. Defense Advanced Research Projects Agency (DARPA) program in 1973 to investigate ways of connecting various existing networks so that they could exchange information. One aim was to develop a common standard to replace the growing number of proprietary ones that were being developed in complete isolation. The work undertaken as part of the DARPA project eventually led to the development of the Internet as we know it today. Oh, and before we go any further, if you've read elsewhere about the primary aim being to create a "nuclear bombproof" network that would still work if X percent of the network was out of action, well, that's a bit of an urban myth— true, the Internet is a robust, routed network capable of withstanding a high degree of outages, but the nuclear angle came up in a document *long after* the DARPA project had started, and is sort of a "realization after the event." If you want to read more about this try the following addresses:

http://www.isoc.org/internet/history/cerf.html
http://www.usatoday.com/life/cyber/tech/ctg000.htm

So what have we got then? An "ancient" protocol from the 1970s that is, at this very moment, responsible for carrying the data passing through the world's high-tech Internet infrastructure? Sounds about right!

Objective 6.01 The TCP/IP Protocol Suite

We already know from Chapter 5 that when we refer to a "protocol" such as NetBEUI or IPX/SPX, we're really referring to a whole suite of protocols, each of which supports a specific task like addressing or connection-oriented data delivery. Well, TCP/IP is no exception; behind the scenes, there are dozens of protocols in the suite all ready and willing to do your bidding, whether sending an e-mail message or reporting the status of your server. In essence, the "TCP" and "IP" bits describe the protocols that can help get all this data to its destination. The reason why there are so many protocols in the TCP/IP suite stems from its origins; at its beginning there were numerous operating systems in use on all sorts of minicomputers and mainframe systems (and not a PC in sight!). These operating systems shared little common functionality, or they did things in totally different ways. So it wasn't possible to guarantee, for example, if you wanted to copy or move a file between two computers, that their operating systems actually had compatible file transfer capabilities. To overcome this problem, protocols were developed that *did* support the functionality required, like FTP, the File Transfer Protocol, which we might well use today for our file copying requirements.

To enable operating system developers to create programs and driver code to support all these "utility" protocols, the standards for the protocols were (and still are) published for all to see and comment upon—and that's where our "designed by committee" statement comes in. Anyone who has a vested interest in the standards associated with TCP/IP can contribute to their development.

RFCs, STDs, and FYIs

TCP/IP standards are developed through documents called *Requests for Comments* (RFCs)—there's an RFC for pretty much every major Internet milestone and related protocol. These RFCs are edited and managed by the Internet Architecture Board (IAB). By looking up the appropriate RFCs, you can find out how a protocol works so that perhaps you can develop a version of it for your system, or you can give your input. As you might expect, there have been many developments in networking technology since the 1970s, and the TCP/IP protocol suite is a dynamic structure, ever changing and ever responding to new technical requirements. It is important to understand this because over time many of the original protocols have been enhanced or revised, leading to the publication of a new RFC describing the new functionality—as opposed to an update of the original RFC. Thus it's vital, if you ever need to look up the RFC for a particular issue or protocol, to ensure you locate the most up-to-date one.

Some of the RFCs aren't actually about protocols but contain useful information and tutorials (and poems—see RFC 1121) about the TCP/IP protocol suite and the Internet—for example, RFC 1118, "The Hitchhikers Guide to the Internet," contains a very useful introduction to the Internet, its concepts, and terminology (even though it was written in 1989, the basics still hold true). Go download a copy today from the following address, if you are able—it may help with your Network+ studies.

Travel Assistance

RFC1118, "The Hitchhikers Guide to the Internet," can be found at various locations, including http://www.ietf.org/rfc/rfc1118.txt.

In addition to the RFCs, there are two other categories of documents:

- **Standards documents (STDs)** represent individual Internet (TCP/IP) standards and are released periodically in order to condense the relevant information from numerous related RFCs into a single document.
- **For Your Information (FYI)** documents contain general information about Internet and TCP/IP-related issues.

There are many lists of RFCs, STDs, and FYIs on the Internet, but the following is a good start point: http://www.faqs.org/rfcs/index.html.

Exam Tip

You will not be expected to remember and quote **RFC numbers** on the exam—they are included here for your reference and optional further study.

Objective 6.02 IP Addressing

The Internet Protocol (IP) handles Network layer issues for all TCP/IP traffic, defining the rules for moving data between *hosts* across a routed network.

Local Lingo

host A *host* is any machine that can send or receive data on the network: clients, servers, printers, and so forth. Every host needs its own IP address.

Every TCP/IP host has a logical address known as its *IP address*. Because IP supports routing, every machine must also have a *network* address (back again to our telephone number + area code analogy) and, indeed, a host's IP address comprises both these elements—as we'll soon see.

Exam Tip

We use the term "logical address" when referring to IP addresses to distinguish them from MAC addresses, which we refer to as "physical addresses".

32-Bit Numbers

IP addresses comprise a 32-bit binary number—there's one in Figure 6-1.

Try quoting that over the phone to a customer! To make things more manageable, we break down IP addresses into 8-bit chunks and write them down in a "dotted decimal notation"—the IP address in Figure 6-1 works out as 192.168.50.2.

Each section of this notation represents 8 bits from our binary number and is known as an *octet*. To know how we get from the binary to the decimal part requires a bit of math—sorry!

First of all, we have to know our binary powers, but let's backtrack and start with decimal powers.

Here's a number in decimal: 548.

As any Nobel prize winning scientist will tell you, this number represents the following values: $(10^2 \times 5) + (10^1 \times 4) + (10^0 \times 8)$. In other words, it's OK if you know that the decimal positions (powers) in that number are hundreds, tens, and units. Applying the same principle to 8-bit binary numbers, where the number positions represent binary powers (base 2), rather than powers of ten, we get the values shown in Figure 6-2.

11000000101010000011001000000010

FIGURE 6-1   A 32-bit binary number

Binary power	2^7	2^6	2^5	2^4	2^3	2^2	2^1	2^0
Decimal value	128	64	32	16	8	4	2	1

FIGURE 6-2   Binary powers

If you split a binary number into 8-bit sections, this instantly makes it more readable:

11000000 10101000 00110010 00000010

Working out the first (top) octet now goes as follows:

$(128 \times 1) + (64 \times 1) + (32 \times 0) + (16 \times 0) + (8 \times 0) + (4 \times 0) + (2 \times 0) + (1 \times 0)$, or simply $128 + 64 = 192$

Exam Tip

The highest number for a single octet is 255 (11111111 in binary).

Fortunately, the Network+ exam doesn't require you to do too much binary math, but understanding the principles is extremely useful in the real (networking) world.

IP Classes, or "Which bit does what?"

We said a short while ago that an IP address (such as 192.168.50.2) contains both a *network* address and a *host* address—so which bit's which? The trick is to have a look at the first octet (the left-most 8 bits—also known as the *top* octet) and compare it with Table 6-1, which shows the predefined "splits" based on a system known as IP classes.

Spotted some gaps? Look carefully!

Class D and E Addresses

If the top octet is between 224 and 247, the address is a *class D* or *multicast* address— used for sending data to a "group" of systems, such as you might want to do for a

TABLE 6.1 IP Class Table

If the top octet is between...	...because the top 4 bits of that octet are...	...then the IP address class is...	...which means that the network part of the address is really...	...leaving the host part as...	...so this split (Network/Host address) is like this...
1 and 126	0000	A	The top octet	The next three octets	N.H.H.H
128 and 191	1000	B	The top two octets	The next two octets	N.N.H.H
192 and 223	1100	C	The top three octets	The last octet	N.N.N.H

videoconference. Addresses with the top octet set between 248 and 255 are *class E*—"experimental" addresses. Where's 127? We'll leave that for later!

Exam Tip

The Network+ exam doesn't cover class D and E addresses.

IP Addresses—Facts, Rules, and Regulations

Now that we've got the basics out of the way, let's delve into the practicalities of addressing. First of all, let's go back to our sample address: 192.168.50.2. Right, question time—you at the back there—class? Well-done, it's a class C address. OK, then, what *is* the actual address of the *network?* Hmm, from the previous table, the network part must be the top three octets, so it's 192.168.50. Correct!

So what's the 2? Well, the entire address refers to (unique) host number 2 on network 192.168.50.

That's it!

Thinking about this address, we have one octet representing the *hosts* portion of the address and (because we are now binary experts!) we know that this (8-bit) octet can range from 0 to 255, but that *doesn't* mean we can have 256 hosts on this network—we have to chop two off:

- The network itself is represented by an IP address with the all hosts bits set to zero.
- Broadcasts on the network are sent to the host represented by a host address of all 1s.

In our case, this means that our IP network is referred to as 192.168.2.0 and broadcasts are sent to 192.168.2.255.

The same rule applies for other IP classes too—for example, we're also not allowed to give a host on a class B network an address of x.x.0.0 (the address of the network itself), nor x.x.255.255 (the broadcast address for that network).

This 0 and 255 rule holds true for the *network* portion of the full IP address too—class A network addresses of 0.x.x.x and 255.x.x.x are not allowed, and neither are class B network addresses of 0.0.x.x and 255.255.x.x. Table 6-2 summarizes the permutations.

This table tells us that if we want to construct a wide area network using just class A addresses, we can interconnect up to 254 networks, and that each network

TABLE 6.2 IP Network and Hosts Address Ranges

Address Class	Number of Bits in Address Part (8 Bits per Octet)	Max Number of Network addresses in That Class	Number of Bits in Hosts Part (8 Bits per Octet)	Max Number of Hosts on That Class of Network
A	8	$2^8 - 2 = 254$	24	$2^{24} - 2 = 16,777,214$
B	16	$2^{16} - 2 = 65,534$	16	$2^{16} - 2 = 65,534$
C	24	$2^{24} - 2 = 16,777,214$	8	$2^8 - 2 = 254$

can have over 16 million hosts on it. In reality, we can interconnect class A, B, and C networks without problems (see Figure 6-3), and so our only dilemma would seem to be deciding which address class to use—for example, if we need to construct a network with 500 computers on it, using a class C address range might not be a good start!

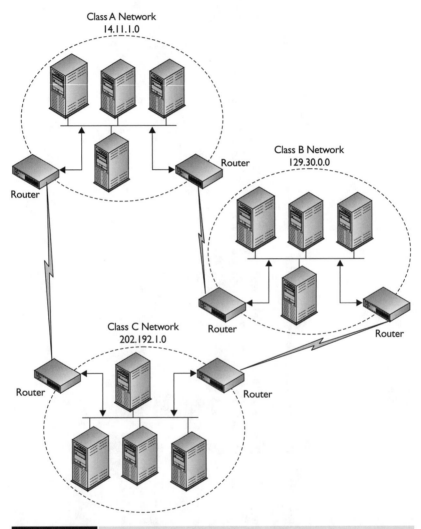

FIGURE 6-3   Any class of network can be linked to any other.

IP Addresses—Classless Notation and Partial Address Range Assignment

The *classful* IP address structures are now often referred to simply by the number of available address bits (the address prefix)—using so-called *classless* or *CIDR* notation, as shown in Table 6-3.

Local Lingo	
CIDR	Classless Inter-Domain Routing

Classless notation makes it easier to see straightaway the number of IP address bits actually assigned to the network address.

Give Me a Network Address

If we have no intention of joining our in-house LAN or WAN directly to the Internet proper, then, in theory, we can pick and choose any IP addresses that suit our needs. If, however, all or part of our network is going to be directly connected to the Internet (as opposed to using something like a simple dial-up connection or a routed NAT connection—this is covered in Chapter 7), we must apply for an "assigned network address" so that we don't happen to pick one that's already in use by a network elsewhere on the Internet.

Address assignment is managed by a central authority known as the Internet Network Information Center, or InterNIC. InterNIC keeps track of all of the

TABLE 6.3	Classless (CIDR) Address Notation	
Example Address	**Class**	**Address in Classless Notation**
14.12.23.244	A	14.12.23.244/8
132.12.23.233	B	132.12.23.233/16
234.123.2.93	C	234.123.2.93/24

addresses currently in use and assigns blocks of previously unassigned addresses to organizations based on their size. InterNIC calls these blocks of addresses *licenses*.

Private Networks

Although you can use pretty much any address range you fancy if you're not connecting to the Internet proper, RFC 1918 defines a range of class A, B, and C addresses that have been declared "non-routable," which means that if you *do* use them *and* you have connectivity to the Internet, your Internet routers (or gateways in proper TCP/IP lingo) won't pass your in-house traffic on elsewhere—and so there's *absolutely* no danger of your IP addressing scheme clashing with anyone else's (see Figure 6-4). These so-called "private IP addresses" are shown in Table 6-4.

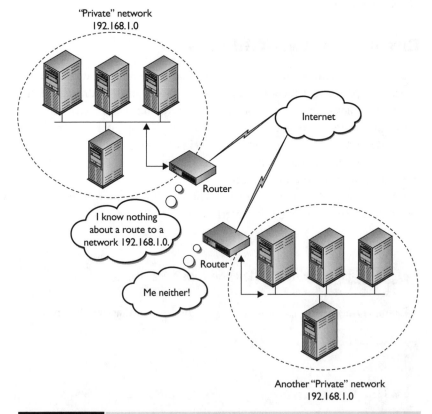

FIGURE 6-4   Private IP addresses don't route.

TABLE 6.4	Private IP Address Ranges
Address Class	**Private IP Address Range**
A	10.x.x.x
B	172.16.x.x to 172.32.x.x.
C	192.168.0.x to 192.168.255.x

Travel Assistance

For a more detailed discussion of IP addressing, consult 3Com's "Understanding IP Addressing: Everything You Ever Wanted To Know" at http://www.3com.com or "Connected: an Internet Encyclopedia" at http://www.freesoft.org.

127.0.0.1: The Loopback Address

Remember that IP network address 127 was missing from our earlier list? Well, TCP/IP sets aside address 127.0.0.1 for internal testing. Referred to as the *loopback address,* messages sent to 127.0.0.1 never leave the sending machine; instead, they are redirected back through the internal software layers to confirm (or otherwise) that TCP/IP has been installed properly. On a correctly installed system, the command-line instruction "PING 127.0.0.1" is used to perform the loopback test—there's more on the PING command later.

Objective 6.03

Subnet Masks and Subnetting

The class of an IP address also determines another important variable: its *default* subnet mask. The *subnet mask* defines which part of an IP address

TABLE 6.5	Default Subnet Masks
IP Class	**Default Subnet Mask**
A	255.0.0.0
B	255.255.0.0
C	255.255.255.0

refers to the network ID and which part refers to the host ID. Table 6-5 shows the various main IP classes and their corresponding default subnet masks.

For each octet, if the corresponding value in the subnet mask equals 255, that octet refers to the network ID. If the corresponding value equals zero, the octet refers to the host ID. On a bit-by-bit basis, if a specific data bit in the subnet mask is a 1, the corresponding bit in the IP address given is part of the *network* address. If a specific bit in the subnet mask is a 0, the corresponding bit in the IP address given is part of the *host* address.

In technical terms, a logical ("comparing") binary operation called ANDing is performed between the IP address given and the subnet mask specified. ANDing compares two binary numbers in a way that always yields a zero result unless the first AND second bits being compared are both 1s. Figure 6-5 shows how ANDing the IP address 192.168.50.2 with its subnet mask of 255.255.255.0 (in binary) arrives at the network address of 192.168.50.0—notice that ANDing any bit with a 1 (the dark gray bits) preserves its original state, but ANDing with a 0 always returns a 0 (shown in light gray).

For the class B address 187.12.54.123, the default subnet mask is 255.255.0.0. Address 187.12.54.123 translates to "host 54.123 on network 187.12.0.0." Table 6-6

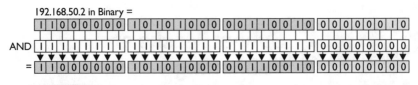

| FIGURE 6-5 | Performing a logical AND identifies the network part of an IP address. |

TABLE 6.6	Translating IP Addresses into Network and Host IDs Using the Subnet Mask		

IP Address	Default Subnet Mask	Network ID	Host ID
210.35.156.198	255.255.255.0	210.35.156.0	198
195.25.210.12	255.255.255.0	195.25.210.0	12
180.220.215.19	255.255.0.0	180.220.0.0	215.19
155.35.123.99	255.255.0.0.	155.35.0.0	123.99
142.98.189.222	255.255.0.0	142.98.0.0	189.122.
85.123.225.19	255.0.0.0	85.0.0.0	123.225.19

shows other examples of translating IP addresses into their equivalent network and host IDs using the subnet mask.

At one level, subnet masks seem pointless because they don't necessarily tell us anything we don't already know, but the reason they're there is so that we *can* change them to "break the rules" and split an IP address into the network and host portion wherever we want; this is known as *subnetting*.

Exam Tip

The Network+ exam does not cover subnetting in any significant depth.

Subnetting Basics

The basics of subnetting allow you to take a single IP-based network address and divide (subnet) it into smaller sections. This is ideal for situations where you want to split a network for traffic reasons or perhaps have a WAN with several locations that, overall, still needs to behave like a single network for management purposes (with routers between the sites, of course). Figure 6-6 shows a subnetted network,

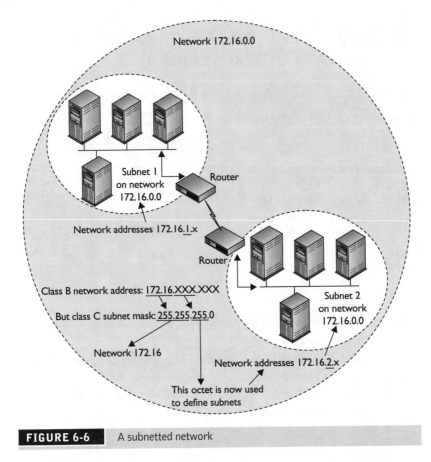

FIGURE 6-6   A subnetted network

and Figure 6-7 illustrates the difference between a regular IP address and a subnetted address.

The first step when subnetting is to decide how many subnets (sections) you want, because this determines how many binary bits of an overall 32-bit address you need to borrow for the subnet address; this is a binary issue so, for example, if you have a need for five subnets, you need to know how many binary bits are needed to represent them. Table 6-7 shows how many bits you need for between 2 and 30 subnets.

How does this work? Well, let's take using our requirement for five subnets—the table says we need 3 bits. The highest binary number you can have with 3 bits is 111, which equates to $(4 \times 1) + (2 \times 1) + (1 \times 1) = 7$, giving eight permutations if you include 000 as a number, but just as with regular IP addressing, you can't have

Standard IP address

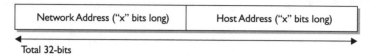

Total 32-bits

Subnetted IP address

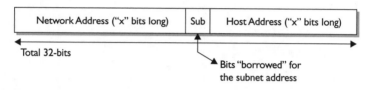

Total 32-bits

Bits "borrowed" for
the subnet address

FIGURE 6-7   A regular IP address has two parts, a subnetted address
has three.

a subnet numbered all zeroes (0) or all ones (111 in our case)—so 3 bits gives us
$8 - 2 = 6$ permutations—as shown in Table 6-8.

Taking a real-world example, let's use a class B network address, say 129.30.0.0.
We need to borrow 3 bits for our subnetting, so we modify the default subnet
mask (255.255.0.0) to show that we've pinched 3 bits from the hosts section as
follows:

```
Original Subnet mask in binary: 11111111.11111111.00000000.00000000
(255.255.0.0)
```

TABLE 6.7   The Number of Bits Required for Various
Numbers of Subnets

Maximum Number of Subnets	Bits Required
2	2
6	3
14	4
30	5

TABLE 6.8	Possible Subnets Using Three Subnet Bits
Subnets Bit Pattern	**Subnet**
000	Not allowed
001	1
010	2
011	3
100	4
101	5
110	6
111	Not allowed

```
Using 3 bits for subnetting:     11111111.11111111.11100000.00000000
(255.255.240.0)
On our class B network, every host must now use the subnet mask
255.255.240.0.
```

When it comes to addressing, we would set our subnet bits on one site to 001, the next would use 010… and so on—so we can refer to network 129.30.0.0, subnet 1 and 129.30.0.0 subnet 2, and so forth.

Now that we've borrowed 3 bits for subnetting, we've reduced the remaining bits left for identifying host machines on each subnet from $2^{16} - 2$ (65,534) to "only" $2^{13} - 2$ (8,190), but that's probably still enough for us!

Well, that's the basics of simple subnetting—and it's certainly enough for the Network+ exam. If you want to read more on the subject, try the following:

Travel Assistance

Useful guides to subnetting can be found at http://support.
microsoft.com/support/kb/articles/q164/0/15.asp.

Objective 6.04 IP Version 6

The word is out (actually, it has been for some time)—the Internet's running
out of spare 32-bit IP addresses. What to do? Simple—use bigger addresses.
Make everything backwards compatible with the existing address scheme? No
problem; here's IP version 6...

Sounds easy, but its taken many years to perfect a replacement for the 32-bit IP
addressing scheme—known, by the way, as IP version 4, or IPv4. ("What happened
to version 5?" I hear you ask. Well, it never really existed! Don't worry about it!)

With a 128-bit address range, IPv6 supports a mind-blowing 340,282,366,920,
938,463,463,374,607,431,768,211,456 addresses, which equates to (so we're reliably informed) approximately 665,570,793,348,866,943,898,599 addresses per
square meter of the surface of the planet Earth.

IPv6 is in use today on parts of the Internet, but it's not quite appearing "at the
desktop" yet (Microsoft aims to have native support for IPv6 in Windows in 2002).
The new addressing scheme was designed to slide in relatively seamlessly in place
of IPv4 and parts of the Internet infrastructure are being upgraded all the time
without us noticing.

Don't worry about the long numbers above—they're just there out of interest and to give you something to talk about next time you're at a party (well, if you want to get rid of somebody who's bugging you perhaps!); you only need to know that IPv6 exists, and that it uses a 128-bit address range, for the Network+ exam—but if you fancy a little extra reading, surf along to the following addresses:

Travel Assistance

Further information on IPv6 can be found at http://playground.sun.com/pub/ipng/html/ipng-main.html and http://www.microsoft.com/ipv6/.

Objective 6.05   Routing

Routers do not grab traffic off the network and forward it automatically; if the data packets you're sending need to be forwarded, your host machine must send these packets to a router, and the router must know how to find every other network within the *internetwork*, the larger "network of networks" within which it operates.

Exam Tip

In a TCP/IP network, a host's nearest router is called its *default gateway*.

The IP address for a host's default gateway must lie on the same network as the host (see Figure 6-8).

For proper routing to take place, all the routers must learn the location of the other networks within their internetwork.

Static and Dynamic Routing

Static routing requires a network tech to sit at each router and manually enter a route to each network within the internetwork. The commands used vary from

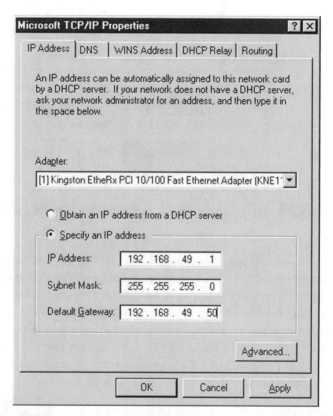

FIGURE 6-8   If you want to internetwork, you must specify the address of your default gateway.

router to router, depending on the brand, but all supply the same essential information. With *dynamic routing* (see Figure 6-9), the routers in an internetwork automatically exchange information with every other router, building their own list of routes to the various networks. The routers build this list, called a *routing table*, by sending out messages to other routers on the network informing them of the networks that they can reach. Although dynamic routing increases traffic between the routers, it relieves network administrators of the task of manually configuring the routers.

Static routing works best for small internetworks that rarely change, while dynamic routing works best in larger internetworks that change frequently. In a small internetwork with relatively few routers to configure, the network tech should take the time to set any necessary routes manually. In addition to eliminating

FIGURE 6-9   Dynamic routing takes place automatically between routers

dynamic routing traffic between the routers, static routing gives the network tech control over the routes used. In a larger internetwork with dozens or hundreds of routers, updating manual configurations becomes so time-consuming that some type of dynamic routing becomes essential. Network architects can choose from a variety of dynamic routing protocols, with names like Router Information Protocol (RIP), Open Shortest Path First (OSPF), Exterior Gateway Protocol (EGP), and Border Gateway Protocol (BGP). Each dynamic routing protocol has advantages and disadvantages in terms of ease of use and efficiency. As a general rule, the larger the network managed by a routing protocol, the more complex its configuration becomes.

Exam Tip

Routers configured with *static routing* require manual configuration of routes; routers configured with *dynamic routing protocols* communicate with each other and automatically calculate routes on their own.

Objective 6.06   **Transport Layer Protocols**

We've kept a secret from you—TCP is not alone! Remember that TCP is the Transmission Control Protocol (TCP), a *connection-oriented* protocol,

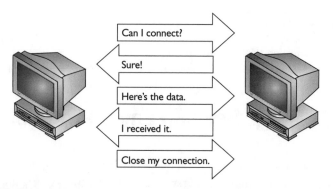

FIGURE 6-10   TCP is connection-oriented and checks every stage of the data transmission process.

establishing a connection between two hosts before transmitting data and verifying the receipt of the data before closing the connection (Figure 6-10). Well, TCP has a Transport layer colleague called UDP—the User Datagram Protocol (UDP).

UDP is a connectionless protocol and is used by applications that don't feel the need for all that connection-oriented mumbo jumbo. We do not concern ourselves with choosing a Transport layer protocol for a particular application–the programmers who designed the applications choose the appropriate protocol. Applications that send short bursts of data typically use UDP because of its low overhead (see Figure 6-11). Applications that send larger pieces of data typically use TCP because the cost of establishing the connection becomes less significant as the amount of data sent over that connection grows.

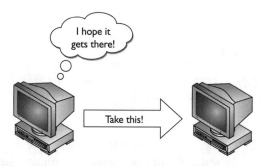

FIGURE 6-11   UDP is a connectionless protocol and sends data without any pre- or post-transmission setup and checking.

Exam Tip

TCP is connection-oriented; UDP is connectionless.

Objective 6.07   # Session Layer Protocols

It's the responsibility of protocols at the session layer to manage the actual connections between communicating systems. TCP/IP networks currently support two distinct Session layer protocols: NetBIOS and Sockets. Microsoft operating systems using TCP/IP employ NetBIOS names to track connections, while traditional Internet functions such as web browsing use Sockets, the traditional TCP/IP Session layer protocol. The way that these two protocols work is radically different, and they require specific configuration and functionality to work properly.

Exam Tip

TCP/IP questions on the Network+ exam generally assume that the client system uses a Microsoft operating system such as Windows 9x or Windows NT.

NetBIOS and Sockets

As you know, NetBIOS manages connections between machines using NetBIOS names—essentially the "computer name." The socket's standard manages connections based on an IP address and a *port number*.

Local Lingo

socket   A *socket* is a combination of a port number and an IP address, uniquely identifying a connection.

The IP address identifies the machine at the other end of the connection, and the port number identifies the function being performed—for example, web browsers use the Hypertext Transfer Protocol (HTTP)—port 80—to transfer web pages between a web server and a browser. The server sends the requested page, using the socket to keep track of the connection.

Table 6-9 lists the most common Application layer protocols in the TCP/IP suite and their corresponding port numbers.

TABLE 6.9	The Most Common Application Layer Protocols		
Application Layer Protocol	**Port(s)**	**Transport Layer Protocol (Typically Used)***	**Description**
HTTP	80	TCP	Web servers use Hypertext Transfer Protocol to send web pages to clients running web browsers such as Internet Explorer or Netscape Navigator.
HTTPS	443	TCP	HTTP over SSL (Secure Sockets Layer) provides a secure, encrypted connection between a web server and a client. Most web browsers display a closed padlock symbol when HTTPS is being used to indicate that a secure connection has been established.
FTP	20 and 21	TCP	The File Transfer Protocol (FTP) transfers data files between servers and clients. FTP uses port 21 for control messages and sends the data using port 20.

TABLE 6.9	The Most Common Application Layer Protocols *(Continued)*		
Application Layer Protocol	**Port(s)**	**Transport Layer Protocol (Typically Used)***	**Description**
TFTP	69	UDP	The Trivial File Transfer Protocol (TFTP) transfers files between servers and clients. Unlike FTP, TFTP requires no user login. Devices that need an operating system but have no local hard disk (for example, diskless workstations and routers) often use TFTP to download their operating systems.
SMTP	25	TCP	The Simple Mail Transfer Protocol (SMTP) sends e-mail messages between clients and servers or between servers.
POP3	110	TCP	The Post Office Protocol version 3 (POP3) enables e-mail client software (for example, Outlook Express, Eudora, Netscape Mail) to retrieve e-mail from a mail server. POP3 does not send e-mail—SMTP handles that function.

TABLE 6.9		The Most Common Application Layer Protocols (Continued)	
Application Layer Protocol	Port(s)	Transport Layer Protocol (Typically Used)*	Description
SNMP	161	UDP	The Simple Network Management Protocol enables network management applications to remotely monitor devices
Telnet	23	TCP	Telnet allows a user to log in remotely and execute text-based commands on a remote host. Techs typically use Telnet to log into UNIX-based systems or managed network devices such as routers and switches.
NetBIOS	137, 138, 139	TCP	Used to route NetBIOS functionality over TCP/IP networks.

*Some Application layer protocols can be used with either TCP or UDP—this table shows the most common implementations to be remembered for the Network+ exam.

Objective 6.08   Name Resolution

If we had to remember the IP address of every computer we wanted to access, we'd probably go nuts! It's much easier to use proper (computer) names, such as DATA1 or web addresses such as "http://www.totalsem.com."

TCP/IP networks require some means of "name resolution" so that people can use names instead of numbers and the computers can determine the IP addresses to which these addresses refer. In a simple network, name resolution is easy; our host can simply broadcast on the network to get the name of a particular system. When routing becomes involved, however, broadcasting is no longer a viable option—remember, routers do not forward broadcasts.

TCP/IP networks have two separate name resolution methods tools—DNS (Domain Name System) and WINS (Windows Internet Name Service)—depending on the types of applications supported on the network. DNS and WINS essentially provide directory assistance for TCP/IP networks. Just as we might call directory assistance to find out someone's phone number, a host on a TCP/IP network contacts a DNS or WINS server to find out the IP address of another host on the network. The two different name services exist because Sockets and NetBIOS applications use names and addresses in different ways.

Sockets, Applications, and DNS

TCP/IP Sockets-based applications, such as web browsers and e-mail client programs, do not require that computers have names in order to function; so when we type in an address such as **www.totalsem.com** or **ftp.usgs.gov**, the Domain Name Service (DNS) standard is used to look up the associated IP address. In very simple terms, DNS is simply an application running on a computer system providing an address look-up service; we may have a DNS server on our local network, or we may use the DNS services available through our Internet Service Provider, the Internet itself, or all three.

A local DNS service (running on, perhaps, an NT server) maintains a database of known addresses, either entered manually or through an association with another DNS server (such as the one provided by our ISP), but the system used by the Internet proper is a bit more complex. Here, DNS management is arranged in a hierarchical structure, with the DNS namespace broken into domains.

A *DNS domain* is a specific branch of the DNS namespace, as shown in Figure 6-12. The DNS namespace starts at the root and this is controlled by InterNIC (Internet Network Information Center). InterNIC does not have to know the name of every computer in the world. Instead, the InterNIC delegates authority for particular subdomains to other organizations. InterNIC contracts with Network Solutions (www.networksolutions.com), for example, to maintain the .com subdomain.

There are a variety of subdomains similar to .com in the Internet world. Table 6-10 shows the common top-level subdomains used in the United States. This first

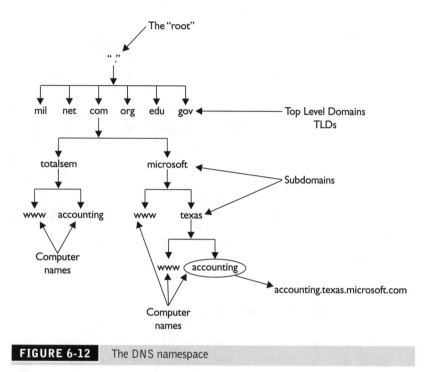

FIGURE 6-12 The DNS namespace

level of subdomains, including the .com, .org, and .net domains, are often referred to as TLDs (top-level domains).

TABLE 6.10 Common Top-Level Subdomains

Top-Level Domain	Refers To
.com	Originally intended for companies involved in commercial activities, but anyone can register a .com address.
.net	Companies involved in providing network access, such as Internet service providers (ISPs), but anyone can register a .net address.

TABLE 6.10	Common Top-Level Subdomains *(Continued)*
Top-Level Domain	**Refers To**
.org	Organizations not involved in commerce, especially nonprofit organizations, but anyone can register a .org address.
.mil	United States military organizations.
.edu	United States educational institutions, especially higher education.
.gov	United States federal government organizations.

DNS Name Resolution

When we enter an address such as www.microsoft.com into our browser, the chain of events used to identify the actual address of the web server is as follows:

1. The host contacts its local DNS server (if present) and requests the IP address, as shown in Figure 6-13.
2. If the local DNS server does not know the address for www.microsoft.com, it will refer to a DNS root server. The root servers, maintained by InterNIC,

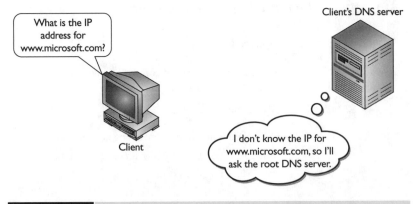

FIGURE 6-13   A host contacts its DNS server

know all of the addresses of the top-level domain DNS servers. The root servers do *not* know the address of www.microsoft.com, but they do know the address of the DNS server in charge of all .com addresses.

3. Our local DNS server refers our request to the DNS server responsible for .com addresses. The .com DNS server identifies the IP address of the microsoft.com DNS server.

4. Our DNS server asks the microsoft.com DNS server for the IP address of www.microsoft.com and then passes this information back to our browser. Figure 6-14 shows the process of resolving a fully qualified domain name into an IP address.

If we don't actually have a local DNS server, the resolution is performed directly by our browser software.

Although this procedure might sound a bit complex, it works very well and provides a great deal of flexibility. Prior to the existence of DNS, every computer

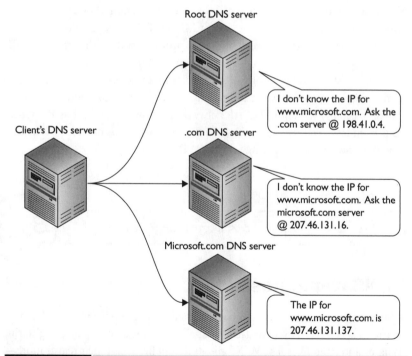

FIGURE 6-14 The host's DNS server resolves a fully qualified domain name using a hierarchy of DNS servers.

that wanted to use domain names had to have a local list—called a HOSTS file— that contained a table of IP addresses and their associated names. Because the HOSTS file changed on a daily basis, network techs had to keep downloading updates from the Internet! You can still use a HOSTS file today if you just have a small number of computers on a local network, but DNS is the way to go for bigger networks.

```
109.54.94.197    stephen.totalsem.com
138.125.163.17   roger.totalsem.com
127.0.0.1        localhost
```

Notice that the name "localhost" appears in the HOSTS file as an alias for the loopback address 127.0.0.1.

NetBIOS Applications and WINS

NetBIOS applications include basically every program that has the word "Microsoft" in front of its name except Microsoft Internet Explorer. Because NetBIOS-based applications can run over protocol suites other than TCP/IP, NetBIOS applications themselves must remain aloof from details like IP addresses that only exist in a single protocol suite; instead, these programs use NetBIOS names instead of sockets when connecting to talk to other computers. The need for compatibility with non-TCP/IP networks prevents NetBIOS-based applications from taking advantage of DNS. NetBIOS applications must find their own way: Windows Internet Naming Service (WINS).

Exam Tip	
WINS servers only exist on Microsoft-based TCP/IP networks.	

WINS Name Resolution

When a WINS client (that is, any machine using WINS) boots up, it sends a message to its specific WINS server (usually specified in the control panel) registering its name and IP address. The WINS clients do not broadcast their registrations— they send them directly to the IP address of their WINS server. After registering with the WINS server, the WINS clients have a means of determining the IP address that corresponds with a particular NetBIOS name; they simply contact the WINS server instead of depending on broadcasts.

WINS performs another vital task on a NetBIOS-based network—ensuring name uniqueness. If a second computer tries to register a duplicate NetBIOS name, the first computer that registered the name will send a message to the second computer, telling it to get off the network. The user of the machine that has its name refused sees the error message shown in Figure 6-15.

In a routed network, NetBIOS can create some interesting problems. A computer's bootup broadcast—"This is my name!"—will not reach machines on the far side of a router, leaving open the possibility of duplicate names on the network. A WINS server solves the problem of duplicate NetBIOS names on a routed network, because it does not allow a machine to register a NetBIOS name that is already in use *anywhere* on the network.

In the absence of a WINS server, a file called LMHOSTS offers another means of resolving names to IP addresses. This is very similar to the way that a HOSTS file functions for DNS host names. Where a WINS server acts much like directory assistance, the LMHOSTS file acts like a little black book of phone numbers. The WINS server provides a centralized database to which every machine can refer, while the LMHOSTS file exists on each machine's individual hard drive and exists for that machine's exclusive use.

```
102.54.94.97    rhino     #PRE #DOM:networking  #net group's DC
102.54.94.102   "appname  \0x14"                #special app server
102.54.94.123   popular   #PRE                  #source server
102.54.94.117   localsrv  #PRE                  #needed for the include
```

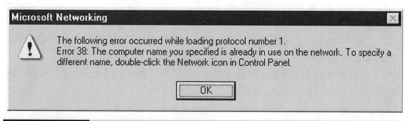

FIGURE 6-15   If a client tries to register a duplicate NetBIOS name, it will receive this message.

Exam Tip

The Network+ exam doesn't require you to know the full syntax of an LMHOSTS file.

Travel Advisory

The LMHOSTS file can resolve NetBIOS names to IP addresses, but it cannot guarantee unique NetBIOS names across a routed network.

WINS servers are the preferred and recommended method for handling NetBIOS name resolution. While LMHOSTS files can be used, they cannot guarantee unique names. In addition, administrators must manually edit the LMHOSTS files of each machine should the network change. Typically, LMHOSTS files are used when a WINS server cannot easily be added to the network because of cost or other factors, and sometimes for remote users dialing in to a network where WINS is not available for remote users for security reasons.

DNS vs. WINS

DNS and WINS serve a similar function on TCP/IP-based networks, providing centralized databases of names and addresses for network hosts to consult, but there are some key differences between them. The DNS namespace is hierarchical, while the NetBIOS namespace used by WINS is flat. Administrators must maintain DNS databases manually, while WINS builds its databases as clients register. The key difference, however, lies in the types of applications that use each service. TCP/IP sockets-based applications (web browsers, e-mail clients, and so forth) use DNS, while Microsoft-based NetBIOS applications (Network Neighborhood, the Save As dialog box in Microsoft Word) use WINS. Table 6-11 summarizes the distinctions between DNS and WINS.

DHCP

With so many settings (IP address, subnet mask, default gateway, DNS servers, WINS servers) to specify, the typical TCP/IP network administrator can spend days properly configuring each host manually. Fortunately, TCP/IP provides a

TABLE 6.11	DNS vs. WINS	
Area of Difference	**DNS**	**WINS**
Used by:	Sockets Applications	NetBIOS Applications
Database built:	Manually	Dynamically
Text file alternative:	HOSTS	LMHOSTS
Name Space:	Hierarchical	Flat

protocol that takes much of the drudgery out of TCP/IP configuration: Dynamic Host Configuration Protocol (DHCP).

DHCP servers distribute settings to other machines on the network, freeing the network tech from the wear and tear on the tennis shoes inflicted by manual configuration. Machines that can handle this automatic configuration are called, appropriately, DHCP clients; most network client software can be set up to accept DHCP (see Figure 6-16).

When a DHCP client boots up, it sends out a broadcast message requesting its configuration. If a DHCP server receives that message, it returns the appropriate values to the DHCP client, as shown in Figure 6-17. The DHCP server keeps track of the addresses it assigns to ensure that it does not assign the same address to two machines.

When using DHCP, network techs may need to check the configuration of specific machines to ensure that the DHCP server has assigned the appropriate configuration. Every operating system that supports TCP/IP will include a utility that displays the current TCP/IP configuration. In Windows 9x, for example, run the WINIPCFG program from a command line to display the screen shown in Figure 6-18.

On a Windows NT or 2000 system, the command IPCONFIG /ALL displays similar information:

```
C:\> ipconfig /all
Windows 2000 IP Configuration
      Host Name . . . . . . . . . . . . : nk-mobile
      Primary DNS Suffix  . . . . . . . :
```

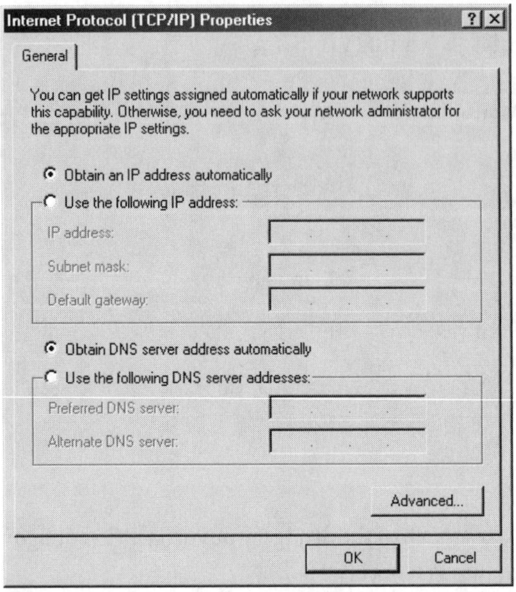

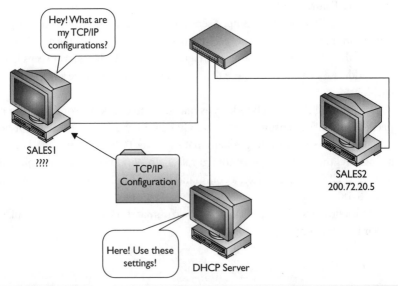

FIGURE 6-16   Windows 2000 set to obtain an IP and DNS address automatically (using DHCP)

FIGURE 6-17   A DHCP server supplying configuration information

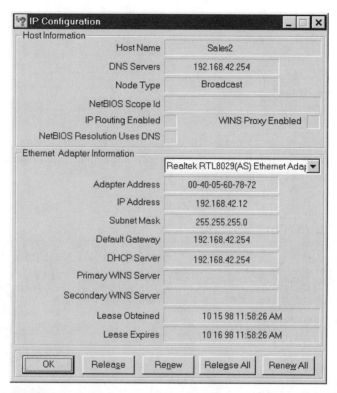

FIGURE 6-18 The Windows 9x WINIPCFG utility

```
        Node Type . . . . . . . . . . . . : Peer-Peer
        IP Routing Enabled. . . . . . . . : No
        WINS Proxy Enabled. . . . . . . . : No
Ethernet adapter Local Area Connection:
        Connection-specific DNS Suffix  . :
        Description . . . . . . . . . . . : Intel 8255x-based PCI Ethernet Adapter
(10/100)
        Physical Address. . . . . . . . . : 00-D0-59-0E-0B-C8
        DHCP Enabled. . . . . . . . . . . : Yes
        Autoconfiguration Enabled . . . . : Yes
        IP Address. . . . . . . . . . . . : 192.168.2.77
        Subnet Mask . . . . . . . . . . . : 255.255.255.0
        Default Gateway . . . . . . . . . : 192.168.2.1
```

```
DHCP Server . . . . . . . . . . : 192.168.2.1
DNS Servers . . . . . . . . . . : 192.168.2.1
                                  192.168.2.1
Primary WINS Server . . . . . . : 192.168.1.10
Lease Obtained. . . . . . . . . : Sunday, October 07, 2001 16:54:00
Lease Expires . . . . . . . . . : Wednesday, October 10, 2001 16:54:00
```

In UNIX, the command used to display this information can vary, but is usually IFCONFIG. Regardless of the operating system, a utility exists that can display the current configuration.

Exam Tip

In pre-DHCP days, other basic protocols were used to provide automatic IP address assignment; these went by the names BOOTP and RARP (the Reverse Address Resolution Protocol). Both these protocols have been superseded by DHCP.

 **Objective 6.09**   **TCP/IP Utilities**

TCP/IP—in all OS flavors—comes with a powerful set of troubleshooting utilities with which all network techs should familiarize themselves.

PING

The PING utility tests connections between two hosts. To test the connection between two hosts, sit at one of them and type in **PING** followed by the name or IP address of the other host. PING uses a special protocol called the *Internet Control Message Protocol* (ICMP) to determine if the other machine can receive the test packet and reply. A host that can be reached will respond back, and the PING command will report success. PING can also be used to test for the availability of Internet-based services using fully qualified domain names, but note that some sites block PING to dissuade their sites from being used for testing—and some corporate Internet security systems will also block PINGs to external sites.

```
C:\>ping 192.168.2.1
Pinging 192.168.2.1 with 32 bytes of data:
Reply from 192.168.2.1: bytes=32 time<10ms TTL=255
Reply from 192.168.2.1: bytes=32 time<10ms TTL=255
Reply from 192.168.2.1: bytes=32 time<10ms TTL=255
Reply from 192.168.2.1: bytes=32 time<10ms TTL=255
Ping statistics for 192.168.2.1:
    Packets: Sent = 4, Received = 4, Lost = 0 (0% loss),
Approximate round trip times in milli-seconds:
    Minimum = 0ms, Maximum =  0ms, Average =  0ms


C:\PING www.google.com
Pinging www.google.com [216.239.33.100] with 32 bytes of data:
Reply from 216.239.33.100: bytes=32 time=270ms TTL=49
Reply from 216.239.33.100: bytes=32 time=271ms TTL=49
Reply from 216.239.33.100: bytes=32 time=270ms TTL=49
Reply from 216.239.33.100: bytes=32 time=271ms TTL=49
Ping statistics for 216.239.33.100:
    Packets: Sent = 4, Received = 4, Lost = 0 (0% loss),
Approximate round trip times in milli-seconds:
    Minimum = 270ms, Maximum =  271ms, Average =  270ms


C:\ping www.madethisup.com
Unknown host www.madethisup.com.
```

Read the messages PING reports back when it cannot reach another machine—they can contain important clues about the source of the problem. If PING cannot turn a name into an IP address, for example, it will report back "Unknown Host" or some similar message, indicating that PING was unable to determine the proper IP address for the name used. (The exact message returned by the PING command varies depending on the operating system.) If PING determines an IP address (either because the tech specified one or because PING resolved it using DNS) but cannot reach the specified address, PING will display a different message, such as "Destination Host Unreachable."

- "Unknown host" means "I don't know the IP address!" (probably you specified an invalid/unused DNS name).
- "Destination Host Unreachable" means "I can't get to that IP address."

(check for possible routing problems—for example, have you specified a default gateway?).

If a (seemingly) valid host is specified but that host doesn't appear to be responding, you will see a sequence similar to the following:

```
C:\> ping 192.168.2.223
Pinging 192.168.2.223 with 32 bytes of data:
Request timed out.
Request timed out.
Request timed out.
Request timed out.
Ping statistics for 192.168.2.223:
    Packets: Sent = 4, Received = 0, Lost = 4 (100% loss),
Approximate round trip times in milli-seconds:
    Minimum = 0ms, Maximum =  0ms, Average =  0ms
```

TRACERT

TRACERT (or TRACEROUTE on some operating systems) traces the route between two hosts. When PING fails, TRACERT can track the problem down to a specific router. TRACERT lists each router between the host and the destination. The listing below shows a trace to the Total Seminars' web server from a machine in the UK:

```
C:\> tracert www.totalsem.com
Tracing route to www.totalsem.com [64.226.214.168]
over a maximum of 30 hops:
  1    <10 ms    <10 ms    <10 ms  192.168.2.1
  2    80 ms     70 ms     80 ms  gyle-du-93.access.demon.net
[194.159.254.93]
  3    80 ms     90 ms     90 ms  tele-core-1-fxp3.router.demon.net
[194.159.254.100]
  4    90 ms     91 ms     90 ms  tele-backbone-1-ge020.router.demon.net
[194.159.252.54]
  5    90 ms    100 ms     90 ms  tele-border-12-e36.router.demon.net
[194.159.36.234]
```

```
 6    90 ms     90 ms     90 ms   sl-gw10-lon-3-0.sprintlink.net
[213.206.130.81]
 7    81 ms     90 ms     90 ms   sl-bb20-lon-8-0.sprintlink.net
[213.206.128.41]
 8   130 ms    131 ms    120 ms   sl-bb21-cop-14-0.sprintlink.net
[213.206.129.38]
 9   130 ms    120 ms    121 ms   sl-bb20-cop-15-0.sprintlink.net
[80.77.64.33]
10   200 ms    200 ms    201 ms   sl-bb21-msq-10-0.sprintlink.net
[144.232.19.29]
11   210 ms    210 ms    211 ms   sl-bb22-rly-15-3.sprintlink.net
[144.232.19.98]
12   210 ms    200 ms    211 ms   sl-bb21-rly-12-0.sprintlink.net
[144.232.7.253]
13   220 ms    211 ms    220 ms   sl-bb20-atl-10-1.sprintlink.net
[144.232.9.198]
14   220 ms    221 ms    220 ms   sl-gw21-atl-9-0.sprintlink.net
[144.232.12.18]
15   220 ms    221 ms    220 ms   sl-il-3-0.sprintlink.net
[160.81.204.10]
16   220 ms    221 ms    220 ms   64.224.0.99
17   230 ms    221 ms    240 ms   totalsem.com [64.226.214.168]
Trace complete.
```

ARP

The ARP utility helps diagnose problems associated with the Address Resolution Protocol (ARP). TCP/IP hosts use the ARP protocol to determine the physical (MAC) address that corresponds with a specific logical (IP) address. The ARP utility, when used with the –a option, displays the IP and MAC addresses currently known by the host:

```
C:\>arp -a
Interface: 192.168.43.5 on Interface 0x1000002
  Internet Address       Physical Address     Type
    192.168.43.2         00-40-05-60-7f-64    dynamic
    192.168.43.3         00-40-05-5b-71-51    dynamic
    192.168.43.4         00-a0-c9-98-97-7f    dynamic
```

NETSTAT

NETSTAT enables the network tech to examine the current sockets-based connections on a specific host:

```
C:\>netstat
Active Connections
    Proto  Local Address        Foreign Address         State
    TCP    brian:1030           BRIAN:1274              ESTABLISHED
    TCP    brian:2666           totalsem.com:pop3       TIME_WAIT
    TCP    brian:2670           totalsem.com:pop3       TIME_WAIT
    TCP    brian:2672           www.cnn.com:80          TIME_WAIT
    TCP    brian:2674           www.nytimes.com:80      ESTABLISHED
    TCP    brian:2460           MARSPDC:nbsession       ESTABLISHED
    TCP    brian:1273           NOTES01:2986            TIME_WAIT
    TCP    brian:1274           BRIAN:1030              ESTABLISHED
```

NBTSTAT

NBTSTAT enables a network tech to check the current NetBIOS name cache, which shows the NetBIOS names and corresponding IP addresses that have been resolved by a particular host:

```
C:\ >NBTSTAT -c
Node IpAddress: [192.168.43.5] Scope Id: []
          NetBIOS Remote Cache Name Table

    Name            Type      Host Address     Life [sec]
    _____

    WRITERS    <1B>  UNIQUE    192.168.43.13      420
    SCOTT      <20>  UNIQUE    192.168.43.3       420
    VENUSPDC   <00>  UNIQUE    192.168.43.13      120
    MIKE       <20>  UNIQUE    192.168.43.2       420
    NOTES01    <20>  UNIQUE    192.168.43.4       420
```

When properly used, NBTSTAT helps network techs diagnose and troubleshoot NetBIOS problems, especially those related to NetBIOS name resolution. NBTSTAT enables the network tech to determine if the WINS server has supplied inaccurate addresses to the WINS client.

Using command-line utilities such as PING, TRACERT, ARP, NETSTAT, and NBTSTAT, an experienced network tech can diagnose most TCP/IP problems quickly and begin working on solutions. If two hosts can PING each other by address but not by name, for example, the wise network tech knows to leave the routers alone and concentrate on name resolution (DNS, WINS) issues instead.

To function effectively as a network tech, learn TCP/IP. Supported by most operating systems, the TCP/IP suite provides excellent tools for integrating multiple operating systems within the same network. Its importance will continue to grow as the Internet continues to increase its importance in both business and everyday life.

CHECKPOINT

✔ **Objective 6.01:** The TCP/IP Protocol Suite   TCP/IP has been around since the 1970s, but it is a dynamic suite of protocols and is still being enhanced today through the use of RFC documents. Underpinning the Internet's functionality has allowed TCP/IP to become universally adopted as networking standard for most computer platforms.

✔ **Objective 6.02:** IP Addressing   The original IP addressing scheme (IPv4) uses a 32-bit address to identify a host address and its network address based on a series of addressing schemes known as IP classes. The associated subnet mask identifies where the boundary between the network and host address lies and also allows us to change this boundary if we wish. Various IP addresses have been defined as nonroutable and so can be used to create "private networks," thus reducing potential WAN configuration issues.

✔ **Objective 6.03:** Subnet Masks and Subnetting   Altering the default subnet mask allows us to subdivide a network into smaller sections, called *subnets*. Subnetting can help with general network management and also traffic management.

✔ **Objective 6.04:** IP Version 6   IPv6 uses a 128-bit addressing scheme to provide a (in effect) limitless supply of IP addresses and is needed because the 32-bit address range of IPv4 is running out of spare addresses. Parts of the Internet are already using IPv6, but it is not generally in use at the desktop yet.

✔ **Objective 6.05: Routing**   You must configure your host PC to know the address of its default router ("default gateway" in TCP/IP-speak); otherwise, it will not be able to communicate with hosts on other networks. Routers also need configuring to know the other networks to which they are able to forward data packets; this can be done manually (static routing) by a network tech, or automatically by the routers "talking" to each other using one of several route discovery protocols (dynamic routing).

✔ **Objective 6.06: Transport Layer Protocols**   The TCP/IP protocol suite supports two main transport layer protocols: TCP (Transmission Control Protocol) provides reliable, connection-oriented packet delivery, whilst UDP (User Datagram Protocol) is a faster, connectionless (unreliable) protocol more often used with applications that send short bursts of data.

✔ **Objective 6.07: Session Layer Protocols**   Session layer protocols manage the connections between devices communicating across a network. Microsoft operating systems using TCP/IP employ NetBIOS names to track connections, while traditional Internet functions such as web browsing use Sockets, the traditional TCP/IP Session layer protocol. The sockets standard uses a combination of IP address and a port address to manage connections; each major TCP/IP-based protocol has its own port address that identifies its functionality—for example, HTTP (the protocol used by browsers to communicate with web servers) uses port 80.

✔ **Objective 6.08: Name Resolution**   Although it's easier for humans to refer to computer systems using computer (NetBIOS) names or fully qualified domain names (such as www.totalsem.com), communication between two systems can only take place if the target machine's IP address is known. In the Microsoft networking world, WINS (Windows Internet Naming Service) is used to resolve IP addresses from NetBIOS computer names, but pure TCP/IP environments (such as the Internet) use a database system called DNS (Domain Name System) to resolve IP addresses from fully qualified domain names, such as www.totalsem.com. DNS uses a hierarchical structure, with separate servers (or groups of servers) managing the resolution of various parts of a domain name.

✔ **Objective 6.09: TCP/IP Utilities**   There are a number of basic TCP/IP and NetBIOS-related utility programs that every tech should know about: PING tests connections between hosts (and can also be used to test the local installation of TCP/IP using the command PING 127.0.0.1 or PING localhost. PING uses a special protocol called the Internet Control Message

Protocol (ICMP). TRACERT (TRACEROUTE) traces the route between two hosts and can be used to identify routing problems. The ARP (Address Resolution Protocol) utility can be used to display the contents of the local ARP cache—this holds a table of IP addresses against their host's known MAC addresses. NETSTAT displays a list of current sockets-based connections active on the local host. NBTSTAT displays the current NetBIOS name cache, which shows the NetBIOS names and corresponding IP addresses that have been resolved by a particular host.

REVIEW QUESTIONS

1. Which of the following correctly defines a TCP/IP host? (Select one answer.)

   A. Any server on a TCP/IP network
   B. Any device on a TCP/IP network that can send or receive data packets
   C. A device on a TCP/IP network that forwards data packets to other networks
   D. A device on a TCP/IP network that resolves names to IP addresses

2. Which of the following is a valid class B host address? (Select one answer.)

   A. 147.28.0.0
   B. 192.168.14.50
   C. 12.12.12.12
   D. 128.14.255.0

3. Which of the following commands would produce the following output? (Select one answer.)

```
Active Connections

  Proto  Local Address     Foreign Address        State
  TCP    brian:1030        BRIAN:1274             ESTABLISHED
  TCP    brian:2666        totalsem.com:pop3      TIME_WAIT
  TCP    brian:2670        totalsem.com:pop3      TIME_WAIT
  TCP    brian:2672        www.cnn.com:80         TIME_WAIT
  TCP    brian:2674        www.nytimes.com:80     ESTABLISHED
  TCP    brian:2460        MARSPDC:nbsession      ESTABLISHED
  TCP    brian:1273        NOTES01:2986           TIME_WAIT
  TCP    brian:1274        BRIAN:1030             ESTABLISHED
```

    A. NBTSTAT

    B. ARP

    C. NETSTAT

    D. TRACERT

4. What is the minimum number of data bits required for subnet addressing to allow a total of four subnets to be created? (Select one answer.)

    A. 1

    B. 2

    C. 3

    D. 4

5. Sue is checking a customer's machine on-site. The machine can access devices on the local network, but nothing else on the WAN. What is the most likely cause of this? (Select one answer.)

    A. The computer has an invalid NetBIOS name.

    B. There is no WINS server running.

    C. The machine does not have a default gateway address set.

    D. The ARP cache is corrupt.

6. What port number does TELNET use? (Select one answer.)

    A. 443

    B. 23

    C. 80

    D. 43

7. Which of the following protocols provides TCP/IP name resolution? (Select two answers.)

    A. WINS

    B. SNMP

    C. TELNET

    D. DNS

8. Jo issues the command PING 127.0.0.1 and receives the reply "Request timed out." What should Jo check first? (Select one answer.)

    A. That the correct default gateway has been specified

    B. The NIC LEDs

C. That DNS is running on the network

D. That TCP/IP has been installed correctly

9. Which of the following will resolve NetBIOS names to IP addresses? (Select two answers.)

   A. A HOSTS file

   B. A WINS server

   C. A router

   D. An LMHOSTS file

10. Which protocol provides automatic host IP address assignment? (Select one answer.)

    A. DHCP

    B. DNS

    C. NetBIOS

    D. BOOTR

REVIEW ANSWERS

1. **B** Any device on a TCP/IP network that can send or receive data packets is called a host.

2. **D** Only D is a valid class B address. Answer A is class B, but has an invalid host address of all zeroes (x.x.0.0).

3. **C** The listing shows the output from the NETSTAT command.

4. **C** Three bits allows a total of six subnets to be created, giving scope for the four we want to create. Two bits (answer B) would only allow two subnets.

5. **C** Since we cannot see past the local network, it sounds like we have a default gateway (router) issue.

6. **B** TELNET uses port 23.

7. **A** **D** WINS and DNS provide name resolution. SNMP is for network management and TELNET provides terminal login functionality.

8. **D** PINGing 127.0.0.1 runs a local loopback test, and if this doesn't work, something's wrong with the installation of TCP/IP on that machine.

9. **B** **D** A WINS server or an LMHOSTS file can be used for NetBIOS name resolution.

10. **A** DHCP—the Dynamic Host Configuration Protocol—provides automatic host IP address assignment.

Wide Area
Networking

	NEWBIE	SOME EXPERIENCE	EXPERT
ETA	3 hours	1 hour	30 minutes

This chapter discusses some of the options available for interconnecting networks to create a Wide Area Network (WAN). It touches on Internet connectivity, but that's not the main focus of this chapter—you *can* link LANs together using the Internet, but that's discussed in more detail in Chapter 10, where we also deal with the security issues that Internet connectivity raises.

WAN interconnectivity boils down to several key issues:

- What sort of speed you want
- What your pattern of usage will be
- What service(s) are available in your area
- How much money you want to spend

The options for interconnecting networks seem to be changing all the time. Historically, the main telecom companies have offered three basic services:

- Use the standard phone lines (analog) or ISDN (digital) for dial-up, on-demand access.
- Rent a circuit that links your sites through the telecom company's equipment for an installation charge and then a fixed monthly/quarterly/yearly fee.
- Rent connectivity on to a switched circuit and be charged for the amount of data you send/receive during the billing periods.

The options available today still fall into these broad categories, but there are many more solutions to your WAN connectivity requirements than ever before. Some of the older technology circuits are still in use today, but, inevitably, they are slowly being replaced by modern alternatives.

Basic Equipment Requirements

Objective 7.01

You should be familiar with the term *router* by now, and you should also know that routers can be used to link sites (networks) together to provide either a direct, point-to-point link or a mesh-type topology with multiple pathways between your network and the destination network. Well, routers and routing *are* one solution, but what are these routers hooking up to for the link between sites? That's a thought! This chapter (naturally!) covers this issue, and it also looks at other, nonrouter-based options.

The basic requirement for wide area connectivity is some device that can interface between the network and the communications circuit in use, as shown in Figure 7-1. Wherever some form of half-decent WAN solution is provided,

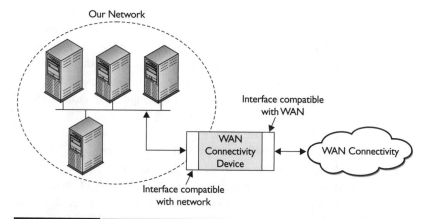

FIGURE 7-1   The generic requirements for a wide area connection

bridging or routing functionality will be needed to provide some form of traffic management to avoid swamping the WAN connection with unnecessary traffic. For most of the options listed here, security and encryption are not usually a major concern because most of the kits discussed can also be purchased with various built-in encryption systems to further protect your data packets from prying eyes. A more general discussion of encryption can be found in Chapter 10.

Figure 7-1 shows a generic WAN connection; the interface between the WAN unit to the network is likely to be simply a connector that matches the existing network topology—for example, a BNC or RJ-45 connector on an Ethernet device or perhaps a pair of fiber connectors. The interface to the communications circuit will depend on what that communications circuit is—it might be just an RJ-11/telecom phone connector or a specialized interface that conforms to a specific datacomm standard.

As soon as the interconnectivity solution strays away from the basic phone-type solution, it is *very* important that you understand what type of interface is required; otherwise, you may be left with a very expensive kit that won't connect at all!

So let's have a look at how you might connect your networks together.

 **Objective 7.02** # PSTN—The Analog Telephone System

The use of dial-up services (phone circuits) for datacommunications is a well-established practice. The two services generally available fall into two easy-to-remember categories: analog and digital.

The public switched telephone network (PSTN—sometimes also known as the plain old telephone system, or POTS) is capable of carrying data, but since the system was originally designed for (analog) voice traffic only, the maximum bandwidth for data is quite limited, even though the systems in most countries now use digital technology for almost everything except the wire between the exchange and your phone socket (sometimes called the *local loop*). Figure 7-2 shows a typical modem setup.

To connect a computer system to the PSTN requires a modem: a device that can convert a computer's digital signals into a PSTN-compatible analog signal (perform MOdulation) and do the reverse for incoming signals (perform DEModulation). Apart from laptop computers that often use PC-card–based modems, most PCs have their modems connected to one of their serial ports or plugged in as an internal card. Figure 7-3 shows an internal and an external modem. The hardware alone doesn't make the network connection, of course, but every modern operating system has built-in support. Figure 7-4 shows the network configuration for a Windows 98 system.

The main limitation of a configuration that uses a modem and serial port for a network connection is the speed. The two current fastest standards for modems are V.90 and V.92, and if your modem is capable of supporting these standards, then under the *best conditions* you will get an *asymmetric* connection (different speeds in either direction), *receiving* at 56 kilobits per second and *transmitting* at 33.6 (V.90) or 48 (V.92) kilobits per second. It's also worth remembering that for a V.9*x* link to work properly, the kit at the main end of the link (usually your ISP, but this would need to be in your computer room if you are setting up for remote access) isn't just another V.9*x* modem—special equipment is needed. If you use a pair of V.9*x* modems to link systems, they will slow down to around 33.6 kilobits per second (to transmit and receive).

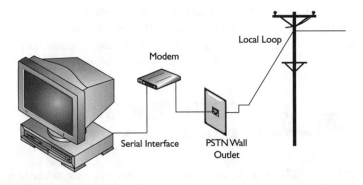

Local Loop

Modem

Serial Interface

PSTN Wall Outlet

FIGURE 7-2 Typical modem setup

FIGURE 7-3   Internal and external modems

Modem Performance

As a rough guide, you divide the modem speed (in kilobits per second) by 10 to
get the approximate throughput in bytes per second. So a 56K link will average

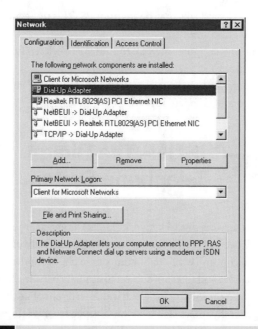

FIGURE 7-4   Windows 98 network configuration showing modem support
(Dial-Up Adapter)

around 5.6 kilobytes per second, or Kbps (actually a bit more when you take data compression into consideration)—not the kind of bandwidth that you'd want to use as a wide area link for a business network with even just a few people on it.

Of course, modems are widely used for remote access to systems by, for example, home workers (teleworkers), but in this case, the limited bandwidth available for a single user is not such an issue, and, of course, setting up a system to accept modem dial-in links is cheap, flexible, and not fixed to a particular remote location.

Under some circumstances, in some countries, local telephone calls are free, and this makes using a modem for local dial-up users very attractive (if the users can live with the 56K bandwidth), but for a permanent connection between distant sites, the cost can be frightening, and other options are definitely worth considering (they'll probably be faster, too!).

PSTN Summary

- The maximum speed under the best conditions is 56 kilobits per second (for receiving data)—probably not suitable for WAN links.
- PSTN is ideal for remote access by a mobile workforce if high bandwidth is not required.
- The cost of (local) calls may be free, but PSTN is not generally suitable for permanent connections.
- PSTN requires support software to route network traffic through the modem link.
- V.9x standards require special equipment at the main end of the link to provide the top supported speed.

Objective 7.03

ISDN—The Digital Telephone System

The integrated services digital network (ISDN) has been around for some time and has long been a favorite for low-end bandwidth network connections, as well as standard telephony (with ISDN-compatible phones and a switchboard kit). Being digital in nature, and thus not subject to as many bandwidth-crushing influences (such as noise on the line or electrical interference) as the analog phone system, ISDN generally offers stable 64 kilobits per second (Kbps) performance for received *and* transmitted data. Many ISDN circuits are run over pre-existing (originally analog) copper phone lines, and the quality of these lines from your office to the central office (CO) is a limiting factor in determining whether ISDN will actually work from your premises; the guideline is that you must be within 18,000 feet (about 3.4 miles, or 5.5 km) of the nearest CO for ISDN to work.

Local Lingo

central office (CO)   The local premises used as a customer connection point by a telecom or data services company—for example, a local telephone exchange.

If you place an order for ISDN, the service provider will perform a survey (possibly just an electronic check down the line) to see whether you're in range.

We've carefully avoided the word *modem* in this section because, although the basic ISDN communications kit *looks* like a modem, it doesn't do any MO-ing or DEM-ing (see the previous section). ISDN is *already* in a digital (not analog) format, and it makes connections through a terminal adapter (TA).

Exam Tip

Many techs refer to ISDN modems, but the correct term is *terminal adapter (TA)*. In reality, a TA does sort of the same job as a modem—it connects you to the communications system—and, so in general-speak, we'd let you get away with "ISDN modem," but not for the Network+ exam, please!

ISDN Bridges and Routers

Because it's more data friendly than PSTN, more data-oriented devices are available for ISDN; in addition to a basic internal or external TA, you can purchase ISDN bridges and routers (Figure 7-5). Some even have a built-in hub so that interfacing to your LAN is as simple as plugging in a patch cable. Many workgroup ISDN routers also have a built-in DHCP server so that a peer-to-peer network (no NT/2000 server to run DHCP) can have all of its IP addresses assigned automatically!

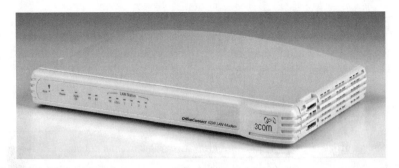

FIGURE 7-5   ISDN TA/router

Basic Rate Interface (BRI)

There are numerous packages available for ISDN (they vary from supplier to supplier and from country to country), but the standard service is called Basic Rate Interface (BRI) and is provided to the user as two 64K data channels, known as the *Bearer*, or B, channels, plus a low-speed (16 kilobits per second) channel that's used for call setup, control and other signaling: the *Delta*, or D, channel. For this reason, Basic Rate Interface is sometimes described as 2B+D.

An ISDN TA might support datacommunications using only one B channel (see Figure 7-6), providing a 64K connection (the other channel could be used at the same time for an ISDN phone), but some can *aggregate* the two B channels to provide a 128K link—provided the kit at the other end (your other office or your Internet service provider) also supports channel aggregation, or bonding (see Figure 7-7). However, remember that each B channel counts as one phone call for charging purposes, and so if your ISDN package doesn't offer unlimited connection time, you will be billed for *two* calls every time you use your 128K link.

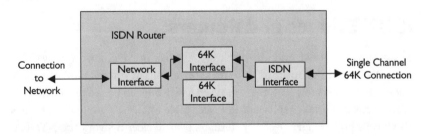

FIGURE 7-6   ISDN router using one channel

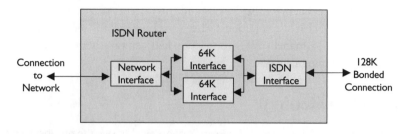

FIGURE 7-7   ISDN channel bonding

Local Lingo

channel aggregation   Channel aggregation is also known as bonding, which stands for Bandwidth On Demand INternetworking (INteroperability) Group.

The ISDN Network Terminator

In the United States, the user must provide the local interface to the ISDN service; this is called a *network terminator*, or *NT-1*, and is built into most ISDN communications equipment. In Europe (for ISDN2e, the European 2B+D service) NT-1 is provided by the telecom company as a wall-mounted box with two RJ45 data outlets, allowing two pieces of equipment to be connected.

Primary Rate Interface (PRI)

Primary Rate Interface provides multiple B channels—the most common configuration in the United States is 23 x 64K B channels + 1 x 64K D channel (23B+D), providing a bandwidth of 1.544 megabits per second. European PRI—known as ISDN30e—can be configured with any number of channels between 8 and 30, with 30B+D providing a bandwidth of 2 megabits per second.

Using ISDN

ISDN-related data technology has been around for some time and is considered stable and mature, making it a popular choice for business use, even when other options are available (see the next sections of this chapter). For general networking, Primary Rate Interface is widely used for interoffice connections (WAN links) and for "fat pipes" between businesses and the Internet service provider (see Figure 7-8). ISDN has also traditionally been used as a fallback service that kicks in if the (faster) permanent WAN connection between two sites fails, and *ISDN fallback* is built into many WAN bridges.

Circuit Switching

ISDN is a dial-up (circuit switching) service: you need to dial the number of the host system to which you want to connect, every time, perform the data transfer, and then close the connection. Although this sounds like a bit of a pain, ISDN dial-up service is very fast (a fraction of a second). It also allows you to dial into different systems according to your need (unlike a fixed WAN link between two sites), and this makes it ideal for connecting computer systems to commercial services, such as printers and graphics design studios, where you can establish a direct PC-to-PC (or Macintosh, or whatever's in the studio) link and upload your (usually very large!) artwork and layouts.

Local Lingo

circuit switching The principle of establishing a connection (circuit) through a communications service, sending and receiving data, and then closing the call.

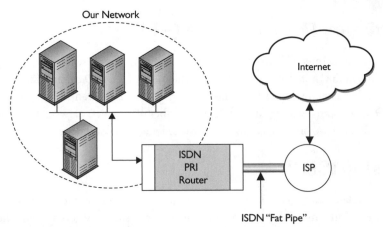

FIGURE 7-8 A Primary Rate Interface fat pipe

Because ISDN is classed as telephony technology, costs can be high if calls are charged by the second/minute/unit, but many service providers now offer flat-rate packages. More recently (especially in Europe), the delay in rolling out more IT-friendly and low-cost services, such as ADSL, has led to widespread use of ISDN for home systems, too.

ISDN Spoofing

If you are *not* on a flat-rate fee scheme, do make sure that your ISDN setup is con-figured correctly. Many network protocols send out regular broadcasts, and if your ISDN kit keeps establishing a link with another site to pass on these broadcasts, you will end up with a huge bill! Many ISDN routers support *spoofing*, where they pretend to establish a link (to keep the broadcasting kit happy), but they don't actually do so (see Figure 7-9).

ISDN Summary

- ISDN is a stable technology providing digital data and telephony ser-vices.
- Basic Rate ISDN (BRI) provides a 64K or 128K data circuit with two bearer (B) channels for data and one delta (D) channel for signaling and control.

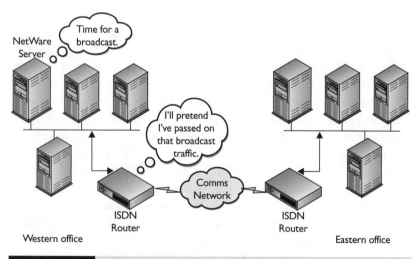

FIGURE 7-9   ISDN spoofing

- Primary Rate ISDN (PRI) provides a 23B+D, 1.544MB (up to 30B+D, 2MB in Europe) circuit for faster connectivity.
- ISDN is a dial-up service, and calls may be charged per second/minute/unit just like regular phone calls.
- ISDN is widely used for low-bandwidth WAN connectivity, as a fallback for faster links, and as a dial-up service between businesses.

Objective 7.04 Fixed-Line (Always-on) Services

If dial-up service doesn't sound like it will suit your situation—either because the call charges would be too high or you want more bandwidth—then you will be looking to rent a fixed line (a leased line) between sites. There are a number of (old-technology-to-new technology) options, which you can choose among according to your needs.

Packet-Switching Circuits

When you use a packet-switching circuit, you rent space on a WAN owned by someone else (usually a telecom company) that's then used to carry your data between sites. Since the WAN won't usually run all the way to your premises, the telecom company will provide lines between local access points (the central office or local exchange) and your premises. The distance between the two COs sometimes defines what is known as the charging distance, and this is used to calculate your rental bill. Some packet-switching options charge by the amount of data transmitted across the network instead.

Although with a packet-switching circuit, from your perspective you appear to have a dedicated, always-on, WAN link between sites, your data is actually mixed with that from all the other customers using the packet-switched network. This may seem like a bit of a mess and also a security risk, but your equipment is set up to establish a *permanent virtual circuit (PVC)* between your site and the CO, giving the appearance that your site is the only one on the network (see Figure 7-10).

As you might gather from the name, data packets are switched (routed) round the network in an arbitrary fashion, ultimately ending up at the correct destination. The route that individual packets take varies according to numerous factors, but all of the packets eventually (we hope—see the following discussion) arrive at

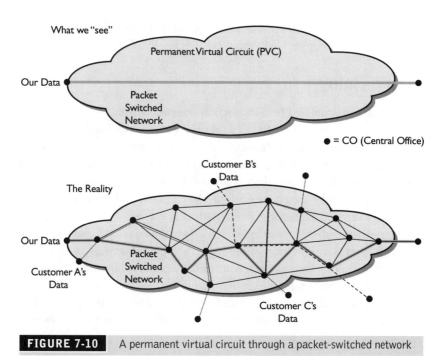

FIGURE 7-10 A permanent virtual circuit through a packet-switched network

their destinations. Although we are concentrating on data links here, the standard telephone system is actually a packet-switching network, as most voice traffic is carried today as digital data.

Some packet-switching networks use fairly old technology and run at speeds of only 9.6 kilobits per second, but this is more than adequate for simple requirements such as linking a network of cash machines to a central location. Obviously, a WAN link running at 9.6K is going to be a bit slow, but there are packet-switching circuits that offer greater speed, as you'll see later.

X.25

One of the oldest commercial packet-switching networks (from the 1970s) goes by the name X.25. This is a connection-oriented (reliable data delivery) analog system that can carry data, interfacing with your networking equipment through a device known as a *Packet Assembler/Disassembler* (PAD). X.25 is generally used for terminals and other low-end devices, and a PAD typically has a standard serial (RS232) interface, not a LAN connection, although X.25 solutions are available for link speeds up to 2 megabits per second. The X.25 spec operates at layers 1 through 3 of the OSI model (physical, data link, and network).

Frame Relay

Frame relay is a simplified (still connection oriented), digital version of X.25. It provides no built-in error control (it works at the OSI physical and data link layers only), and so external, higher-level (OSI layer) protocols are used to ensure data integrity. Because the transmission protocols are stripped down to the basics (packets may make it to their destination, or they may not), frame relay is faster than X.25 and can be used successfully for WAN (data) and voice applications; speeds up to around 50 megabits per second are available.

One other main difference between X.25 and frame relay is that with X.25, your data packets are sent individually across the switched network to their destination. With frame relay, data packets are mixed together (multiplexed) for transmission, and this maximizes the use of available bandwidth, further contributing to frame relay's high performance (see Figure 7-11). Many of the general high-speed circuits used for WAN interconnectivity today are based on frame-relay technology.

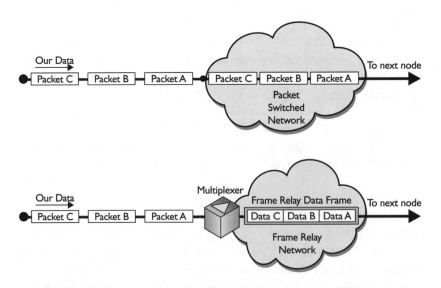

FIGURE 7-11   A frame-relay network multiplexes data packets to maximize bandwidth

Exam Tip
Frame relay networks use multiplexed data to maximize bandwidth. Packet-switching networks send every data packet individually.

Quality of Service

Unlike X.25, frame relay provides a Quality of Service (QoS) facility, which simply means that the bandwidth a connection gets depends on what that connection is doing. If it's sending general data, this data may be carried at normal speed, but a videoconferencing link can be given greater bandwidth to ensure the best possible link (sound and video) quality.

At the low-speed end, frame-relay networks can be accessed via ISDN, and this allows for *switched virtual circuits,* where you choose a specific destination for the task at hand. In fact, if you have ISDN for connecting to an Internet service provider, you may find that when you dial into the ISP, your data is routed to the ISP via a frame-relay network owned by your telecom provider.

ATM

Asynchronous transfer mode (ATM) is the technology used for modern, digital, switched networks. ATM was developed from the technology first implemented on digital voice circuits and, in fact, it is also possible (but expensive!) to implement a "to-the-desktop" ATM LAN using ATM NICs and hubs, with standard speeds of 25, 50, 155, and 622 megabits per second, the latter using fiber media. The performance of ATM WAN links varies according to the carrying media, but speeds into the gigabits per second are available.

ATM also supports Quality of Service to provide optimized bandwidth on demand, but its main claim to fame is its use of very small, fixed-size data packets—called *ATM cells*—only 53 bytes in total (48 bytes of data) per packet (Figure 7-12). When originally implemented for carrying voice traffic, the loss of the odd cell in transit wasn't a problem because 48 bytes of digitized speech is barely a click and won't be noticed by the listener. When it comes to data, however, losing the odd 48 bytes of a database would be a tad worrisome, and this was one of the main challenges for ATM data network designers. Thankfully, they got it right, and the whole thing works, delivering all the packets safely, with control protocols in place to ensure reliability.

Header: 5 bytes	Payload: 48 bytes

FIGURE 7-12   ATM cell—that's it!

Local Lingo

cell switching   The switching technology used on ATM networks with very small data packets (cells).

ATM can easily be bridged to existing networks and is very popular for high-performance WAN connectivity.

The small packet size implemented in ATM can cause problems under some circumstances, where larger data packets (such as those used by protocols such as IPX/SPX and TCP/IP) are fragmented for transmission, but modern ATM bridges and routers have mostly overcome these problems, using various techniques to accommodate the fragmentation.

Switching Circuits Summary

The basic points to remember about switching circuits are:

- Switching circuits typically provide an always-on connection between sites and are very popular for WAN links.
- Some services provide only a point-to-point *permanent virtual circuit* between two sites, but others also support a *switched virtual circuit*, which allows you to choose the destination, as required.

Modern switched networks, based on frame-relay and ATM technology, are capable of providing high-speed WAN connectivity.

General Fixed-Line Services

Sometimes we don't worry about the nature of the network providing our WAN connectivity—we just want to pay for (lease) a fixed bandwidth between sites and have it installed; whether our data goes via copper, fiber, ATM, or frame relay, we don't care, as long as everything works.

Many telecom companies and WAN solution providers offer a generic connection to their service, and one of the most popular options is a 1.544-megabits-per-second circuit (24 x 64K channels) known as a T-1 (or DS-1) carrier. T-1 provides a service akin to Primary Rate Interface and often uses the same interface equipment. Many of the services behind the scenes are, in fact, based on frame-relay technology, although ATM is becoming increasingly popular. The following table lists the two most popular T-carriers (see if you can work out which is the most expensive to lease).

Carrier	Bandwidth	Channels
T-1 (DS-1)	1.544 megabits per second	24
T-3 (DS-3)	44.736 megabits per second	672

In Europe, a different carrier system is available, offering other levels of performance. The principle is the same, though: multiple 64K channels are provided according to your needs and budget.

Carrier	Bandwidth	Channels
E-1	2.048 megabits per second	32
E-3	34.368 megabits per second	512

To connect to your T- or E-circuit, you use a pair of devices known as a Channel Service Unit (CSU) and a Data Service Unit (DSU). Often, but not always, these items are built into one module, providing a CSU/DSU, which, for all intents and purposes, can look just like a humble modem. Keeping things simple, the CSU provides the interface to the network, while the DSU provides an interface to the T-x or E-x carrier circuit. The actual interface to your T-x/E-x connection will depend on how the service is provided: it may be a copper or fiber connection.

Travel Advisory

Some information sources state that the designator **T-*x*** is for copper-based circuits, and the designator **DS-*x*** for fiber. Technically, the term *T-x* refers to the *copper transmission medium,* while *DS-x* refers to the *service* rather than the medium, but these terms frequently are used interchangeably.

SONET and SDH

The Synchronous Optical NETwork (SONET) is an American National Standards Institute (ANSI) standard for data transmission over optical fiber, and it's very popular for telecommunications and WAN connectivity and with Internet service providers. SONET is also used extensively for metropolitan area networks (MANs) because of its ability to carry a mix of services, including: data, voice, and video. SONET is widely used in the United States, Canada, and Japan, and it provides a range of services (speeds), known as *Optical Carrier (OC) levels* (see Table 7-1).

The European equivalent of SONET is the Synchronous Digital Hierarchy (SDH). There are some minor speed differences between SONET and SDH at the

TABLE 7.1	OC-*x* Carrier Speeds
OC-1	51.84 megabits per second
OC-3	155.52 megabits per second
OC-12	622.08 megabits per second
OC-24	1.244 gigabits per second
OC-48	2.488 gigabits per second
OC-192	10 gigabits per second
OC-256	13.271 gigabits per second
OC-768	40 gigabits per second

lower end, but the European SDH speed standard STM-1 closely maps to OC-3, which also closely maps to the 155-megabits-per-second ATM standard, making OC-3 a very popular connectivity option because it fits so many requirements.

Exam Tip
You don't have to remember all of the OC-*x* speeds, but it *is* worth noting that OC-3 is a popular option.

SONET backbones form part of many of the connectivity options we have discussed here, so your PSTN voice traffic, ISDN, ATM, T-1, or switched-circuit data may well make its way toward its ultimate destination via a SONET/SDH pathway (see Figure 7-13). Some top-end service providers can also provide you with a direct, point-to-point SONET connection (so-called private SONET) between offices, using their main SONET network to create a permanent virtual circuit.

Other WAN Services

This chapter has covered the mainstream wide area networking connectivity options, starting with the slowest first. Other wide area services are also available

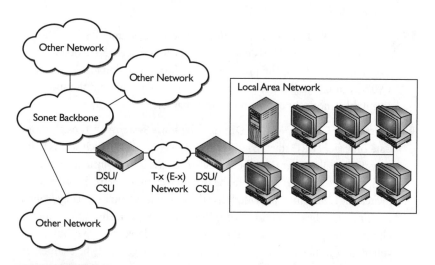

FIGURE 7-13   SONET backbones often carry other data services between destinations.

if you have the need, the business case, and the cash: services such as satellite links and national wireless networks. Although the focus of the Network+ exam is on wide area networking, to link LANs together, remember that in the real world there are often wide area requirements that don't need 10+ megabits per second WAN performance; we've already mentioned cash machines, and we can add to that list other services such as the updating of stock levels overnight in retail stores, the transmission of financial information, and the transmission of data from traffic monitoring stations. If you don't need to send megabytes of data instantaneously, some of the slower, and therefore cheaper, wide area networking options may be perfectly suitable.

CHECKPOINT

✔ **Objective 7.01: Basic Equipment Requirements** At the most fundamental level, your wide area networking kit must provide two interfaces: one to your network and one to the communications circuit you are using for the WAN link. The equipment may also do other things, such as compress and encrypt data, and will almost certainly provide routing or bridging functionality.

✔ **Objective 7.02: PSTN—The Analog Telephone System** PSTN is the least attractive option for a WAN connection due to its speed: 56 kilobits per second on a good day, and probably only 33.6K if you don't have the full V.90/92 setup. For dial-in remote users, it is a viable option if the speed is acceptable (more about this in the next chapter).

✔ **Objective 7.03: ISDN—The Digital Telephone System** Although Basic Rate Interface (BRI) starts by offering only a 64K link—which seems to be only marginally better than the PSTN—this 64K is pretty much guaranteed, and you can also aggregate the two 64 B channels actually provided to create a 128K link—provided that the terminal adapter or bridge/router equipment at the other end of your WAN link supports this option, too. Flat-rate charging options for ISDN also make it look attractive, but if you're not on such a scheme, remember that you'll generally be charged by the second/minute/unit for each channel in use, and that incorrect network setups can make a lot of regular calls just to exchange routing and other information, so check your kit's ability to block these regular calls using a

procedure called spoofing. Primary Rate Interface (PRI) offers up to 23
(30 in Europe) B channels and so can offer a bandwidth of up to 1.544
megabits per second (2 megabits in Europe). PRI ISDN is widely used for
interoffice links and connectivity to ISPs where there's need for a "big"
connection (well, bigger than BRI anyway!).

✔ **Objective 7.04: Fixed-Line (Always-on) Services**   The fixed (leased) line
options are best suited to site-to-site links, and they generally provide a
packet-switched, permanent virtual circuit between sites through the communications company's. The old, analog X.25 system is not designed for
today's high-speed demands, but it is still suitable for slow-speed links and
is mainly used for applications that don't transfer a lot of information.
Frame-relay, switched networks, on the other hand, can provide decent
bandwidth and are often used for WAN connectivity. ATM technology also
provides a high-speed, switched option using small, 53-byte data packets
called cells. Among the most popular switched solutions are those defined
by the designations T-1 and T3 (E-1 and E-3 in Europe); these provide
connectivity at 1.544 and 44.736 megabits per second, respectively (2 and
34.368 megabits in Europe). The SONET (SDH in Europe) standards provide very high bandwidth and are generally used by telecom carriers and
network service providers to form their main backbones. SONET speeds
are referred to as Optical Carrier (OC) levels, with OC-3 (155 megabits
per second) being a very popular choice.

REVIEW QUESTIONS

1. Which of the following provides the fastest service? (Select one answer.)

    A. BRI ISDN
    B. PRI ISDN
    C. PSTN
    D. V.92

2. John wants to connect his laptop computer to an ISDN port. Which of the
   following will probably be suitable? (Select one answer.)

    A. V.90 modem
    B. V.92 modem
    C. NIC
    D. A terminal adapter

3. You have been asked to provide a wide area network between two offices. The primary objective is to provide data connectivity, and a secondary objective is to allow your videoconferencing system to receive optimum bandwidth. Your proposed solution is a 128K BRI using channel bonding and ISDN routers. What goals does this solution meet? (Select one answer.)

    A. Both the primary and the secondary objectives
    B. The primary objective only
    C. Neither of the above

4. Which of the following applies to an ATM WAN? (Select all that apply.)

    A. The ATM WAN uses packet-switching technology.
    B. ATM offers a QoS facility.
    C. The WAN supports kilobyte-sized, variable-length packets.
    D. ATM uses small, fixed-length data packets called cells.

5. Which of the following services provides the greatest throughput? (Select one answer.)

    A. T-1
    B. V.90
    C. OC-3
    D. E-3

6. Which of the following is not an optical WAN standard? (Select one answer.)

    A. X.25
    B. STM-1
    C. SONET
    D. SDH

7. What type of interface is required to connect to a T-1 circuit? (Select one answer.)

    A. X.25
    B. PAD
    C. 2B+D
    D. CSU/DSU

8. Harry has just been asked why the company's telecomm bill for the WAN link is so high, and he has noticed that the bill includes a significant number of short-duration dial-up calls. What is the most likely cause? (Select one answer.)

A. The ATM interface is faulty.

B. The V.90 modem has been set to dial a not-in-service number.

C. ISDN spoofing is not configured correctly.

D. Harry has set the wrong ATM frame format.

9. What is the maximum distance allowed to the CO for a BRI link? (Select one answer.)

A. 100 meters

B. 2,048 meters

C. 1,800 feet

D. 18,000 feet

10. Which of the following is a packet-switching network? (Select one answer.)

A. ISDN

B. ATM

C. X.25

D. V.90

REVIEW ANSWERS

1. **B** Primary Rate Interface provides the fastest service: BRI = 128K max, PRI = 1.544 megabits max, PSTN = 56K, V.92 = 56K.

2. **D** John needs an ISDN Terminal Adapter.

3. **B** The ISDN connection will provide connectivity but no Quality of Service and so will not give any form of priority to the videoconferencing data.

4. **B** **D** ATM provides QoS and also uses small packets called cells.

5. **C** OC-3 = 155.52 megabits per second, T-1 = 1.544 megabits, V.90 = 56K, E-3 = 34.268 megabits.

6. **A** X.25 is provided over a copper wire circuit, and so it not an optical standard.

7. **D** A CSU/DSU combination is required for a T-x interconnection.

8. **C** Since the WAN link is clearly working, all of the answers that relate to

configuration problems (A, B, and D) are unlikely to be true. In any case, since we're talking about a dial-up problem, we're not looking at an ATM issue since we're not even using ATM (A and D), and if we were dialing a not-in-service number with a V.90 modem (answer B), we would not be charged.

9. **D** ISDN works only if you are within 18,000 feet of the nearest CO.

10. **C** X.25 is a packet-switching network.

Remote
Access

	NEWBIE	SOME EXPERIENCE	EXPERT
ETA	3 hours	2 hours	1 hour

Local area networks (LANs) provide organizations with the services essential for today's business needs: access to important databases, e-mail, printers, fax machines, and so on—all of the stuff needed to get a job done. In the vast majority of organizations, most of the employees are office-based and access the LAN from a desktop computer. Some people, however, need access to the LAN no matter where they are working—at home, in an airport, or from a hotel room. In particular, they need access to the company's data, and most people want to be able to access the network exactly as though they were sitting at a local system on the LAN. Chapter 7 touched on the hardware needed and service options available for WAN connections; this chapter covers remote user access options in more detail, including the software side of things.

Objective 8.01   Defining Remote Connectivity

The L in LAN stands for "local," and in the classic LAN all of the systems (clients and servers) are said to be local to each other—all connected together via some type of *dedicated* connection, usually a cable. A remote system, in contrast, accesses your LAN via a connection that your organization does not own—for example, a telephone line.

Dial-up remote access requires two devices: a client and server (see Figure 8-1). The remote access server has a dedicated connection to a LAN and some type of modem or modem equivalent. It has special software that works with the modem to listen for rings, authenticate the user, and provide network access. The remote access client has a modem or equivalent, plus software to enable it to link into the server.

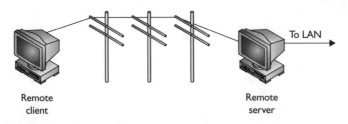

FIGURE 8-1   Remote client and server

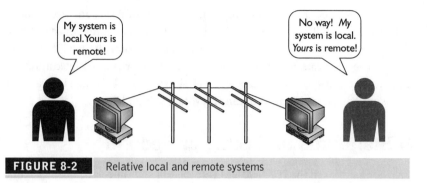

FIGURE 8-2   Relative local and remote systems

Remote or Local?

If you have a remote access server and a remote access client, which is local and which is remote? Two different definitions exist. Many people define the terms "remote" and "local" in a relative way, from their own viewpoint: their local system is the one with them, and the remote system is the one elsewhere (back at the office, perhaps). For remote access terminology, however, the office-based server is always the local system and the users *out there somewhere* are always remote. This second definition is the preferred way to define a local and remote system, but you should be prepared for Network+ to throw questions at you from either perspective (see Figure 8-2).

Objective 8.02   Dial-In Remote Access

This section expands on the communications services options discussed in Chapter 7. By far the most popular option for remote access communications is a dial-up service—the PSTN or ISDN. Although these options only provide an access speed of around 56/64 Kbps, the equipment is cheap and the service is flexible because all you need to use it is a compatible telephone outlet wherever you happen to be. (ISDN may be a bit more restrictive in this respect, as not every hotel or airport provides ISDN services to its customers.)

Client Hardware Requirements

In order to use a dial-in remote access server, your PC, notebook, or whatever will need a compatible (ISDN) TA or (PSTN) modem. The speed standards (protocols) for ISDN are fixed, but modems come in a variety of shapes and sizes—internal, external, USB, serial, and so forth—and support different standards. Fortunately, all the important modem standards (protocols) have been well defined over the years and are now managed by the International Telecommunications Union-Telecommunication (ITU-T, sometimes abbreviated to just ITU) to ensure that a Brand X modem can always talk to Brand Y.

V Standards and Bits per Second

I already mentioned the ITU V.90 and V.92 (56 Kbps) protocols in Chapter 7, but there are three other (non speed-related) protocols that all decent modems will support:

- V.42 for error checking
- V.42bis for data compression
- MNP5, which defines error correction and data compression protocols

It can almost be taken for granted that a modern modem will support these protocols, and it's pretty much essential that they be used both to maximize throughput and to cope with data transmission errors. Fortunately, once you have a modem that supports these protocols, they are generally enabled by default, so there's nothing you have to do to switch them on.

One of the most misused datacomm terms is "baud rate," or "baud," often incorrectly used to refer to the operating speed of a modem.

Exam Tip
The correct way to describe the speed of a modern modem is in bits per second (bps), not baud.

For modems, the baud rate and the bps *are* the same until the data transfer between the modems surpasses 2,400 baud. After this point, the technical definition for *baud* does not apply to the way the data signals are processed (modulated) to yield higher throughputs, and the term "bits per second" takes over. The Network+ exam doesn't want you to worry about the ins and outs of this issue (that's why I've kept it simple here); just remember it's *bits per second* and not baud.

In order for two modems to run at their fastest, it is critical that they modulate signals in the same fashion. The two modems must also query, or negotiate with, each other in order to determine the fastest speed of each modem. The ITU-T (V.)

standards define a series of common speeds (over the years getting faster and faster), and a pair of modems will negotiate the best common standard they both support. The most common speed standards are as follows:

- **V.22**   1,200 bps
- **V.22bis**   2,400 bps
- **V.32**   9,600 bps
- **V.32bis**   14,400 bps
- **V.34**   28,000/33,600 bps
- **V.90/V.92**   57,600 bps

Serial Port Speeds

Many people get a little confused on the concept of port speed and modem speed. All versions of Windows give you the opportunity to set the port speed, which is the speed of the data between the *serial port of your PC and the modem*—not between the modems. As a rule, always set this speed to 115,200 bps, regardless of the capabilities of your modem, to allow for the most efficient transfer of data. Setting a slower speed is likely to result in slower modem performance.

The Serial Port Interface

Just a quick note here—the chip or chipset functionality that makes up the electronics of a serial port is known as a Universal Asynchronous Receiver/ Transmitter, or UART (see Figure 8-3). The original IBM PC (and many clone machines) used a design based on an Intel UART chip known as the 8250. The 8250 UART runs out of steam very quickly above 9,600 bits per second, and a newer chip design based on an Intel chip called the 16550 is now used for all modern applications. If you happen to stumble across an old PC and you set its modem serial port to 115,200 bps, Windows will probably let you do this, but modem performance will be dire—if it works at all. Faced with this problem, all you can do is either install a new serial port card (with a 16550-based design) or use an internal modem, which will include its own serial port circuitry. If you think you have encountered this problem, the modem icon in the Windows Control Panel includes a diagnostics option that tells you your UART type.

Windows Modems or *Soft Modems*

There is a breed of low-cost modem called a Windows modem (Winmodem) or soft modem. These units do *not* have a UART, and instead rely on the PC's processor

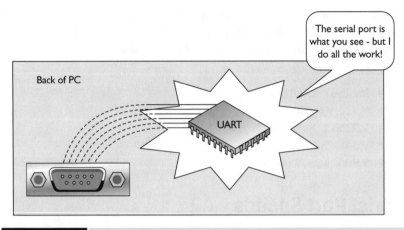

FIGURE 8-3   PC serial ports are controlled by a UART chip.

to perform some of the data processing tasks normally associated with this chip. Although many people will never notice that they are using a Winmodem, you should be aware that these devices can eat into the PC's processing power and generally slow things down during heavy data transfers. If you are experiencing problems with a PC as soon as it goes online, it's worth checking the brand and type of modem being used.

Objective 8.03   Dial-In Software Requirements

OK, so you have the hardware for dial-in. Now, what's going to make it work? You need some software!

Client Side: Microsoft Dial-Up Networking

On the client side, the most popular of all remote access clients (because it's free!) is Microsoft's Dial-Up Networking (DUN), configured through Network and Dial-Up Connections on Windows 2000. DUN allows you to configure your communications device (modem or TA) to dial into a remote access server (or the Internet). Also, subject to you providing an acceptable login user name and password, you can then use the network as if you were directly connected to the LAN, albeit at a severely reduced speed.

Like all remote access clients of this type, the setup for DUN requires you to specify a device to use (modem or TA), a phone number to dial, and, depending on the network protocol used, special settings like IP address, gateway address, and so on (see Figure 8-4).

Setting up DUN is fairly straightforward and intimate details are not required for the Network+ exam, except for one important issue: the protocol used to provide you with a network connection through a telephone line. This is covered later.

Server Side: Microsoft Remote Access Service (RAS)

If you are using Microsoft Dial-Up Networking to connect yourself to your organization's network, you may well then be using Microsoft's Remote Access Service (RAS) on your NT/2000 server to manage your dial-in services. You do not need to know the ins and outs of RAS for the Network+ exam, but you should be

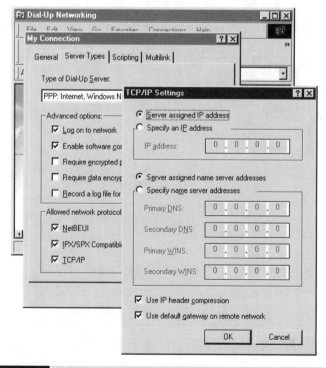

FIGURE 8-4   Configuring DUN

generally aware that you need to configure the server to accept calls, provide the necessary passwords (many RAS servers have a separate logon password just to allow the user to access the remote access server), and set the dial-up user's rights/permissions on the server. (Many remote servers have a separate set of permissions for dial-up users). Figure 8-5 shows Remote Access Service being configured.

Remote Access Protocols

All of the Data Link layer networking protocols you have encountered in previous chapters are designed for use with networks using proper media like coax or UTP wiring. Telephone lines and serial port network connections also need a Data Link layer protocol to handle the nonvoice data sent between computers, but the existing protocols, like Ethernet and Token Ring, simply won't work. Many years ago (well before the first PC landed in a receiving department somewhere), network

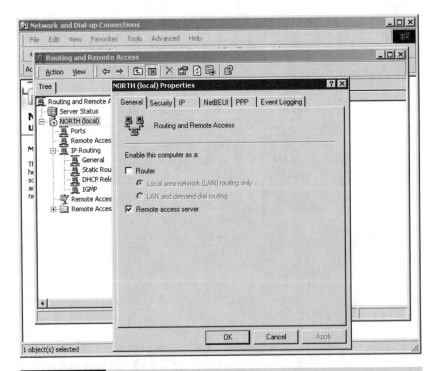

FIGURE 8-5   Configuring RAS

techs were trying to link (mainly UNIX) systems together. They did this either directly through their serial ports, or using a pair of modems and a phone line, so they could exchange data (such as simple e-mails). This led to the development of a protocol called SLIP: the Serial Line IP.

SLIP

SLIP was the first effort to make a Data Link protocol for serial interfaces, and it shows. About the only thing good you can say about SLIP is that it works, but it has a couple of major limitations. First, SLIP only supports IP; it's no good for network connections using NetBEUI or IPX. Second, any system that used SLIP required a static IP address. This wasn't too big an issue in the early days of direct system-to-system connections, or when the Internet was in its infancy, but today's shortage of IP addresses makes SLIP unacceptable. SLIP continues to be supported by most remote access programs, primarily as a backward-compatibility option, but it's not a good choice for today's requirements. In a few words—don't use SLIP.

PPP

PPP, the Point-to-Point Protocol, fixed all of SLIP's shortcomings and has totally replaced SLIP in all but the oldest connections. While PPP has many powerful features, its two strongest are the ability to support IPX and NetBEUI in addition to IP, and the ability to support dynamic IP addresses. All remote access software comes with the PPP protocol. PPP is the one to use, as shown in Figure 8-6.

Remote Control Software

Using DUN and RAS extends your organization's network to your remote PC. A network connection that runs at (let's hope!) around 56 Kbps is not going to be much fun if you have to retrieve and work on a large spreadsheet. Let's say you have 1Mb (1,024KB) of data to download; assuming your modem connection makes 56K, that's around 6KB of data transfer per second. That spreadsheet's going to take about 1,024/6 seconds to get to you—that's about 170 seconds, or nearly 3 minutes!

An alternative to a DUN-type link is to dial into a computer on your in-house network and take it over, operating it remotely. This way, all that comes down the wire is the screen information, and all that goes up the wire is the data for your keyboard and mouse operations. This way of working forms the basis of a number of remote access options where the applications that are involved are data-heavy.

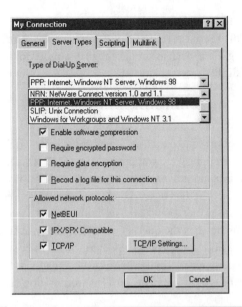

FIGURE 8-6   Use PPP for your remote access requirements—everyone else is!

Various remote access products of this type are available. Common ones include Symantec's pcAnywhere and Altiris' Carbon Copy.

Heavy Duty Remote Access: ICA and RDP

The third main option for remote users (alongside DUN and remote control software) is a high-performance solution based on a Windows NT/2000 Server that runs a virtual PC for every remote user on top of its core operating system (see Figure 8-7). In effect, this solution shares the hardware of the server amongst the remote users, which is a bit like the remote control software described above but without the need for physical PCs. The two main products in this field are Citrix MetaFrame, with what they term their *Independent Computing Architecture* (ICA), and Microsoft's Windows Terminal Server (WTS) with its *Remote Desktop Protocol* (RDP). Both of these solutions can be used with remote (dial-up or via the Internet) access or for local users on the LAN. Because all the users' processing is done by the central server (which has to be fairly powerful because of its workload), the desktop PCs do not need to be that high-end. In fact, many users are now installing cut-down systems that are barely more than a NIC, keyboard, monitor, mouse, and printer port in a single unit—a so-called *thin client*.

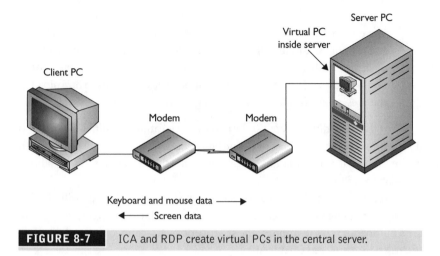

FIGURE 8-7   ICA and RDP create virtual PCs in the central server.

Travel Assistance

For an overview of Citrix ICA, see http://www.citrix.com/press/
corpinfo/ica.asp.

For an overview of Microsoft WTS, see http://www.microsoft.
com/ntserver/ProductInfo/terminal.

Access Through the Internet

So far, all of the remote access options discussed have been dial-up services available from wherever there's a suitable connection point (probably PSTN) directly
to your organization's network. Products such as DUN can also connect you to the
Internet, so if your organization's server (or whatever you want to connect with)
is also on the Internet, you can take this route. In fact, this would be a very flexible
option because you could get to your systems from anywhere there's an Internet
connection. Cost-wise, there may also be benefits; for example, imagine the following scenarios:

- John is on a business trip to London, UK, and needs to download a
  PowerPoint presentation from the corporate server in Atlanta, USA. John
  hooks his notebook PC to the hotel room's telephone line and dials the
  remote access server in Atlanta, logs in, and begins to download the presentation—all 12MB of it!

- Isabel is on a business trip to Paris, France, and needs to download a PowerPoint presentation from the corporate server in Phoenix, USA. Isabel hooks her notebook PC to the hotel room's telephone line and dials the number of a local Internet service provider, fires up her remote access software, logs in to the corporate server, and begins to download the presentation—all 12MB of it!

Spot the main difference? OK, the names and locations are different, but who do you think will have the biggest phone bill, Isabel with her local call or John with his international call to Atlanta? If you're not sure, then you've never seen a hotel room phone bill—ouch!

Connecting through the Internet raises many issues, mostly to do with the fact that you're sending possibly sensitive information across an open network. There are a number of ways to improve the security of such a connection, and these are discussed more fully in Chapter 10.

Objective 8.04   Fixed-Point Remote Access

If there's a need for remote access from a fixed location—say an employee's home—then other, faster, nondial-up options may well be suitable. The options below will connect you to the Internet through an Internet service provider (ISP)—so, provided that the systems you need to access are available through the Internet, you have a potentially viable solution to your remote access requirements.

ADSL

Asymmetric digital subscriber line (ADSL) is the next great leap forward for telephone lines. ADSL is a fully digital, dedicated (no phone number) connection to the telephone system that provides always-on (no dial-up) download speeds up to 9 Mbps and upload speeds up to 1 Mbps *over PSTN lines*! That's right—the phone company can take your PSTN line and make it go at speeds approaching that of 10BaseT! To make it even more attractive, the same ADSL line that you use for data can also work with your telephone, allowing simultaneous data and voice over the same line (see Figure 8-8). The only downside to ADSL is that your ISP must also support ADSL. As of this writing, there is a mad scramble by ISPs to provide that support.

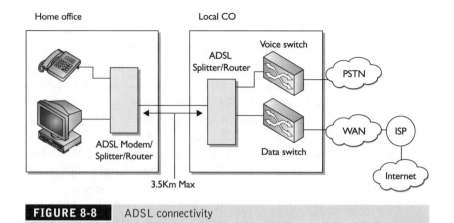

FIGURE 8-8 ADSL connectivity

ADSL is actually only one type of a group of similar technologies known as xDSL. The fact that the upload and download speeds are different is the *asymmetric* part of ADSL; other xDSL technologies provide equal upload and download speeds. ADSL seems to be the xDSL that has become by far the most common.

ADSL has roughly the same distance restrictions as ISDN (18,000 ft, 3.5 km), so if you are too far from the local CO, you might not be able to use the service. ADSL has many variations in upload/download speed, according to the service provider and the country you're in; the more basic service gives a download speed of 512 to 2,048 Kbps maximum and an upload speed of 128 Kbps. The faster (and a lot more expensive) service gives a download of 9 Mbps maximum, and an upload of 384 Kbps.

ADSL shares a high-bandwidth local distribution point, provided by your local telecom or cable services company, between premises in your area. This sharing arrangement (known as *contention*) can lead to a slowdown in performance if the local area has a lot of ADSL users. Overall, though, performance is often significantly greater than a dial-up or ISDN connection.

ADSL providers should tell you what their contention ratio is. Typically, it's 50:1 for home users and 20:1 for business users—that's 50 or 20 connections (not necessarily all in use at the same time) sharing a local 512-, 1,024-, or 2,048-kbps download connection. In reality, this *doesn't* mean that each user gets, say, 512/50-Kbps performance, because it's the overall load at the local exchange—where all the connections to the groups of 50/20 users are linked together—that actually limits the available per-user bandwidth.

ADSL Hardware

The most common installation for ADSL consists of an *ADSL modem* that connects to the wall jack. This device is not a modem—it's more like an ISDN terminal adapter—but the term has stuck, and even the manufacturers of the devices now call them ADSL modems. The ADSL modem connects to a standard NIC, providing the ADSL service. If you want to use the ADSL line for your regular telephone service, you must add a *POTS splitter* to the line between the ADSL modem and the wall outlet (see Figure 8-9). Of course, there are also ADSL cards that connect to the PC, combined ADSL/hubs, USB adapters, and ADSL-capable routers. Which equipment you choose is simply a question of money.

The one place where ADSL might bite you in cost is the ISP link. Most ISPs add a significant surcharge to use ADSL. Before you choose ADSL, make sure that your ISP provides ADSL links at a reasonable price. Most telephone companies bundle ISP services with their ADSL service for a very low price.

ADSL Summary

- ADSL is generally faster than PSTN or ISDN connections for Internet connectivity.
- Depending on how much you want to pay, it typically offers an upload speed between 128 and 384 Kbps and a *shared* download speed of 512, 1,024, or 2,048 Kbps.

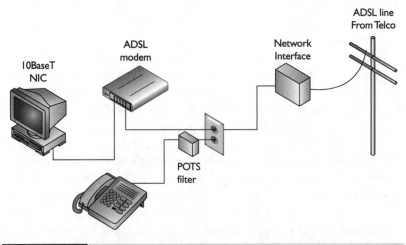

FIGURE 8-9   ADSL modem and telephone sharing one line

Cable Modems

The big competition to ADSL comes from the cable companies. Cable modems also provide an always-on service, but the single most impressive aspect of cable modems is their phenomenal top speeds. These speeds vary from cable company to cable company, but most advertise speeds in the (are you sitting down?) 10 to 27-Mbps range! Now don't get too excited. You have to share that massive throughput with all of your neighbors who also have cable modems. As more people in the neighborhood connect, the throughput will drop. How significant will that drop be? Well, it varies and can be difficult to predict; a heavily used cable line's throughput can drop to under 100 Kbps, but a typical figure is more like 1-3 Mbps. Like ADSL, performance is asymmetric, and upload speeds are generally fixed at between 256 Kbps to 2.5 Mbps. A cable modem installation consists of a cable modem connected to a cable outlet. In most cases, the cable modem gets its own outlet separate from the one that goes to the television. This is the same cable line—it's just split from the main line as though you were adding a second cable outlet for another television. Like ADSL, the cable modem connects to a PC via a standard NIC (see Figure 8-10).

Cable modems are a very popular choice in many areas because the cable companies generally offer their service for a fixed monthly charge. Some service providers limit the amount of contiguous online time to dissuade people from leaving an active connection open 24 hours a day. Often there is a regular disconnect time, say after 2-4 hours of full use, but you can always reconnect and resume your work, often without any disruption.

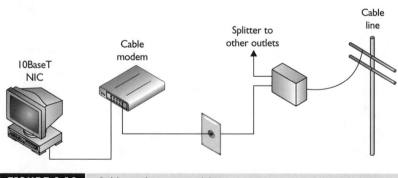

FIGURE 8-10   Cable modem connectivity

Cable Modem Summary

- Cable modems offer very high performance, but the bandwidth is shared so exact speed you attain will vary.
- Typical speeds are 1 to 3 Mbps (download) and 256 Kbps to 2.5 Mbps (upload).
- It is only available if your location has a cable service *and* the service provider offers Internet access.

Satellite Modems

One exotic solution remains for your Internet connectivity: satellite! But forget massive dishes and powerful beams of energy radiating from your own personal satellite transponder towards the sky—it doesn't quite happen like that! Satellite comms use a regular modem for your uplink, usually via the PSTN or ISDN, but the data you request is beamed to you via satellite using an encoded MPEG2 (a video compression standard) data stream (see Figure 8-11).

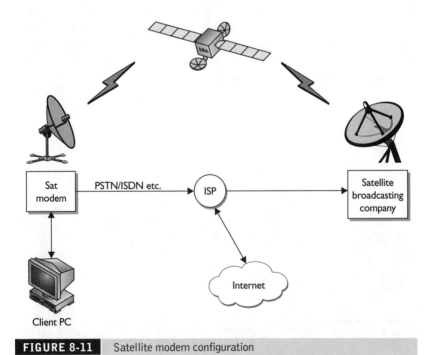

FIGURE 8-11 Satellite modem configuration

The satellite modem system offers asymmetric performance—different upload and download speeds—and the actual speed in the downlink direction can be anywhere up to 52 Mbps (although 400 kbps is more the norm) and the uplink speed will vary according to the service you use (PSTN, ISDN, and so forth).

Obviously, you are unlikely to be the only one using the service at any particular instant, so the downlink protocol manages your data to ensure that you are the only one who picks it up.

Satellite modems are popular for high speed LAN/Internet access where there's no alternative service, and where there's no particular need for a fast upload speed.

The secret to succeeding on the remote access questions on Network+ is to keep it simple. What do you need to make remote access work? You need a communications link, hardware, a data link protocol, and the correct software. Make sure you know the difference between PSTN and ISDN and the other options covered. Know that you want to use PPP instead of SLIP. Finally, know the types of remote access software available and you'll do fine!

CHECKPOINT

✔ **Objective 8.01: Defining Remote Connectivity**   Remote connectivity means being able to access resources on an organization's network from a remote site. In order to establish remote access using a dial-up (PSTN or ISDN) connection, you need client software on the remote machine and also a remote access server product running on a system in your office.

✔ **Objective 8.02: Dial-In Remote Access**   Dial-in remote access is very popular for two main reasons: first, it's a well-established way of doing things, and second, it's very flexible because it can be used anywhere, provided that you have access to a compatible phone socket. International modem standards—known by their V. prefix—ensure that you can use your modem anywhere in the world. Just watch those call costs, even with a modem, fast V.90 modem capable of up to 56 Kbps. Take care to remember to use bps/Kbps rather than the term "baud" when referring to the speed of a modem. Baud is not technically correct, but is widely misused. One common problem with older PCs is that their serial port chip (a UART) is based on an older design and cannot cope with modern, fast modems; if your modem's struggling, make sure that the serial port to which the modem is connected is using a 16550-type UART. If not, install a replacement serial interface or fit an internal modem. A cheap type of modem, called a

Winmodem or soft modem, doesn't have a UART but can cause your PC to slow down during heavy data transfers because they require the PC's main processor to perform some of the UART's functions.

✔ **Objective 8.03: Dial-In Software Requirements**   The most common dial-in software is Microsoft Dial-Up Networking (DUN). DUN is simple to configure and allows you to establish a connection to a remote access server or an Internet service provider (ISP). On the server side, Microsoft's Remote Access Server (RAS) is also easy to set up and provides a degree of access control for remote users. One important point to watch is the choice of data link protocol for your serial port/phone line (PSTN or ISDN) link. SLIP is an older standard that supports TCP/IP only, using a fixed IP address, and has been largely replaced by PPP, which supports TCP/IP using a dynamically assigned IP address and/or IPX/SPX and/or NETBEUI. Dial-up networking extends a LAN to your location, but the speed of your link is limited to that of your modem, meaning it's v-e-r-y slow compared to a regular connection through a NIC. An alternative approach is to connect to a PC on the LAN and just send the screen, keyboard, and mouse information across the link. This type of remote access can be done on a PC-by-PC basis using programs such as PC Anywhere and Carbon Copy, or with heavy-duty products such as Citrix MetaFrame and Microsoft Windows Terminal Server, which create virtual PC environments inside a central server on the network. All of the access options discussed in this section can also be implemented via a dial-up connection to the Internet; while this opens up the possibility of local-call access to your systems from anywhere in the world, it also raises important security issues, which are tackled in Chapter 10.

✔ **Objective 8.04: Fixed-Point Remote Access**   Dial-up services are flexible—they can be used from almost anywhere—but they're also slow. If you don't need the mobility of a dial-up solution (for example, you're providing remote access from a home worker's house), then faster Internet-based solutions are available. Asymmetric Digital Subscriber Line (ADSL) provides an always-on digital connection through a regular phone line (provided you're close enough to the local CO), and cable modems provide similar services through a local cable TV connection. If you don't have the luxury of such services in your location, it may be possible to install a satellite modem system. All these systems offer greater speeds than PSTN/IDSN dial-up connections, but ADSL and cable performance varies according to the number of other users sharing your local bandwidth.

REVIEW QUESTIONS

1. Which of the following is a data compression protocol?

   A. V.90
   B. V.42bis
   C. V.92
   D. V.40

2. What is the name of Microsoft's remote access client?

   A. Microsoft Client for Networks
   B. Dial-Up Networking
   C. ICA
   D. RAS

3. Kyle is having problems getting good performance from his new V.90 modem on his trusty old PC. Everything seems to connect properly, and he has set his serial port speed to 115,200 bps, but file transfers often grind to a halt. What might be the cause of his problem?

   A. Wrong brand of modem.
   B. V.42 has been disabled.
   C. Faulty NIC.
   D. Old UART type.

4. Which of the following protocols are supported by Microsoft Dial-Up Networking? (Choose all that apply.)

   A. TCP/IP
   B. NETBEUI
   C. IPX/SPX
   D. XNS

5. Which of the following is not a data link protocol for telephone lines? (Select all that apply.)

   A. SLIP
   B. IP
   C. PPP
   D. ICA

6. Joe needs to provide a dial-up service for a home worker. Which of the following options are viable? (Select all that apply.)

   A. ISDN
   B. ADSL
   C. Cable modem
   D. PSTN

7. Alex works from a remote, converted farmhouse approximately 5 miles from the nearest town and telephone exchange. Alex needs some form of Internet access and would prefer a high-speed connection for downloading information. Which of the following would provide the best solution, if actually available in the area?

   A. Satellite modem
   B. ISDN
   C. ADSL
   D. PSTN

8. Which of the following statements about ADSL are not correct? (Select two.)

   A. ADSL provides a dedicated connection running at approximately 2 Mbps.
   B. ADSL provides contention-based asymmetrical bandwidth.
   C. ADSL provides a high-speed, dial-up service.
   D. ADSL routers are available.

9. Which of the following V standards defines error checking?

   A. V.42
   B. V.42bis
   C. V.22bis
   D. MNP 8

10. Which of the following UARTs is required for high-speed modem use?

   A. 8250
   B. 82550
   C. 16550
   D. 80486

REVIEW ANSWERS

1. **B** V.42bis is a data compression protocol.

2. **B** Microsoft's remote access *client* is Dial-Up Networking.

3. **D** Kyle should check the UART type on his trusty *old* PC. If it's an 8250, that's the problem.

4. **A** **B** **C** DUN supports the three main network protocols (TCP/IP, NETBEUI, and IPX/SPX). XNS is an old Xerox protocol from which IPX/SPX was developed, but it is not supported by DUN.

5. **B** **D** SLIP (A) and PPP (C) are data link protocols, while IP (B) and ICA (D) are not.

6. **A** **D** Joe needs a *dial-up* service and so ADSL (B) or a cable modem—both always-on services—will not meet the requirement.

7. **A** Using a satellite modem (with a PSTN uplink) would provide the best option. ISDN and ADSL won't be available due to the distance from the nearest town, where the CO (exchange) is located.

8. **A** **C** ADSL does *not* provide a dedicated connection (A), and is *not* a dial-up service (C).

9. **A** V.42 is an error-checking standard.

10. **C** The 16550 UART is the modern, high-speed version.

Network
Security

	NEWBIE	SOME EXPERIENCE	EXPERT
ETA	4 hours	2 hours	1 hour

233

If data security makes you think of user IDs, passwords, and access control, then that's great—you're in the right area. But what you must do for both the Network+ exam and real life is consider other equally important issues that help secure your data from unwanted events such as equipment failures, accidental erasure, and general network problems—not just the attention of unwelcome visitors.

Objective 9.01 Protecting Your Server

Your servers are under potential attack 24 hours a day—and we're not talking about hackers; your servers are the target for power-related problems, environmental issues (heat, dirt, being kicked, and so on), mistakes by the users, the laws of physics, and plain, simple theft! All of these are potential sources of data loss, and so you must do all you can to prevent a major catastrophe.

Protecting Against Power Problems

All of the components in a PC run on electrical power; without a clean, steady supply, they stop working. There are a number of stages through which electrical power must travel between the power company and those components. At any given moment, if there is failure at any one of those stages, the PC will no longer work. You can take several actions to safeguard your hardware to make sure this doesn't happen, starting with the power company.

In most developed countries, you can count on a good electrical supply *most* of the time; it's those other times that will get you. Electrical power sometimes stops (because of power outages) and sometimes goes bad (because of spikes caused by nearby electrical storms or the operation of heavy motors and sags caused by supply equipment failures or other equipment being switched on nearby), as illustrated in Figure 9-1. Additionally, techs (and non-techs) can mess up perfectly good electricity on their own by overloading circuits with too much equipment. You can protect your servers from problems of power outages, electrical spikes, and overloaded circuits using several important technologies: dedicated circuits, surge suppressors, uninterruptible power supplies, and backup power.

Dedicated Circuits

A *dedicated circuit* is an electrical supply circuit that runs from a building's central power distribution point to specific power outlets—perhaps directly (and only)

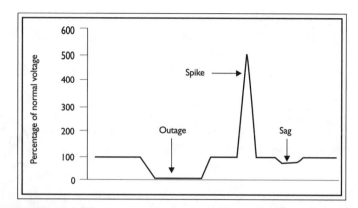

FIGURE 9-1 Power problems

to the computer room. Compare this to a general power circuit that supplies many outlets, feeding copiers, water coolers, PCs, printers, and the occasional vacuum cleaner or floor polisher. Using too many devices on one circuit causes the power to sag (dip), and these sags can cause computer systems to lock up or sponta-neously reboot, depending on how lucky (or unlucky) you are at that moment. Dedicated circuits keep this from happening. They will (theoretically) prevent some uninformed person from plugging a room heater into the circuit and bring-ing down the entire corporate computer system.

Surge Suppressors

An electrical surge—a sudden increase in the voltage on a circuit caused, for example, by a nearby lightning strike—can (and will) destroy an unprotected computer. All modern PCs and other equipment have a degree of built-in protec-tion, but additional, external suppressors add an extra layer of security for not much money.

> **Exam Tip**
>
> Suppressors are also called passive filters or just filtering.

UPS

A uninterruptible power supply (UPS) is standard equipment for servers. A UPS contains a bank of batteries and a DC-to-AC converter circuit so that the batteries

(DC) can provide AC power for the server in the event of a main power failure (many UPSs also provide protection from spikes and sags). UPSs often provide only a few minutes of power, but that's enough to enable the server to shut down cleanly or the backup power supply to kick in (see Figure 9-2).

Exam Tip
All servers should be connected to a UPS.

Ironically, a power failure caused by a local high-voltage cable fault occurred while this book was being written, and office power was lost for nearly two hours—the first such major outage in the area since a bad storm in 1997. Fortunately, the office server was protected by a UPS, which shut down the system safely, and work on the book was being done using a local file on a laptop PC at the time, so we carried on by flashlight!

Backup Power

If your business cannot function without its computer systems, it will need a backup power system, which will kick in when the electricity supply fails completely for a long period of time. This will usually be in the form of a gasoline or diesel generator. A generator can supply power to your main systems, the networking equipment, and key computer systems, if not the whole building. It is *vital* that backup power systems be tested regularly to ensure that they will fire up when needed. Make sure your standard operating procedures include such a check.

FIGURE 9-2   Typical UPS

Environmental Issues

All of this wonderful protection is useless if someone walks off with your mission-critical server. It has happened!

- Keep the server room locked at all times, install a card lock or combination lock doorknob, and make sure that only the right people have access.
- The closed environment of a computer room also allows you to reduce the thermal stress on the system. This will prolong the life of sensitive components, especially the power supply and hard disks.
- Use air conditioning to keep the humidity low, but not too low—around 40 percent is about right for most electronics.
- Keep the room a little on the cool side—about 68°F (20°C) is just about perfect, although most PCs can handle up to 80° or 85°F (26°C or 29°C) before overheating becomes a problem.
- Check with the system's manufacturer for recommendations.

Finally, be aware of the potential hazards from sources of electromagnetic interference (EMI). For example, documented reports have indicated that the signals radiated from cell (mobile) phones can interfere with sensitive electronic equipment, so many organizations ban cell phones from their main computer rooms.

Travel Advisory

Cell phones can crash computers—see http://catless.ncl.ac.uk/Risks/18.60.html#subj4.

Objective 9.02 ## Reliability and Fault Tolerance

Ever seen a bathtub? No, sorry, we're not questioning your bathing habits—maybe we should have said bathtub *curve*! What's that? Well, to find out, see Figure 9-3.

The bathtub curve is a classic figure, often used when discussing the reliability of any item—it shows how, for any manufactured object, there will be a number

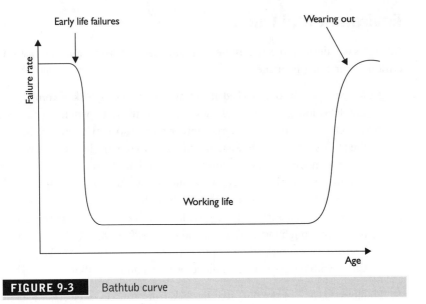

FIGURE 9-3 Bathtub curve

of early life failures due to component defects and manufacturing-related issues, then a period of low defects during the life of the unit, followed by a rise in failures as the item and its components come to the end of their life (wear out). Nothing is immune to the bathtub effect, which means that at some time or other you *will* experience a PC equipment or network failure—it's unavoidable!

A sudden loss of data—or the ability to get to their data—would cripple most organizations. Computers can be replaced and new employees hired, but the data is what makes most organizations function.

Providing Redundancy

One of the ways to reduce the impact of a failure is to install redundancy in a system: duplicate the bits that might fail. Many components inside a system can be made redundant. It is very common to find servers with redundant power supplies, where a power supply can be removed without even shutting down the PC. You can buy NICs that work together in the same PC, covering for one or the other if one dies; there are even NICs you can replace without rebooting the PC. There are also methods for making the entire server redundant—two or more servers can be mirrored, providing the ultimate in reliability, assuming the cost is bearable.

Protecting Disks

One of the most unreliable components inside a PC is the hard disk. That's because hard disks are so mechanical in nature and because of the fine manufacturing tolerances required to make everything work. OK, let's say you need to come up with a way to install multiple hard disks *and* have them manage data storage. How do you do this? Well, you could install a fancy hard drive controller that reads and writes data to two hard drives simultaneously. The data on each drive would always be identical. One drive would be the primary drive, and the other drive, called the mirror drive, would not be used unless the primary drive failed. This process of reading and writing data at the same time to two drives is called *drive mirroring* (Figure 9-4).

If you really want to make data safe, you can use two separate controllers for each drive. With two drives, each on a separate controller, the system will continue to operate even if the primary drive's controller stops working. This super drive mirroring technique is called *drive duplexing* (Figure 9-5). Drive duplexing is also much faster than drive mirroring since one controller does not have to write each piece of data twice.

The third, and most common, way to create redundant data is a process called *disk striping with parity*.

Disk striping by itself (without parity) is the process of spreading data among multiple (two or more) drives. Disk striping by itself provides no redundancy. If you save a small text file, for example, the file is split into multiple pieces; some of the pieces are stored on one drive, some on the other (Figure 9-6).

The one and only advantage of disk striping without parity is speed—it's a very fast way to read and write to hard drives. But if either drive fails, *all* the data

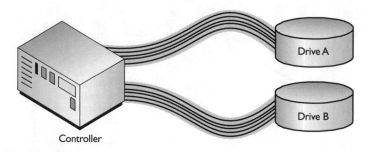

FIGURE 9-4   Mirrored drives

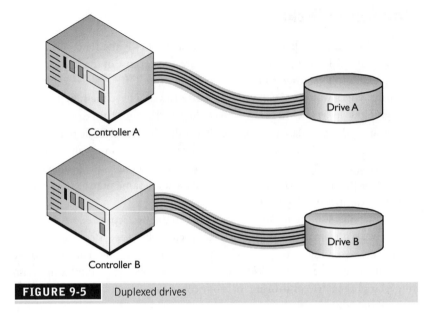

Controller A

Drive A

Controller B

Drive B

FIGURE 9-5   Duplexed drives

is lost. Disk striping is not something you should ever want to do—unless you simply don't care about your data. Nobody does *just* disk striping!

Disk striping *with parity*, by contrast, protects data. It adds an extra drive, called a parity drive, that stores information you can use to rebuild data should one of the data drives fail. Let's look at that same text file we used earlier. The data is still stored on the two data drives, but this time a simple, but very accurate,

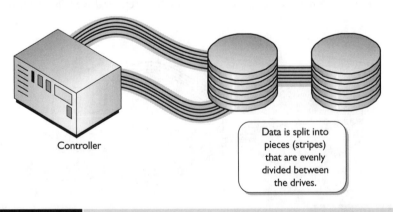

Controller

Data is split into pieces (stripes) that are evenly divided between the drives.

FIGURE 9-6   Disk striping

Making Tape Backups

Think about how much work you have done to create your nice, stable servers, workstations, and network. Imagine how many hours your users have spent creating data and storing it on those servers. Now imagine a virus (or user!) that deletes critical data or configuration files. As you can also imagine, this situation is not good for either your blood pressure or your job security.

Common sense dictates that you create backups of your data—and this will usually mean a *tape* backup; simply because tape offers high capacity, fast speed, and low cost (Figure 9-7). If your needs are simple (and your amount of vital data small), you *might* consider alternatives, such as burning a CD or using a Zip-type drive, but the capacity of these devices is limited, and they can be relatively slow compared to tape.

A variety of tape backup types (all noninterchangeable, of course!) are available. You don't have to know the full technical specs, but they may be mentioned in the Network+ exam so here's an overview of the most common types:

- **QIC—Quarter Inch Cartridge**   This is an old technology that's been surpassed by many of the others listed here. Tape capacities up to 15GB are available.
- **Travan**   This is magnetic tape similar to QIC but it supports higher densities—it's very popular with home users and small businesses. Capacities up to 20GB are available. Travan drives can read and write (some) QIC tapes/formats.
- **DAT (4mm)**   This very popular tape type is based on a data-grade version of the digital audio tape format known as the digital data specification (DDS). It's now showing its age a bit, and new, sexier technologies are trying to steal the market. Capacities up to 40GB per tape are available.

FIGURE 9-7   An 8mm backup tape

- **8mm** This is another spin-off from a consumer product (8mm video tapes), but using a higher-quality tape system. Capacities up to 150GB per tape are available.
- **DLT—Digital Linear Tape** This tape type is very popular due to its speed and tape capacities—it's quite a whizzy system, and a tape can pack up to 80GB.
- **AIT—Advanced Intelligent Tape** AIT is a (relatively) new kid on the block. It is fairly fast, with high capacity—up to 100GB per tape. It's a bit pricey at the moment.
- **ADR—Advanced Data Recording** ADR is a low-cost digital tape format that's popular with home users and small/medium businesses. Capacities up to 60GB per tape are available.

Schedule Your Backups

You can't use a backup tape created several weeks ago to restore a file if the missing live file was updated yesterday. To make sure that you always have current data available, you should create a backup schedule that ensures that your data is backed up regularly and can be restored easily. The best way to start is to make sure that you have a backup plan in place. The backup plan should include answers to the following questions:

- When will backup occur, and what will the tape rotation schedule be?
- What types of backups will be performed at each backup time?
- Where will the backups be stored?
- Who is responsible for managing the backups, and what should be done if that person is not available?

Perhaps the most important details are the types of backups and the backup schedule, or strategy.

Types of Backups

The goal of backing up is to ensure that whenever a system fails, a recent backup will be available to restore the system. At first thought, you might simply back up the complete system at the end of each day, or whatever interval you feel is prudent to keep the backups fresh. This can work if the amount of data to be backed up is small enough to be copied to tape during an available off-hours timeslot, but if you are responsible for a massive repository of data, this may not be possible. And if you are running a 24/7 operation, there may be no after-hours time, so you might want to avoid arranging a mass backup of everything that would slow down the system noticeably for those currently using it.

> ### Exam Tip
>
> Avoid running backups during live system hours as they will slow down the network for all users.

Most backup software solutions have a series of backup options available other than the old Complete (usually called Full or Normal) backup.

The Archive Bit

The key to understanding how backups are managed and performed is knowing about the existence and use of a file attribute called the *Archive* attribute. All files have a series of attributes (or archive bits) that act as on/off or set/unset indicators for the status of the file. The most common attributes are:

- **Hidden**   Don't show the file in normal directory listings.
- **System**   The file is a critical file for the system.
- **Read-Only**   The file can be read but not written to or erased.
- **Archive**   The file is new or has been opened or changed since the archive bit was last cleared.

Backup programs can use the archive bit to decide whether a file should be backed up or not; if the archive bit for a file is set (on), then the file is a likely candidate for backup. If a file's archive bit is turned off, there's likely a backup of that file on some tape (because the backup process is configured to copy a file to tape and then clear the archive bit). Figure 9-8 shows two files: one with the archive bit on, and one with it off.

Using the archive bit allows a complete range of backups to be performed, as shown in Table 9-1.

> ### Exam Tip
>
> Remember the different types of backups, including which ones clear the archive bits and which ones do not.

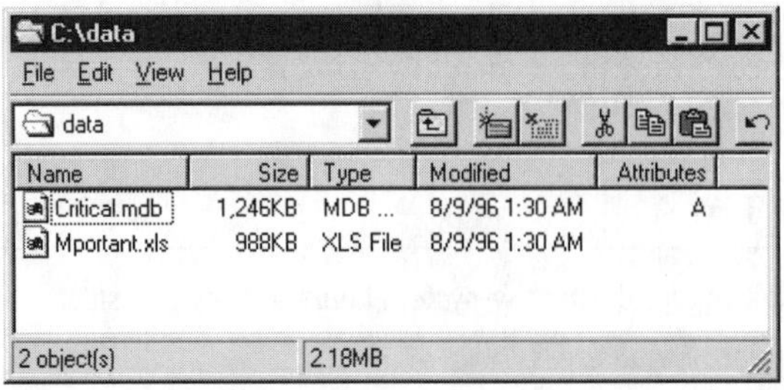

Name	Size	Type	Modified	Attributes
Critical.mdb	1,246KB	MDB ...	8/9/96 1:30 AM	A
Mportant.xls	988KB	XLS File	8/9/96 1:30 AM	

2 object(s)   2.18MB

FIGURE 9-8   Archive bit

The motivation for having both incremental and differential backups is not always clear—they seem to do pretty much the same job. Incremental seems the better option at first. If a file is backed up, you would want to turn off the archive bit, right? Well, maybe. But there is one scenario where that may not be too attractive a choice. Most backup procedures include a big weekly normal backup, with daily incremental or differential backups at the end of every business day. Figure 9-9 shows the difference between the two types.

Notice that a differential backup is a cumulative backup. Since the archive bits are not set, it keeps backing up all changes since the last normal backup. Clearly, the backups will get progressively larger through the week as more files are changed.

TABLE 9.1   Types of Backups

Backup Type	Description	Archive Bit Status
Full/Normal	Backs up everything regardless of the archive bit setting.	Cleared
Copy	Makes copies of all data regardless of the archive bit setting.	Unchanged
Incremental	Backs up all files that have the archive bit set.	Cleared
Differential	Backs up all files that have the archive bit set.	Unchanged

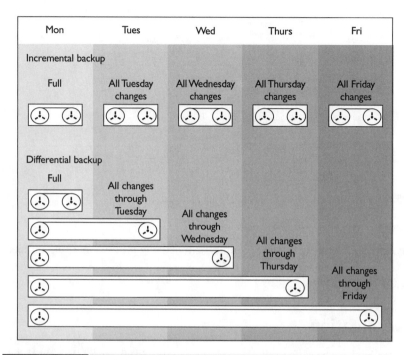

| Mon | Tues | Wed | Thurs | Fri |

Incremental backup

| Full | All Tuesday changes | All Wednesday changes | All Thursday changes | All Friday changes |

Differential backup

Full

All changes through Tuesday

All changes through Wednesday

All changes through Thursday

All changes through Friday

FIGURE 9-9   Incremental versus differential backups

The incremental backup, in contrast, backs up only the changes since the last backup. Each incremental backup will be small and also totally different from the previous backup. Now assume that the system is wiped out on Thursday. How will the system be restored? Well, with an incremental backup, you need first to restore the weekly backup, then the Tuesday backup, and then the Wednesday backup before the system is restored. If you use a differential backup, on the other hand, you need only the weekly backup and then the Wednesday backup to restore the system. The greater the distance between normal backups, the more incremental backups you need to restore. With a differential backup, you will always need only two backups to restore the system (Figure 9-10). Suddenly, the differential backup looks better than the incremental!

Backup Strategies

Putting your data onto tape is one step in the right direction, but managing your backups is also a vital issue. How are you going to store them? Where are you

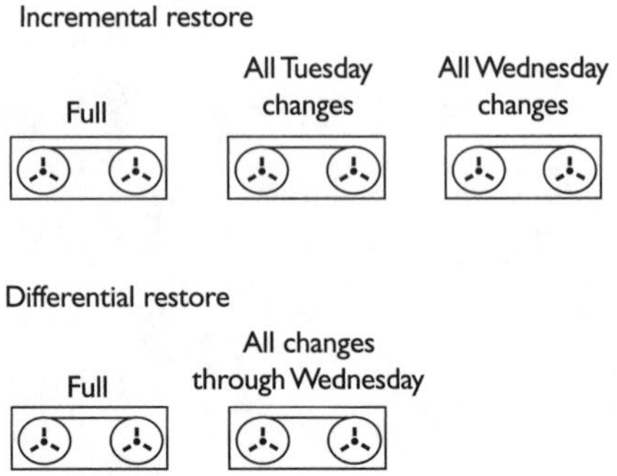

Incremental restore

| All Tuesday | All Wednesday |
| Full | changes | changes |

Differential restore

| | All changes |
| Full | through Wednesday |

FIGURE 9-10   Recovering from Thursday's crash

going to store them? Is the backup system actually putting anything on tape? Backing up to tape is not a fit-and-forget exercise. Consider, and remember, the issues discussed here.

Verification

After you have backed up all of your data, you should give some thought to data integrity on the backup tapes as well as to the safekeeping of those tapes. To verify data integrity, test the restore procedures on a regular basis. All that entails is performing a restore operation on some of the files from a tape to an alternate location and then comparing the data to make sure it is usable and correct. Many organizations have religiously backed up their systems on a daily basis only to discover sometime down the line (during a crisis) that there's nothing on the tapes.

Tape Reliability

Tapes do wear out. If you have used the same tapes for a long time, buy some new ones. Set a schedule for taking tapes out of production and either archiving them or destroying them and replacing them with new tapes. Also, you do not want to store all of your backups on a single tape. You should rotate tapes so that you always have the tapes necessary to run a full restore back to your last full backup. Depending on the type of backup you have chosen to perform, this may entail having a full week's worth of tapes that you rotate—maybe more; some organizations, for example, keep their Friday tapes for a month and their monthly tapes for a year, just in case. Figure 9-11 shows a comprehensive tape backup set.

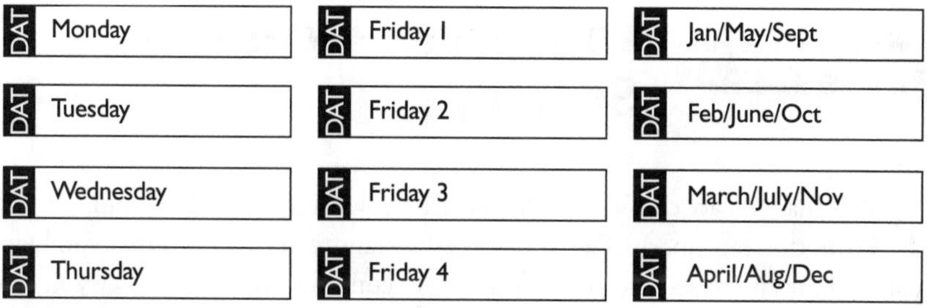

DAT	Monday	DAT	Friday 1	DAT	Jan/May/Sept
DAT	Tuesday	DAT	Friday 2	DAT	Feb/June/Oct
DAT	Wednesday	DAT	Friday 3	DAT	March/July/Nov
DAT	Thursday	DAT	Friday 4	DAT	April/Aug/Dec

FIGURE 9-11   One example of a tape rotation policy

With the tape setup in Figure 9-11, differential backups are stored on the daily tapes, and full backups are stored on the Friday tapes, with the tapes rotated throughout the month, and a month-end backup on the last Friday of the month that's kept for three months before being reused.

Storage

If possible, you should always store backups off-site, in a secure location so that they are not damaged by catastrophic events such as a fire or flood. The next-best solution is a fireproof safe, and this should ideally be located in another part of the building (*not* in the computer room), preferably somewhere secure on the ground floor. Why not in the basement? Basements fill with water if the building floods or is pumped full of water during a fire.

Disaster Recovery

Always plan for the worst. It's a depressing thought, but we all know, realistically, that bad things *do* happen. Every IT department should have a disaster recovery plan that includes the relocation of equipment to a suitable off-site location or the hiring of replacement equipment—some disaster recovery companies have mobile computer rooms in freight containers that they can bring by truck to your site. Your plan should also include procedures for the retrieving and restoring of backups; using backup power supplies; and setting up a network for users, telecom facilities, cell phones, links for homeworkers, and so on. Decide how key techs will be contacted and what their responsibilities will be. Finally, *test* the plans—see how quickly everything can be brought back to functionality. Yes, it's tedious; yes, it takes time and money; and yes, your business may fail if you have an emergency and you haven't planned for it.

Objective 9.03

Logon and Access Security

Now that you are confident that your servers will stay up and running (or will shut down properly if a major electrical failure occurs) and that you have planned for all foreseeable events, it's time to consider how unavailable you can make your servers to the "wrong" people.

Basic security issues common to all networks include the level of security, the proper use of passwords, and the centralization of control. Most decent computer systems won't let you get very far unless you can prove you are a recognized user—you need either a password for the resource you are trying to access, or a user name and a password.

Implementing Share-Level Security

A network designer can choose from two levels of security: share level and user level. With share-level security, a network administrator assigns each shared *resource* a password (see Figure 9-12). These resources are generally either *shared folders*, where data or programs are stored, or *shared printers*. All users attempting to access the resource must supply a password. Network administrators usually consider share-level control to be weak and difficult to manage. It's the kind of security used most often with simple peer-to-peer networks using Windows 9*x* or Me.

Figure 9-13 shows the share-level security options under Windows 9*x*; you can choose to have a password (or not), and it can be for read-only or full access to the resource—and that's it!

Because share-level passwords aren't personal, they tend to be treated as less important than they are (many a resource password has been spotted on a sticky yellow note fixed to the corner of someone's monitor!). Worse yet, the poor users may need to remember dozens of different passwords for all the resources they use. While share-level control can provide some benefit for small, trusting companies with few computers and few users, they can be a pain to manage because there's no centralization—for example, a peer-to-peer network with 20 computers each sharing resources will have 20 locations at which share-level security needs to be set up and managed. Large networks require a more sophisticated scheme, such as user-level security.

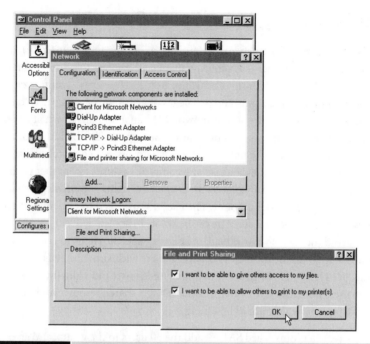

FIGURE 9-12 Turning on share-level security under Windows 9x

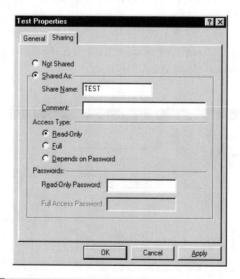

FIGURE 9-13 Share-level security options under Windows 9x

Implementing User-Level Security

With user-level security, a network administrator creates an account for each user, usually on a central server that can itself manage the access to resources on other systems—in other words, the first benefit of user-level security is centralization. A *user account* defines the rights and privileges of a specific person when that person accesses a computer system or network. When a user sits down at the computer, that user supplies an account name and password, which the computer checks against its security database. If the password specified matches that listed for that user account in the database, the computer assumes from that point forward that the user is valid and grants the user all the rights and privileges that have been assigned to that user account. The user doesn't need to remember a share-level password for each resource he or she wants to access.

To avoid the excessive workload of assigning specific rights to each user individually, network administrators organize users with similar needs into *groups* (Figure 9-14). It *would* be possible to manage each user individually, but suppose that 30 users need access to both the SALESDOCS shared resource and the SALESPRINT printer; which would be easier:

- Create a group called SALES, add the 30 users to the group, and give SALES access permission to the two resources; by virtue of their membership in that group, the 30 users can now access both resources.

or

- Give 30 user accounts permission to access SALESDOCS and then repeat the same exercise for SALESPRINT.

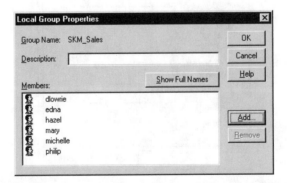

FIGURE 9-14   Group management on a Windows NT 4 server

Think what would happen if you now needed to give the users access to SALESDATA—you either go through the 30 accounts again or just change the group permission once (Figure 9-15).

Take your pick—either approach will work, but one's much less effort (and who doesn't fancy an easy life?). In large organizations with hundreds of employees with similar needs, the time and effort saved quickly becomes significant. In most instances, a user's rights are cumulative, meaning that a user receives the sum of the rights granted to his or her user account and the rights granted to any of the groups to which that user belongs.

Using Passwords

Of course, user-level security only works well when users keep their passwords secure. Passwords, for example, should never be written down where another user might find them, and users should never reveal their passwords to anyone, even the administrator of the network. In most cases, the administrator can reset a user's password without knowing the old password. Many end users, however, remain unaware of this and fall prey to one of the oldest hacker tricks in the book: the fake tech support phone call. In a large organization, most users will not know every network support technician. A hacker simply phones one of these hapless users and says, "This is Bob from tech support. We're upgrading the forward deflector grid, and we need your password so we can reset it when we're done." A

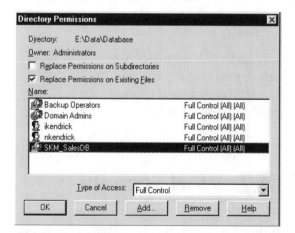

FIGURE 9-15   The SKM_Sales team can get to their favorite database.

shocking number of users will simply give out their password when asked over the phone. A large part of password security is educating network users about the proper care of their passwords.

A good password cannot be guessed easily. A password should never be based on any information about the user that can be easily obtained, such as elements of a user's name, address, relatives' name, or pet's name. Strangely enough, hackers also know about "qwerty" and "letmein".... Ideally, a password should not be a simple real word at all. Hackers probing a network often run password-guessing utilities that simply try common dictionary words at random, but network administrators can reduce the effectiveness of such password-guessing programs by requiring all passwords to be longer than six or eight characters. Hackers have a more difficult task when guessing longer passwords because there are many more possible combinations.

The most secure passwords contain a combination of letters (some in upper-case) and numbers. The following list contains examples of strong passwords:

- Jar56oPtimum
- RhjPop11
- 100bobotw

A good network administrator should assume that, over time, some users' passwords will become public knowledge. To limit the impact of these exposed passwords, a careful network administrator sets passwords to expire periodically, usually once every 30 days or less. Should a password become public knowledge, the gap in network security will automatically close when the user changes the password.

In summary, a strong password should

- Be longer than six or eight characters
- Contain both letters and numbers
- Not be based on easily guessed information
- Be changed on a regular schedule

Objective 9.04   WAN Security

If you're going to extend your network outside the boundary of your building, *expect* and *plan* for third-party attempts to hack their way in. Maybe your organization isn't a likely target for industrial espionage, but that's not the only problem—remember that hacking is "fun," and some people do it simply for the challenge. Also remember that viruses, worms, and other such malicious programs may find their way to the borders of your system—*don't let them in!*

All remote users should be equipped with a secure account with access via a user name and secure password, but this data needs to be passed across the WAN to be verified. If the data is in plain-text format, it's a fairly simple job for a hacker to snare it and have a look. Data packets can be easily read using diagnostics equipment (or suitably equipped PCs) running so-called *promiscuous drivers*, making picking up unencrypted passwords easy.

> ### Local Lingo
>
> **promiscuous mode drivers** NIC drivers that allow a host PC to read *every* data packet regardless of the actual destination MAC address.

Common Connection and Encryption Standards

There are a number of common standards and protocols related to network connectivity, user authentication (logon), and data encryption. Setting up and using these standards and protocols is fairly straightforward: you simply enable the right features in your software or install the appropriate add-on. The following sections tell you all you need to know for the Network+ exam; they cover the common standards you will encounter and where they are used.

> ### Travel Advisory
>
> For an in-depth overview of encryption, see http://www. rsasecurity.com/rsalabs.

Layer 2 Tunneling Protocol (L2TP)

L2TP is used for connecting virtual private networks (VPNs) over public lines and networks, such as the Internet. L2TP itself doesn't provide encryption, but it combines the functionality of PPTP with a protocol called Layer 2 Forwarding (L2F), developed by Cisco Systems, and CHAP (see the next section), which provides encrypted user authentication. Many modern VPN connectivity packages support L2TP. For example, Figure 9-16 shows the VPN configuration options under Windows 2000.

PAP and CHAP

The Password Authentication Protocol (PAP) and Challenge Handshake Authentication Protocol (CHAP) are used by dial-up networking connections (and some VPN configurations) to verify login details. Essentially, they are the password and user verification protocols used with PPP/PPTP connections. All Windows dial-up connection utilities support both PAP and CHAP.

PAP   PAP is a very simple protocol. After a PPP link has been established, a user name and password pair is repeatedly sent (in plain text) until authentication is acknowledged, or until the connection is terminated (Figure 9-17). Although we're talking here about encryption and security, PAP doesn't do either, but is included because it is still widely used.

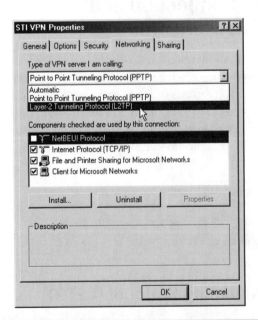

FIGURE 9-16   Configuring a VPN connection to use L2TP under Windows 2000

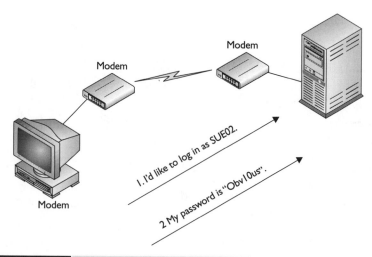

FIGURE 9-17   PAP checking a password

CHAP   CHAP is more secure than PAP. After a remote connection is established, the server sends a *challenge message* to the system dialing in (the *requestor*) for confirmation of the user's password. The requestor generates a response using a one-way hash function—called MD5—and the server compares the response to its expected hash value (Figure 9-18). If the values match, the connection is acknowledged; otherwise, it is terminated. In this way, a server can ask you if you know what your password is without your actually having to send it to the server for comparison. The server can generate a new challenge message at any time, and this makes CHAP very secure because the authentication can be refreshed at any time. Instead of using MD5, CHAP can also encrypt its messages using the Data Encryption Standard (DES) algorithm—a very popular way of encrypting information using a long binary key, but not as secure as MD5.

Local Lingo

one-way hash function   A computing function that takes a variable-length string as the input and produces a fixed-length binary value (hash) as the output. The process is irreversible—it is extremely difficult to find a string that produces a given hash value (hence, it's a one-way function). Message Digest 5 (MD5) is a common hash algorithm.

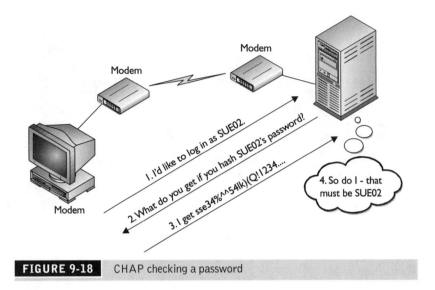

FIGURE 9-18   CHAP checking a password

Although it would seem that PPP links should be configured for CHAP authentication, you can do so only if the remote end also supports CHAP.

IPSec

IP Security (IPSec) is a collection of open standards for ensuring secure private communications using a VPN over the Internet. Because IPSec works at the network layer, it can be used with many different (higher level) protocols without modification. Once enabled, IPSec will authenticate and encrypt all data crossing an IP WAN. IPSec is now built into Windows 2000 (Figure 9-19) and is available for use with other platforms, such as UNIX and Linux.

Travel Advisory

For a comprehensive, easy-to-follow guide to IPSec and VPNs, see http://www-4.ibm.com/software/network/library/ whitepapers/vpn/.

Kerberos

Kerberos is a network authentication protocol, providing authentication for client/server applications using secret-key cryptography. Kerberos was developed

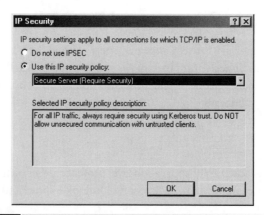

FIGURE 9-19 Turning on IPSec under Windows 2000

by the Massachusetts Institute of Technology. MIT publishes free versions of the protocol, and many commercial and open-source products also now support it. The Kerberos protocol allows a client to prove its identity to a server (and vice versa) across an insecure network connection. After a client and server have established an authenticated connection, they can also encrypt all of their communications to guarantee privacy and data integrity.

Local Lingo

secret-key cryptography An encryption system that uses a common unlocking code (key) that is known only to the sender and recipient of the encoded message.

Microsoft has adopted the Kerberos standard as a feature of the login authentication and resource access system for Windows 2000 servers, albeit with a few custom tweaks here and there that have upset open standards supporters.

Objective 9.05 Internet-Specific Security

We can't avoid it, I'm afraid—some people will insist on using the Internet! This opens the floodgates to potential evildoers intent on stealing the latest copy of your résumé from your personal folder—or worse.

Using Proxy Servers and Firewalls

Putting an intermediary between your main network and the Internet is one way of adding a control mechanism that allows you to monitor what's going on and attempt to block any nastiness. The most common forms of border control are proxy servers and firewalls

Firewalls

Remember that each TCP/IP application layer protocol had its own port number? Figure 9-20, for example, shows Microsoft's Outlook Express and its POP3 and SMTP settings.

A firewall lets you fine-tune the services (by port number) allowed in either direction on and off your network (Figure 9-21). Firewalls can also often block functionality by IP address; for example, you could allow incoming access from a

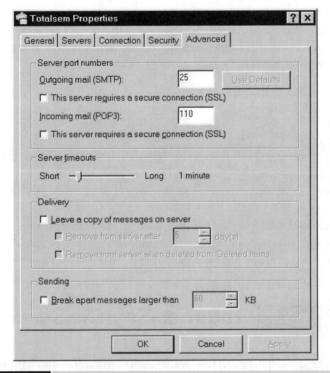

FIGURE 9-20   POP3 and SMTP settings

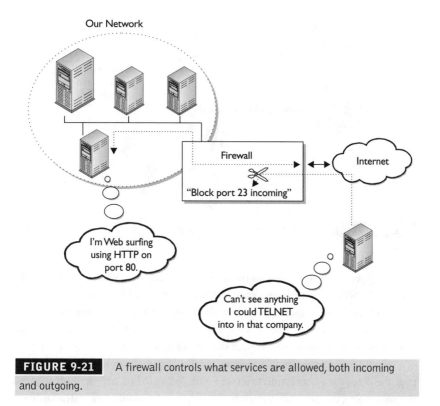

FIGURE 9-21   A firewall controls what services are allowed, both incoming and outgoing.

range of known, fixed IP addresses (used by your remote workers), but from nowhere else. The reverse is also usually true; for example, you could allow web surfing (HTTP, using port 80) from only certain machines in your organization.

Proxy Servers

Most proxy server software offers functionality similar to that of a firewall, but a *proxy server* also acts as a go-between, fetching data from servers on the Internet on behalf of clients on the local network. When you use a proxy server, the client application does not try to connect directly to the server; instead, it sends a request to the proxy server, asking it to get what it wants (Figure 9-22). Proxy servers typically accept requests for web (HTTP), FTP, and e-mail (POP3 and SMTP) resources, but do not support requests for other TCP/IP application protocols unless the proxy server vendor specifically adds support. Proxy servers can enhance both the performance and security of a network.

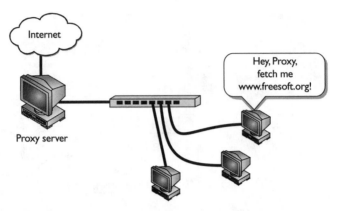

FIGURE 9-22   A client application asks the proxy server to fetch what it wants.

Proxy servers improve the performance of a network by reducing the traffic that results when multiple users request the same data. For example, without a proxy server, if three users on Sherman's network all go to www.cnnsi.com to check the latest baseball scores, Sherman's network downloads the same information from the Internet three times, as shown in Figure 9-23.

When you use a proxy server, however, the proxy server keeps a copy of the page the first time a user requests it (see Figure 9-24). When another host requests the same page, the proxy server gives the client that cached copy instead of contacting the web server again, reducing the amount of traffic going across the Internet and providing a faster response to the client (see Figure 9-25).

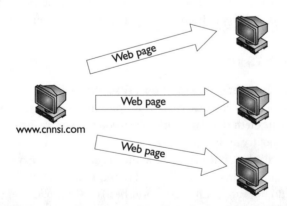

FIGURE 9-23   If three users request the same web page, it's fetched three times.

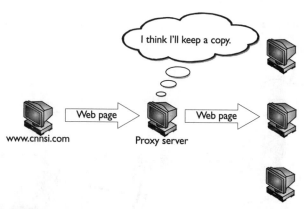

FIGURE 9-24   A proxy server retrieves and caches the web page so it's fetched only once.

Proxy servers enhance the security of a network by hiding individual hosts on the local network from hosts on the Internet at large. Figure 9-26 shows three computers, MO, LARRY, and CURLEY, protected behind a proxy server. As far as the evil hacker lurking somewhere in the dark recesses of the Internet with his computer NEO can tell, MO, LARRY, and CURLEY do not exist. The evil hacker can see only the proxy server. By limiting the number of machines that directly connect to the Internet, wise network techs ease their own workloads. Properly securing a single machine, the proxy server, consumes much less time and effort than properly securing hundreds of individual machines on a network.

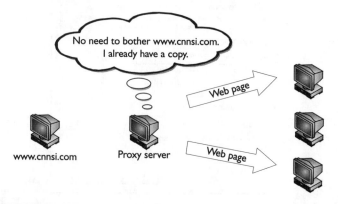

FIGURE 9-25   A proxy server delivers a page from the cache, if the page has already been accessed.

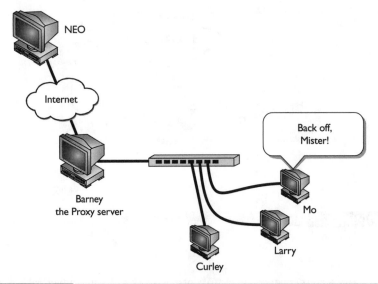

FIGURE 9-26 A proxy server can also act as a firewall.

If you have installed a proxy server, your web browsers will need to be told about it because they will no longer access the Internet directly (they will ask the proxy server for all that they want), as shown in Figure 9-27.

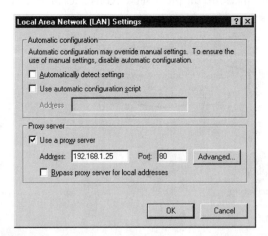

FIGURE 9-27 Microsoft Internet Explorer being told about a proxy server

Using HTTP and SSL

Ever wondered what that padlock-thingy was at the bottom of your web browser (Figure 9-28)? Well, when it's open (Netscape) or hidden (Microsoft IE), it's telling you that you are using plain-text HTTP to exchange information with a web server. When it's locked (Netscape) or present (Microsoft IE), however, you have switched, by magic, to Hypertext Transfer Protocol over SSL (HTTPS), a protocol that uses an encryption algorithm called RC4 that offers much better security, especially when you need it—for example, when you're paying for an online transaction using a credit card. HTTPS (port 443) uses the Secure Sockets Layer (SSL) protocol for its encryption. Many web sites will jump to and from HTTPS mode as required, so there's no need for you to worry about whether it's on or off, but some sites let you choose whether or not you want to access them using HTTPS (Figure 9-29).

Using Network Address Translation (NAT)

Network address translation (NAT) was intended to provide a temporary reso-lution to the problems caused by the shortage of spare IP addresses. Commonly implemented in IP routers, NAT allows multiple computers on a network to connect to the Internet through a single IP address (Figure 9-30). The function of NAT is to ensure that incoming data packets are actually passed to the correct machines. One considerable benefit of a NAT Internet connection is that from the outside it is not at all easy to see what's inside—it's very hard to determine the actual IP address of a host on the LAN. One drawback of NAT is this same feature: machines on the inside are not directly visible to the outside world and so can't easily be used, for example, as Internet web servers. In fact, some ISPs use NAT with their ADSL offerings for just this reason: to stop someone from becoming an amateur ISP with a direct IP connection from their server to the Internet. Many NAT routers also include basic firewall functionality (Figure 9-31).

FIGURE 9-28   Padlock (Netscape) unlocked

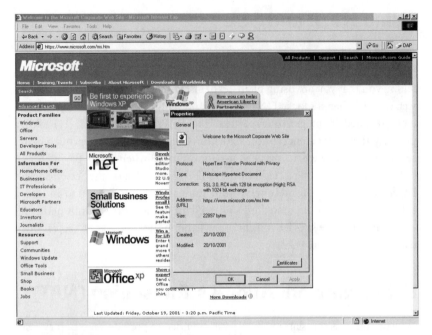

FIGURE 9-29 Microsoft's home page via HTTPS (Microsoft Internet Explorer) — notice the padlock

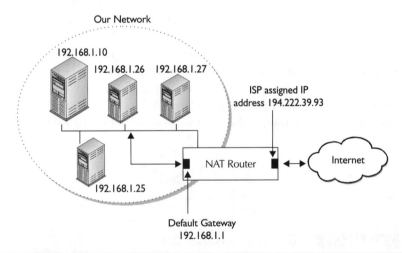

FIGURE 9-30   Using a NAT router to connect to the Internet

FIGURE 9-31   Configuring a NAT router's firewall services via a web browser

CHECKPOINT

✔ **Objective 9.01: Protecting Your Server**   It is important to remember that data protection goes well beyond user name and password control. These issues are certainly important, but you must also consider what might happen to your server in the event of a system failure or power problem—or, indeed, if someone walks off with it! Physical protection, such as a locked computer room or a UPS, is just as important as the access controls that you set up and manage.

✔ **Objective 9.02: Reliability and Fault Tolerance**   Computer systems *will* break—it's unavoidable—but you can take steps to ensure that system failures do not bring down the entire network and that the system can be fixed with minimal disruption. Redundant power supplies and NICs can be installed to keep the system going in the event of a single failure, RAID systems can be used to reduce the chance of a disk failure, and you can plan for the inevitable by implementing a formal tape backup procedure.

✔ **Objective 9.03: Logon and Access Security**   The simplest level of access control is reserved mainly for peer-to-peer networks and is called share-level security. This allows you to choose which folders and printers are available to your user base, and you can restrict access by setting up common passwords for these shares. The downside of this scheme is that the one resource password has to be known by everyone who is allowed access to the resource—there's no concept of validating a user's specific identity. A better setup is to have servers manage their resources on a per-user basis, controlling access to resources by verifying a user's logon name and password. Users can also be placed in groups, which further simplifies access management. The key to good user-level security is the proper management of user passwords which, oddly enough, comes down to educating the system's users. Proper password management means not using obvious words or phrases, not writing passwords down, and changing passwords on a regular basis.

✔ **Objective 9.04: WAN Security**   As soon as your network makes its way into the world at large, you must assume that someone will try and break into it. There are several levels of protection that can be added to your VPN to minimize the risk of intrusion: data can be encrypted using standards such as IPSec, and user authentication can be checked using protocols such as CHAP and Kerberos.

✔ **Objective 9.05: Internet-Specific Security**   The Internet is a real melting pot—it's a professional tool, a means of sending e-mail, a means of linking systems together, and a hunting ground for hackers. Protecting your systems from outside attack involves installing a firewall or proxy server of some type to filter IP traffic by address and/or port number. A proxy server can also help to speed up web browsing by locally caching frequently accessed pages. Sites that use network address translation (NAT) Internet connections have a high degree of inherent protection due to the way the system works.

REVIEW QUESTIONS

1. Which of the following will protect a network server from power outages? (Select all that apply.)

    A. A dedicated power circuit

    B. A UPS

    C. A filter

    D. A surge suppressor

2. John has allowed Tracy, Kyle, and Neil access to the SALES01 printer and has told them what password to use. What type of security system is being used? (Select one answer.)

    A. Peer-to-peer

    B. User-level

    C. Kerberos

    D. Share-level

3. Which RAID level provides disk mirroring only? (Select one answer.)

    A. 0

    B. 1

    C. 3

    D. 5

4. Your servers are configured with dual disk controllers each hosting an independent disk. Data is automatically copied to both disks in its entirety. What fault-tolerant system are you using? (Select one answer.)

    A. Disk duplexing

    B. Disk mirroring

    C. RAID 2

    D. RAID 5

5. Which backup scheme uses a daily tape backup for all files that have changed since the last full backup? (Select one answer.)

    A. Normal backup

    B. Incremental backup

    C. Differential backup

    D. Copy

6. Which backup scheme uses a daily tape backup for all files that have changed since the last daily backup? (Select one answer.)

    A. Normal backup

    B. Incremental backup

   C. Differential backup

   D. Copy

7. Which of the following protocols or standards does *not* provide secure password authentication? (Select all that apply.)

   A. CHAP

   B. PAP

   C. L2TP

   D. Kerberos

8. You have been asked to improve Internet security on your network. As a secondary requirement, you have been asked to improve web browsing performance. You choose to install a firewall. Which of the following requirements does this fulfill? (Select one answer.)

   A. The main requirement only

   B. The secondary requirement only

   C. Both the main requirement and the secondary requirement

   D. Neither

9. Which of the following is *not* a feature of a proxy server? (Select one answer.)

   A. Web caching

   B. Port blocking

   C. Cache mirroring

   D. IP address filtering

10. Which protocol is used by HTTPS to encrypt data? (Select one answer.)

   A. Kerberos

   B. MD5

   C. CHAP

   D. RC4

REVIEW ANSWERS

1. **B** Only a UPS can provide power in the event of an outage.

2. **D** John is using share-level security. We can tell because he has to give a common password to all users of the shared network resource.

3. **B**   Disk mirroring is also known as RAID level 1.

4. **A**   Using multiple disks on independent controllers is known as duplexing.

5. **C**   Differential backups store on tape everything that has changed since the last full backup.

6. **B**   Incremental backups store on tape everything that has changed since the last daily backup.

7. **B**   PAP does not provide secure password authentication. It passes plain-text passwords to the host system.

8. **A**   A firewall will improve security but will not speed up web browsing because a firewall does not have a web cache.

9. **C**   Cache mirroring is a made-up term. All the others refer to proxy server features.

10. **D**   HTTPS uses the RC4 encryption algorithm.

The Complete Network

	NEWBIE	SOME EXPERIENCE	EXPERT
ETA	2 hours	1 hour	30 minutes

273

This chapter starts with an insight into the features of the mainstream network operating systems and clients and then covers topics on the administrative side of networking, including one essential job that everyone hates—paperwork! Don't ignore this stuff—it's important information for the Network+ exam and may help you back at the office, too!

Objective 10.01 Network Operating Systems

There used to be a time in PC networking when you were *either* a Microsoft Windows NT *or* a Novell NetWare server groupie and maybe, just maybe, you might acknowledge the existence of the opposition if really, really pushed! Times have changed, and both camps (and network operating systems) will now talk to each other quite happily, so choosing a network operating system is now much more about suitability for purpose rather than brand loyalties.

All NOSs share the same fundamental goal: to enable *users*, the human beings that sit at the computers, to get work done. The routes to that goal vary, of course, depending on the nature of the work. Some networks simply enable users to share files and printers, while others supply users with access to sophisticated applications that execute on a server. Before choosing the right network operating system or systems for a network, evaluate the roles that need filling for the clients, file and print servers, and application servers (see Figure 10-1).

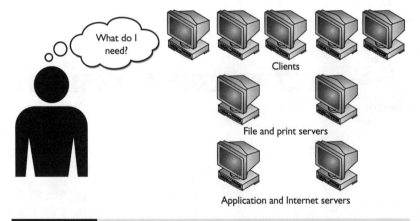

FIGURE 10-1   Evaluate the key roles for your network hardware.

Roles

The majority of most networks consists of *clients*, the machines at which users sit and do work. Client systems run applications such as word processors, spreadsheets, and web browsers while providing access to resources on the network. Most networks today use a Microsoft operating system such as Windows 9*x*, 2000, or Windows NT Workstation as their client operating system, although UNIX workstations and thin clients (remember them from Chapter 8?) are also popular in some settings. The next main section in this chapter deals with client-related issues.

File and print servers, as the name implies, provide access to printers and stored data. In small environments that require little or no security, such as a home network, a single system frequently acts as both a client and a server—a *peer-to-peer* network. In *server-based* networks, one or more systems act as dedicated file or print servers. A *dedicated server* does not function as a client—it exists to serve the needs of other systems. Because they can be physically isolated from the end users, dedicated servers can offer far greater security.

Application servers perform specific tasks or sets of tasks rather than just serving up stored files. Examples of application servers include web servers, e-mail servers, and database servers. Think about how a web site like www.whois.net operates; you key in all or part of a web site address for which you want further information and the site searches its database to find any matches and displays the results (see Figure 10-2). All of the searching takes place on the server; you (on your client PC) just receive the results.

Using an application server rather than performing actions on the client systems offers three key advantages. First, application servers make efficient use of network traffic. Rather than having each client download the entire database and perform its own search, the database stays on the server. Only a minimal amount of network bandwidth traverses the network. Second, only a single copy of the database exists, making maintaining and backing up the database a snap. Third, a single, very powerful server can provide access to a large database for much less expensive, less powerful systems, thus reducing costs—even a 386- or 486-based computer running a client application such as a web browser can access the database.

Local Lingo

client/server   Client/server has at least two distinct meanings. A *client/server network* has dedicated server machines and dedicated client machines. A *client/server application* performs some part of its processing on an application server rather than on the client systems.

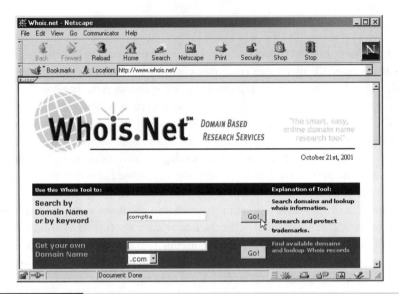

FIGURE 10-2 Searching www.whois.net for web site information

Windows NT Server and Domain-Based Networking

Windows NT Server and Windows 2000 Server, Microsoft's main server products, offer all of the features of Windows NT Workstation and Windows 2000 Professional, plus enhancements that strengthen them as network operating systems—essentially, Microsoft optimized the server versions so that they put a higher priority on serving requests over the network rather than on those of a user sitting at their keyboard.

Travel Assistance

For the sake of simplicity, from now on we will refer to both Microsoft Windows NT Server and Windows 2000 Server as "Windows Server," unless we're discussing a feature specific to a particular version.

One key feature that differentiated Microsoft's Windows NT network operating system from Novell NetWare versions 2.*x* and 3.*x* was Microsoft's *domain*-based security management system; servers could be grouped together (in a *domain*), to share a common security database controlling user access, configuration, and access to shared resources (folders and printers). With Novell NetWare versions 2.x and 3.x, like many other "classic" network operating systems and systems such as Linux and UNIX, a user needing to access more than one system would need a separate user account on each server. Maintaining multiple user accounts for each user created a huge burden on both administrators (who had to create and maintain all those accounts) and end users (who had to remember multiple user account names and passwords). Fortunately, some forgotten genius came up with the idea of a *single login*, which enables a user to log in once and access all of their resources, regardless of the server on which the resource resides. Microsoft implements their single login through domains.

In a domain, a group of special servers known as *domain controllers* store a common security database called the *Security Access Manager (SAM)* database. When a user logs in to the domain, they log in to a domain controller that checks their user name and password. When a user logs in successfully to the domain, the domain controller issues them an *access token*, the electronic equivalent of an ID badge. Whenever the user attempts to access a resource on any server on the domain, their computer automatically shows the server the access token (Figure 10-3). Based on the access token, the server then decides whether or not to grant access.

> ### Exam Tip
>
> For Windows Servers, all computers within a domain share a common security database. Each user logs in once to access all of their resources within the domain.

Give me my stuff!

Penelope
Authenticated by the domain controller

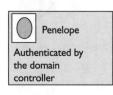

If the domain controller believes this is Penelope, that's good enough for me!

FIGURE 10-3   Once you are authenticated by a domain controller, you can present your credentials to other systems.

Novell NetWare

The continued use of older versions testifies to the power and stability of Novell NetWare. Many organizations upgrade their client software, but continue to use their existing NetWare 3.*x* and 4.*x* servers, following those ancient words of wisdom: "If it ain't broke, don't fix it." Network techs should familiarize themselves with three significant versions of NetWare: NetWare 3.*x*, NetWare 4.*x*, and NetWare 5.*x*.

NetWare 3.*x* and the Bindery

NetWare 3.*x* offers solid file and print sharing capabilities using the IPX/SPX protocol suite, but lacks a centralized security database—each NetWare 3.*x* server maintains its own independent security database, called the *Bindery*. When a user logs in, the NetWare server compares the user name and password to its Bindery database and then determines which resources it will share with the user. NetWare 3.*x* works best in small networks, and even though there are tools available to synchronize user account information (such as passwords) between servers, general user administration is still very much done on a per-server basis; a user wishing to access resources on three different servers will require three separate user accounts and passwords (see Figure 10-4). Keeping account details (user name and password) the same on each server simplifies things a bit for login purposes, but doesn't do much for the poor network supervisors. NetWare 3.*x*'s reliance on IPX/SPX also limits its use as more and more networks adopt TCP/IP as the protocol of choice.

NetWare 3.x
Server

NetWare 3.x
Server

NetWare 3.x
Server

I have to log in to each server separately? What a drag!

FIGURE 10-4   NetWare 3.*x* servers maintain independent Bindery databases.

Exam Tip

While it *is* possible to add TCP/IP support to a NetWare 3.*x* server, this configuration is not common. For the purposes of the Network+ exam, assume that all NetWare 3.*x* servers use IPX/SPX as their sole networking protocol.

NetWare 4.*x* and NDS

NetWare 4.*x* built on the success of NetWare 3.*x* by adding two key features: Novell Directory Services (NDS) and TCP/IP encapsulation. *Novell Directory Services (NDS)* organizes all user and resource information in a database, referred to as the NDS tree. The *NDS tree* acts as a centralized security database, enabling users who "log in to the directory" to access all of their resources anywhere on the network. The general structure of NDS and the naming conventions used are based on an OSI standard called X.500.

NetWare 4.*x* also supports TCP/IP, allowing NetWare servers and clients to place IPX packets inside of TCP/IP packets, a process known as *encapsulation* (see Figure 10-5). NetWare's basic design assumes the use of IPX/SPX, and encapsulation enables Novell to use TCP/IP without massively redesigning the NOS. Encapsulation, however, degrades performance by adding an additional layer of protocol information to each packet.

Exam Tip

Windows servers enable users to log in once and access all of their resources by logging in to the *NT domain*.
NetWare 4.*x* (and 5.*x*) enable users to log in once and access all of their resources by logging in to the *NDS tree*.

NetWare 5.*x*

NetWare 5.*x* (and 6) removes the need for TCP/IP encapsulation, enabling NetWare to run TCP/IP natively. *Native TCP/IP* means that NetWare 5.*x* no longer needs to use IPX/SPX at all (although it can for backward compatibility). Because

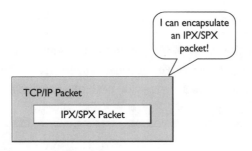

    NetWare 4.*x* and TCP/IP encapsulation

NetWare 5.*x* can "speak" TCP/IP natively, it performs far more efficiently when using TCP/IP than NetWare 4.*x*.

NetWare Summary   For the Network+ exam, familiarize yourself with the protocols and security databases used by each version of NetWare, as shown in Table 10-1.

Microsoft Active Directory

Microsoft Active Directory (or Directory Services) is a new model for centralized server management and was introduced with Windows 2000 Server. Like NetWare Directory Services, it is also based on the X.500 standard and allows you to store information related to your entire network resources in a single database that's stored and updated (replicated) regularly on a number of designated servers. Active Directory includes backward support for NT domains and greatly simplifies the management of multiple servers (which was always the boast of Novell's NDS).

TABLE 10.1 NetWare Security Database and Protocol		
NetWare Version	**Security Database**	**Protocol(s)**
NetWare 3.*x*	Bindery	IPX/SPX
NetWare 4.*x*	NDS	IPX/SPX or TCP/IP
NetWare 5.*x*	NDS	IPX/SPX or TCP/IP

UNIX and Linux

UNIX, the mainstay of universities, scientific computing, and Web servers, becomes more important for the average network tech in the trenches as the importance of the Internet continues to grow. Originally, the Internet consisted of a few UNIX-based systems at a few universities spread around the world. The basic Internet protocols (FTP, HTTP, DNS, ARP, and so forth) originated in the world of UNIX and were only later ported to other operating systems. UNIX comes in many flavors, but they generally share certain features. The flexibility of UNIX and the rise of open source variants such as Linux and Free BSD make UNIX an NOS that network techs ignore at their own peril. From the network tech's point of view, all versions of UNIX look more alike than different, although occasionally you will find differences in command syntax that can keep you scratching your head if you originally learned the command you want to use on a different version of UNIX!

Exam Tip

The Network+ exam does not cover the differences between versions of UNIX.

Travel Assistance

A useful set of UNIX tutorials can be found at http://www. matchstick.com/unix/.

Sharing Files

UNIX systems can share files across a network in a variety of ways, including File Transfer Protocol (FTP—covered in Chapter 6), SAMBA (Chapter 5), and Network File System (NFS).

The *Network File System (NFS)* protocol enables an NFS client to treat files and directories on an NFS server as though they were located on the client system. NFS was originally developed for UNIX-to-UNIX file and directory access requirements, but it has since been implemented on many other platforms—Figure 10-6 shows how a UNIX directory called /data/sales/can be "seen" on an NFS client PC. Windows-based machines don't come with NFS support as standard but there are many third-party NFS client and server options available. Although NFS is a

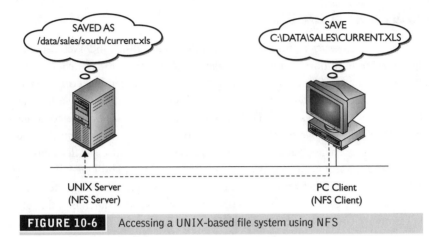

FIGURE 10-6 Accessing a UNIX-based file system using NFS

useful way of accessing data and programs stored on "foreign" systems, it does not support file and record locking (essential features for multiuser database access) and so it is not suitable for absolutely every situation.

Web Applications

Although facing increasing competition from Windows 2000, UNIX remains the server of choice for providing Internet-based services such as Web and e-mail; the September 2001 Netcraft survey shows UNIX-based web servers with about 62 percent of the market and Microsoft Internet Information Server with about 27 percent.

Travel Assistance

The Netcraft survey can be found at http://www.netcraft.com/ survey/.

Open Source UNIX

Linux is an *open source* operating system, meaning that anyone who purchases a copy receives full access to its *source code*, the building blocks of the operating system. Free access to the source code gives software developers tremendous power to modify the operating system to meet their needs, and has led to the rapid development of a wide variety of applications, including some of the most commonly used web and e-mail servers on the Internet—Apache and Sendmail. In most cases, both the Linux operating system and Linux applications are available for free download from the Internet, although vendors such as Red Hat, SuSE, and Caldera charge for support services. For all intents and purposes, Linux is a full-featured clone of UNIX.

Networking Apple Computers

Although we've concentrated on the world of PC networking, we mustn't lose sight of the fact that there are other desktop systems out there—and they, too, can be networked. As well as being known for their non-PC desktop computers, Apple Computer Inc. also developed their own networking protocol way back in the mid 1980s. AppleTalk (the current implementation, first seen in 1989 is known as "AppleTalk Phase II") can run over Ethernet, Token Ring, and Fiber Distributed Data Interface (FDDI) topologies as well as Apple's proprietary twisted-pair cabling system known as LocalTalk (bandwidth 230 Kbps). Access to Mac-based file and print services was performed using a protocol called AppleShare.

Apple systems can be connected to NetWare (NetWare Client for Mac), Windows (Windows NT Services for Macintosh), and Linux/UNIX servers (various solutions) either via an Ethernet or a LocalTalk NIC, but the latter is not so well supported these days. The ideal Mac connectivity solution is to use Ethernet and TCP/IP. You cannot run TCP/IP directly over LocalTalk, although it *is* possible to encapsulate TCP/IP packets in AppleTalk packets over LocalTalk (see Figure 10-7).

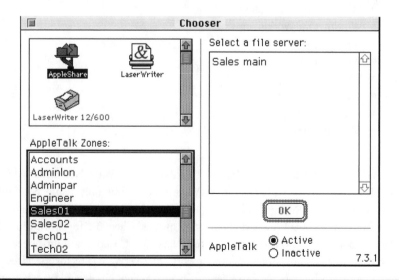

FIGURE 10-7   Navigating around an AppleTalk network

Objective 10.02　Network Clients

Microsoft products dominate the role of desktop client—with built in peer-to-peer networking functionality, too. Generally, all of Microsoft's desktop OS offerings provide similar network client functionality, with minor cosmetic differences between the ways that the network basics are set up.

Window 9x

Microsoft Windows 95, 98, and ME collectively known as Windows 9x, provide basic file and print sharing functions, but little security by themselves. A network tech can configure a Windows 9x system as simply a client, or as both a client and a server. As a server, however, Windows 9x uses share-level control, making it significantly less secure than more sophisticated server operating systems. Windows 9x's key feature lies in its ability to connect to virtually any other kind of server, including Windows 9x, Windows NT, Novell NetWare, and UNIX.

Because Microsoft maintains a high degree of compatibility with their older network operating systems, their network client services enable a Windows 9x system to communicate with any of the following types of servers (client/server or peer-to-peer):

- Microsoft LAN Manager
- Windows for Workgroups
- Windows 95
- Windows 98
- Windows ME
- Windows NT 3.x
- Windows NT 4.x
- Windows 2000
- Windows XP

Windows 9x ships with Microsoft Client for NetWare Networks, which enables connectivity with Novell NetWare servers, but only using NWLink (Microsoft's IPX/SPX-compatible protocol). If you want to use TCP/IP, you need to install Novell's own Windows client kit, known as "Client 32" for short. You will also need to use Novell's client for full NetWare 4/5 compatibility because Microsoft's version does not recognize or work with NetWare Directory Services—it only supports bindery mode. In general, Novell's client kits provide much more functionality than Microsoft's equivalents.

Travel Assistance

The latest Novell client kits can be found at http://www.novell.com/ download/.

Windows NT Workstation

Windows NT Workstation offers the same user interface as Windows 95, but with greatly enhanced security and stability. A knowledgeable "power user" can often defeat most security measures on a Windows 9x machine by directly accessing the registry—the database that defines all settings, including security settings, on a Windows 9x system. Windows NT Workstation, in contrast, follows a more robust security model and an able network administrator can prevent even power users from digging into the internals of the system. Windows NT Workstation also provides a more stable platform for running applications. While applications can still lock up, Windows NT Workstation does a better job of protecting programs from each other—rarely will the failure of one program on an NT Workstation crash other programs.

Windows NT Workstation can also function effectively as a NetWare client. Microsoft provides its own NetWare client software, Client Services for NetWare (CSNW). As with Windows 9x's Client for NetWare Networks, CSNW cannot connect to NetWare servers via TCP/IP and does not fully support NDS, so it's time to switch to Novell's Client 32 for Windows NT/2000.

Windows 2000/XP

Windows 2000/XP combines the friendliness (plug and play, good hardware autodetection, snazzy interface, cozy slippers,and so forth) of Windows 9x with the robust core OS features of NT. Being the most recent high-tech client product from Microsoft, Windows 2000/XP incorporates all of the latest security and connectivity features that may or may not be available as bolt-on functionality for 9x and NT, such as support for the latest encryption standards.

User Profiles and System Policies

Windows 9x, NT, and 2000/XP support the use of user profiles, which enhance both the usability and security of a network. *User profiles* are a collection of settings that correspond to a specific user account, and they allow each user to customize their working environment so that their wallpaper, desktop layout, and so forth remain consistent from session to session. Storing a user's profile on a network server (NT, NetWare, or other NOS) creates so-called *roaming* profiles that will "follow" a user from desktop to desktop, so it doesn't really matter where they sit to work—ideal for so-called "hot desking" environments. Profiles and *system policies* also allow network administrators to customize and restrict desktop settings, and many other Windows features (see Figure 10-8). An administrator can prevent users from running other programs, changing their desktop icons and wallpaper, and loading new programs.

User profiles and system policies offer both a consistent look and feel to the end user and control to the network administrator.

Exam Tip

The Network+ exam doesn't expect you to know *how* system profiles and policies are configured, just that they exist and what they do.

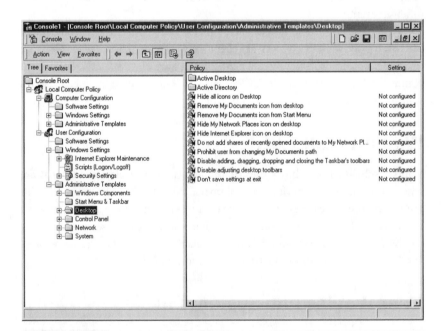

FIGURE 10-8   Configuring a user's desktop in Windows 2000

Objective 10.03 Maintaining the Network Infrastructure

The other key element of any network is its infrastructure. We've already covered the basics in previous chapters, so here's a consolidation of the key issues to consider when putting it all together.

Topology

The core of most business networks today is going to be based on a structured UTP system, but you may need to consider how legacy systems are going to connect in to the system—you may need bridges or routers to integrate older cabling standards and other networking protocols, or take the decision to upgrade the older stuff to the new standard.

Always think ahead and plan your network infrastructure to cope with expansion (networks have a tendency to grow, rather than shrink!)—is it really worth saving such a small amount to get a 12-port hub when a 16- or 24-port is the same physical size and just a fraction more to purchase? Sure, we don't want to go mad and buy "top of the range" for everything, but going for the cheapest in all circumstances can be a false economy (and we haven't even mentioned build quality yet)—many a tech's been asked to hook up a couple of new ports "right now" for the new starters and found themselves in amongst the spaghetti hanging out of the wiring cabinet desperately searching for someone (something!) they can disconnect to make room for the newbies! Oh, and if you *have* got such an untidy setup, why not plan an "out-of-hours tidy up and document" session; it will sure help with future management and troubleshooting—on one site this actually helped identify the source of a previously untraceable network slowdown that was caused when the last hub in a rack was accidentally patched back to the first, creating a "ring" of hubs!

Documentation

Following the last chapter, you should all know to have procedures in place to ensure that regular backups are made and that UPSs and backup power systems are tested regularly. Your life will also be made much easier if you document key activities that take place on the network—your maxim should be "if in doubt, document it!"

Documentation is a broad category that encompasses not only the manuals and read-me files from the manufacturer, but also your own documentation, such as network maps, change logs, and network history. You need to get and create this documentation, and then you need to find a way to store, manage, and update it as necessary.

Manufacturer's Data

The first category of documentation to hoard in your network library is the information you can get from the manufacturers—items such as the following:

- "Read me" files (often called README.TXT or README.DOC) from setup CDs and diskettes.
- Official software and hardware documentation, such as user's manuals. These manuals often give in-depth installation instructions, frequently asked questions, and troubleshooting suggestions. These manuals also provide direction to more updated information, patches, or additional drivers.
- The addresses of relevant web sites. On web sites, you can find searchable troubleshooting databases (often called "knowledge bases"). These databases are compiled based on the questions and problems that other customers have brought to the attention of the manufacturer. When the issue is resolved, it gets added to this database for your benefit.
- The addresses of relevant newsgroups on Usenet. Usenet has many newsgroups that discuss specific types of hardware and software, as well as general hardware and networking topics. These groups are a good place to visit regularly, just to keep an eye on the current topics. They are also a good place to go when you have a problem—someone else may have already solved a similar one.

Read the Fine Manual

Although technical manuals can sometimes get a bad press, it *is* worth reading the documentation that comes with a new piece of software or hardware—the last situation you want to find yourself in is one where you are halfway through a product installation or upgrade and *then* you discover you need a specific update or additional item for *your* specific setup—look specifically for installation instructions and known bugs or incompatibilities.

After glancing through this provided documentation, many network administrators simply stick it in a pile and assume they can sort it out later. Unfortunately, when "later" comes, that same administrator is probably running around with his or her shirt on fire because the main e-mail server is down and they can't find the documentation for that server's NIC. It is best to organize your documentation by machine, or class of machine. If all of your servers, for example, are built to the exact same specification, with the exact same components, you should keep a file for all the documentation for the server-class machines. When any server has even one piece of hardware that is not standard, that server should have its own file, with all the documentation for all its components. This allows you, when you are preparing for upgrades or doing troubleshooting, to take one binder or file folder and have all of the information for that machine at your fingertips.

All Your Own Work

The list of documentation about your network that you should create yourself is even longer and broader reaching than the documentation you obtain from other sources. This documentation must accurately reflect the configuration of the hardware and software installed, as well as any changes that get made to it. Your documentation should have the following elements:

- Each piece of hardware and software has a variety of numbers associated with it, such as serial numbers, part numbers, and license numbers. It is important to keep a list of all the numbers associated with the hardware and software installed in each machine.
- Each of the machines in your environment was built at some point by somebody who put certain pieces of hardware and software into it. You should know what pieces of hardware and software are in the machines, when they were installed and configured, and by whom. This allows you to check back with that person for more information or assistance, if it becomes necessary. Look at Figure 10-9 for a sample of a log that might give all the necessary details on a particular machine.

B	C	D	E
Function and software	**Location/Phone**	**TCP/IP Settings**	**Harware**
PDC; Houston_WRT domain	Houston Server Room	IP=223.190.190.1	Standard Compaq Proliant 7000
OS = NT 4 Service Pack 3	713-999-9999	subnet = 255.255.255.0	inventory number SRVC7x01
Added SP 4 3/99		Gateway = 223.190.100.1	Video Card=S3 Verge DX
Added SP5 6/99			inventory number VCS301
			NIC=Intel 10/100
			inventory number NICI01

FIGURE 10-9 Sample log

- The folder for each machine should also reflect each time one of the machines is changed in any way, including hardware and software upgrades, upgrades to BIOS or drivers, or changes to location.
- A network map, created with a program such as Visio, is often useful. Figure 10-10 shows an example of a network map created with Visio. This map would include the servers, workstations, printers and other peripherals, cables and cable closets, patch panels, hubs, routers, and any other elements of your network. This enables you to find the connections between problems as well as locate specific pieces of your hardware.
- Each time a new procedure is created for installing, fixing, or configuring an element of your network, it must be documented and made available to anyone in your organization that might perform that task.
- Each time a new policy is set—for issues such as password length, login times, available storage space, or other issues—it must be documented.
- All domains, servers, or accounts that require an administrator's account should have a superadministrator account created and documented. This account information and password should not be available to most administrators. You might store it with the network manager or with the other sensitive network documentation.
- Most network operating systems have the ability to configure groups and permissions or rights. You should document what users are members of

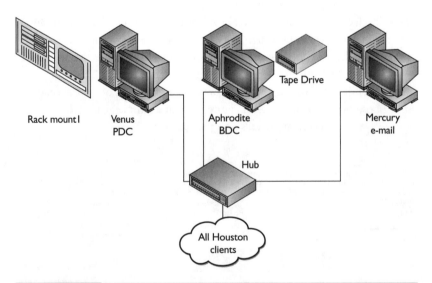

FIGURE 10-10   Sample Visio network diagram

which groups. Then, document which groups and users have which level of permissions or rights to which resources.

- Each network has mapped drives, servers that contain special data or have special functions, and other details. These details are important to document. New employees or consultants need this information when familiarizing themselves with your network.
- As you begin to create special configurations, batch files, or collect special drivers, these should be documented and backed up—what does that strange JOEBOB.BAT do on the primary domain controller machine? Is it necessary? If you were a new network administrator just coming in to an environment that had no documentation, you might be tempted either to run the batch file or to delete it. In one case, it might be a destructive program left by a disgruntled former administrator to delete your most important configuration files; in the other case, it might be the file that runs the nightly backup. Neither scenario bodes well for your stress levels. If all the batch files were documented, however, you would know when each one could be run.

This list of suggested documentation for your network, while long, is just the tip of the iceberg. Each organization has elements of its network configuration that are unique—these are the elements that must be documented and available to the administrators, contractors, or consultants working on your systems.

Document Management

All the hours spent on documentation will be wasted if you allow elements of the network to be changed without updating the documentation. Similarly, no amount of documentation can help if the server that stores it all is the one machine that is irrevocably fried. Managing your documentation is as important as creating it—this consists of ensuring that changes made to the systems or networks are reflected in the documentation and that all the documentation is available when it is necessary.

First, you should ensure that all changes to machines get logged. Similarly to the original log of how the machine was configured, the change log should include the who, when, what, and why information, as shown in Figure 10-11. This enables you not only to keep track of how your machines are currently configured, but also to ensure that you can return to the original configuration if necessary.

Next, you need to ensure that the documentation you've created and organized and updated is available when you need it. While it makes a great deal of sense to use a software-based knowledge management system for your documentation,

Change Log				
Name	Added Software	Date/Who	Added Hardware	Date/Who
Venus	NT Service Pack 4	3/1/99		
		John X. Tech		
	NT Service Pack 5	6/1/99		
		John X. Tech		
			Additional 10/100 NIC	John X. Tech
			inventory number NICI07	6/2/99

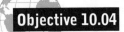

FIGURE 10-11   Sample change log

make sure you can immediately put your hot little hands on at least one hard copy and a software backup of the documentation. This ensures that even if your network or the server that stores the information is unavailable, you have the information you need to troubleshoot that problem.

Objective 10.04   Planned Maintenance

Considering that your network infrastructure (media, servers, clients, and so forth) is vital to your business, it is important to treat it with respect. Upsetting the (sometimes) delicate balance between elements of the system (and we include the users in this!) is not a good idea, so any work that is likely to disrupt service—or even has the potential to do so—should be planned to occur after hours, or if that's not possible, at a time that's known to the users likely to be using the system during that period (see Figure 10-12). Planned maintenance includes the following events:

- Adding or removing network media or equipment
- Installing updates or patches on the servers

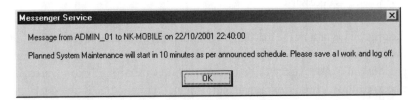

FIGURE 10-12   Plan and announce scheduled maintenance

- Downloading software updates to client systems (known as a *software push*)
- Performing scheduled backups
- Performing diagnostics or testing on the network

Many a network tech has gotten away with pulling a cable out and quickly replugging it to perform a check or move a connection to another hub, and this leads to an atmosphere of complacency—it only takes that one time that you *do* bring down the whole network to make you realize how important it is to do things properly—it may be inconvenient to have to wait to perform what might seem to be a simple, quick repatching task, but it's the *professional* way to behave!

Software Updates and System Patches

Many network operating systems and other applications allow software updates and patches to be dynamically installed—sometimes without a need to reboot. Tempting as it might be to do an '"invisible" update on your servers or for a particular application, these fixes should *always* be tested on a nonlive system before being released into the wild—every serious network support team should have access to a lab area with test servers and client PCs where they can check for potentially unpleasant side effects—we've all heard the one about the software patch that fixes six problems and introduces four new ones!

Exam Tip

Software patches should be tested in a lab environment before live implementation.

Standard Builds and Self-Healing Systems

Having a fixed basic configuration for your client PCs means that you can reinstall easily from the network or CD, or just replace an entire hard disk with one holding a clean setup. This can save a considerable amount of time if you encounter a major problem with a machine—you can get it back to "square one" very quickly without having to install individual packages. A standard build also helps you test patches and updates because you know the target software environment very well. Software products are also available that will take snapshots of client PCs at regular intervals so that they can be rolled back to pre-problem (pre-patch) times in the event of a problem—these systems are known as *self-healing.*

Objective 10.05   # Viruses and Vulnerabilities

The greatest problem in today's sharing, networked computer society is the virus (see Figure 10-13). Viruses today can be executable files, Java or JavaScript applications, and macros that run in other applications (macro viruses currently account for about 80 percent of all viruses). These viruses can be transmitted in a variety of ways, including downloading documents from the Web, receiving viruses or infected documents via e-mail, or through more traditional means such as accidentally booting from an infected disk or running a Trojan horse (a program that claims to do something useful but actually contains a virus). The first step toward protecting your network from these unwanted critters is buying good network-based virus protection software. For protection from downloaded viruses, you might also invest in a firewall that has the ability to screen out unwanted visitors. Firewalls can also be configured to block certain files or types of files from being downloaded. While you probably would not want to block the download of all .DOC or .EXE files, you might block specific, known virus files.

A variety of companies, such as Network Associates, Symantec, Trend Micro, and Sophos offer virus protection suites to help protect your network. These software suites enable scanning and cleaning of viruses on the servers and work-

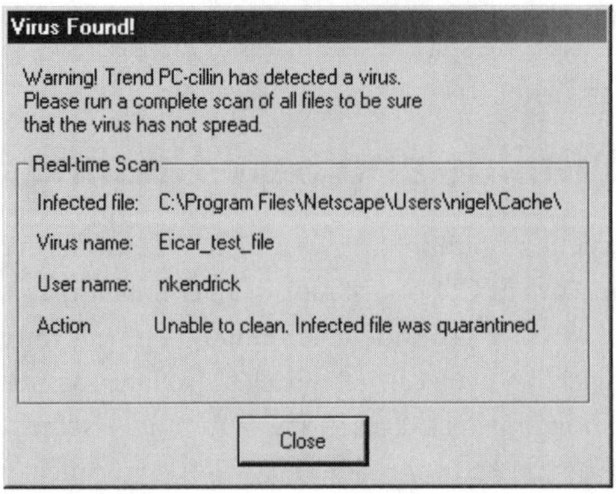

Virus Found!

Warning! Trend PC-cillin has detected a virus.
Please run a complete scan of all files to be sure
that the virus has not spread.

Real-time Scan

Infected file: C:\Program Files\Netscape\Users\nigel\Cache\

Virus name: Eicar_test_file

User name: nkendrick

Action   Unable to clean. Infected file was quarantined.

Close

FIGURE 10-13   Detecting a (test) virus

stations in your network. You have two important tasks to make this work. First, buy and install the virus protection software. Second, *make sure you keep it updated*. Most virus protection software depends on often-updated files—usually called *data, definition*, or *signature files*—that search for and clean particular viruses. If you have good virus software but an out-of-date definition file, the newer viruses can have a field day in your systems. It is best to check for new data files on a regular basis (once per week, but once a day is better) and have a prede-termined method for making sure all the proper locations get updated (see Figure 10-14). This is the only way to protect your machines from infestation. The virus protection suite is the best all-around method of protection for your network. It enables you to scan not only your servers, but also your workstations, and in some cases specific downloaded files and e-mail. The more complete a suite you are able to buy, the more protected your network can be. Once again, don't forget to *test* all virus updates before letting them "go live"—even patches from well-respected antivirus companies have caused unexpected problems.

Exam Tip

Remember how important it is to update the virus definitions regularly.

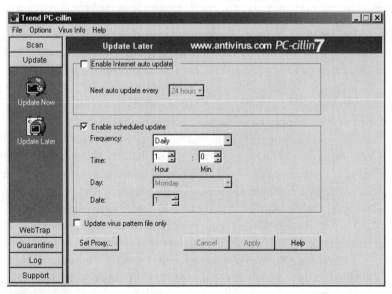

FIGURE 10-14   Scheduling virus protection updates

Application Vulnerabilities

Although antivirus programs will help prevent malicious code from entering your systems, potential damage can also be caused by software vulnerabilities—unplanned program features that can be exploited to break systems or used as "back doors" to gain high-level access to systems and networks. Always keep an eye out for manufacturer's bulletins and announcements from advisory groups about the software you are using—always test and implement security fixes as soon as possible.

Travel Assistance

Advisories about software-related vulnerabilities are published regularly by CERT—www.cert.org—and Security Focus—http://www.securityfocus.com/.

CHECKPOINT

✔ **Objective 10.01: Network Operating Systems**   The two rivals for the hearts and minds of your network servers are Microsoft Windows NT (or 2000) Server and Novell NetWare. Both operating systems provide the same basic functionality, but differ in the way that they are administered and in the performance they offer under different working conditions. It is always best to install the right NOS for your requirements—if necessary, seek advice from other network techs and managers that have installed similar systems—you may even be surprised to find that UNIX/Linux is the best fit for your needs, especially if you are planning to install an Internet-type service, such as an in-house web server. On the management side, Microsoft has always been associated with the domain-based security model and Novell with Bindery files and now Novell Directory Services, but Microsoft introduced their own version of Directory Services (call Active Directory) with Windows 2000. We must also remember that there are other non-PC systems out there, and so this section ended with a brief overview of how Apple computer systems do their network thing.

✔ **Objective 10.02: Network Clients**   Microsoft predominates in the client operating system world with their various flavors of Windows, but at least they do recognize that you may wish to connect to other systems and so provide client software for other environments, such as Novell NetWare, but you generally get better functionality by installing the client kits supplied by the NOS manufacturers—"client 32" kits in the case of Novell NetWare. One delightful task a network tech can perform is to "lock down" a user's configuration so that they have fewer opportunities to mess with their system—in our case, this generally means using Microsoft's User Profiles and Systems policies features to curb their enthusiasm.

✔ **Objective 10.03: Maintaining the Network Infrastructure**   One of the worst things that can happen is for a network to evolve—instead, it is better to plan ahead and document how the network works today and think ahead about how it will work in the future. No one likes managing documentation, let alone reading it, but *do* be a bookworm and show how much importance you place on getting things right—ultimately, downtime due to lack of planning costs a business money (sometimes a *lot* of money), so don't take this responsibility lightly. Planning for expected system events, such as installing a new patch, should also be treated as a formal exercise: test the patch in the lab area, schedule an update for a convenient moment, inform the users, establish contingencies to deal with unexpected results and then install the patch, test again and "go live." This may sound like extra workload, but it's part of the job—it's unavoidable, but it is *not* unnecessary nor time wasting.

✔ **Objective 10.04: Planned Maintenance**   Planning ahead can prevent problems and also reduce downtime and inconvenience. All system changes or updates that *might* have an impact on the network or its users should be performed after hours if possible, with plenty of warning and only after proper testing in an offline (lab) environment. Having a standard build for your client PCs will help you recover quickly from problems and when setting up new PCs. Self-healing software can save considerable time when problems occur by rolling back machines to earlier (configuration) times.

✔ **Objective 10.05: Viruses and Vulnerabilities**   Coping with potential virus attacks and software vulnerabilities is part of a network tech's implied job description. Do install a good antivirus package for your servers and clients. Do ensure that the virus definition files are updated regularly, and do remember to check the appropriate web sites and news groups for virus bulletins and known vulnerabilities that could be exploited to disrupt your systems or to gain unauthorized access.

REVIEW QUESTIONS

1. What is the name of the security management system used by Microsoft Windows NT Server? (Select one answer.)

   A. NTSEC

   B. MDS

   C. Peer to peer

   D. Domain-based management

2. Which of the following are associated with user management with Novell NetWare? (Select all that apply.)

   A. Bindery files

   B. Active Directory

   C. Domains

   D. NDS trees

3. Which of the following protocols can be used for wide area connectivity and performance with a NetWare 5 server? (Choose all that apply.)

   A. NetBEUI

   B. IPX/SPX

   C. TCP/IP

   D. X.500

4. Which of the following can be used to share files between a UNIX system and a PC client? (Choose all that apply.)

   A. NFS

   B. DNS

   C. FTP

   D. SAMBA

5. What is the name of Apple's proprietary network cabling system? (Choose one answer.)

   A. LocalTalk

   B. LocalLink

   C. AppleShare

   D. AppleTalk

6. Which of the following can be used to allow John to see his customized desktop, whichever office computer he uses? (Choose one answer.)

   A. SAMBA

   B. Roaming profiles

   C. Policies

   D. Standard builds

7. Which of the following should be part of your network documentation? (Select all that apply.)

   A. Patches

   B. Drivers

   C. Network map

   D. Change log

8. Which of the following file types can be used to spread viruses? (Select one answer.)

   A. Program files

   B. Macros

   C. JavaScript

   D. All of the above

9. Novell's NDS and Microsoft's Active Directory are based on which standard? (Select one answer.)

   A. X.400

   B. X.500

   C. X.25

   D. None of the above

10. Which of the following security systems is used by NetWare 3.*x*? (Select one answer.)

   A. NDS

   B. Bindery

   C. Binary

   D. Active Binary

REVIEW ANSWERS

1. **D** NT uses domain-based management.

2. **A** **D** NetWare 2.*x* and 3.*x* use Bindery files (A) and NetWare 4 onwards use NDS (D).

3. **B** **C** NetWare 5 supports both IPX/SPX (B) and TCP/IP (C).

4. **A** **C** **D** DNS (B) is a name resolution protocol, but all the others can be used to transfer files between UNIX systems and other machines.

5. **A** Apple's proprietary cabling system is known as LocalTalk.

6. **B** Roaming profiles allows your customized desktop to be loaded from a central location, whichever PC you use.

7. **C** **D** Your documentation should include a network map and a change log. Patches and drivers should be downloaded regularly from the supplier's web site.

8. **D** All of the file types listed can be used to spread viruses.

9. **B** NDS and Active Directory are based on X.500.

10. **B** NetWare 3.*x* uses Bindery-based security.

Troubleshooting
Basics

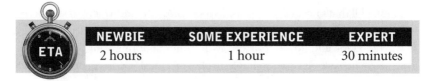

	NEWBIE	SOME EXPERIENCE	EXPERT
ETA	2 hours	1 hour	30 minutes

Back in Chapter 9 we taught you the facts of life. Really! Remember? No? OK, to save your flipping back, we'll go over it one more time: One day, when you least expect, it will hit you; out of the blue someone comes in to your life and utters those immortal words…"Something's wrong with the server" …and as the phone rings to report the same problem for the fifteenth time, the words of Agent Smith from the film *The Matrix* run through your mind: "Hear that, Mr. Anderson? That is the sound of inevitability."

Having good, methodical troubleshooting skills is essential for every network tech, but you must also be able to tell when things are "not right"—when the network's running slowly or the server's disk system seems to be a bit sluggish. You need a "nose" for the merest hint of a potential problem.

Exam Tip

Watching *The Matrix* is not essential for the Network+ exam.

Objective 11.01 General Network Troubleshooting

Troubleshooting is not something that can be easily described in a nice neat list of ten easy steps. It is more of an art—an ability to be "one with the network" and have a feeling where the problems are hiding. The best troubleshooters are those who have a huge amount of knowledge about each of the elements of the network—hardware, software, connections, and so forth. These people can then synthesize all that knowledge into some good guesses about where to start looking for the problems. All of these steps should serve to give you a theoretical idea of where to look and how to proceed with troubleshooting your own network. The theory, however, is easier to implement in real life if you have some examples to give you the feel of the art of troubleshooting.

Simple human error and lack of proper planning leading to basic faults are the two root causes of local area network (LAN) downtime and inefficiencies. The following list shows the ten most common causes of downtime or ineffective LANs that required urgent maintenance, based on a six-week survey of calls taken by a customer support center:

- **Misconfigured routers**   Devices installed incorrectly in the first instance.
- **Faulty Ethernet cards**   Poor-quality cards that fail soon after installation, but take some time to detect.
- **Broadcast storms**   Caused by legacy applications on legacy servers, which should have been taken out of commission.
- **Unwanted protocols**   Many networks suffer from having had Windows terminals, printers, and other peripherals installed along with extra protocols, but these are left on the network when they are no longer in regular use.
- **Poor switch allocation**   LAN bottlenecks caused by too many devices being allocated to run through one overloaded switch.
- **Server overloading**   Poor ongoing maintenance of file servers, causing slow spots on the network.
- **Faulty devices**   Fundamental faults with devices attached to the network, which can be difficult to detect initially.
- **SNMP management tools**   The design of Simple Network Management Protocol (SNMP) is such that it can impact the performance of the devices being managed and add to the traffic burden on the network.
- **Rogue equipment**   Unauthorized connection of illegitimate or inappropriate devices to the network.
- **Power outage**   The total failure of power supplies to networked devices.

Exam Tip

The list above is for general information—it's useful stuff, but don't worry about memorizing it for the exam.

The art of network troubleshooting can be a fun, frolicsome, and usually frustrating skill to gain. By applying a good troubleshooting methodology and constantly increasing your knowledge of networks, you can develop into a great troubleshooting artist. This takes time, naturally, but stick with it. Learn new stuff, document problems and fixes, talk to other network techs about similar problems. All these factors can make your life much easier when crunch time comes and a network disaster occurs—and it *will*, even in the most robust network.

Objective 11.02   Establishing a Baseline

The best way to know when a problem is brewing is to know how things per-form when all's well with the system. You need to establish a baseline—a sta-tic picture of your network and servers when they are working correctly. One of the common tools used to create a baseline is the Performance Monitor utility that comes with Windows NT/2000/XP (but you can also create baselines using most network management utilities).

PerfMon

Administrators use Performance Monitor (PerfMon) to view the behavior of hardware and other resources on NT/2000/XP machines, either locally or remotely. PerfMon can monitor both real-time and historical data about the performance of your systems. To access the Performance Monitor applet, choose Start | Programs | Administrative Tools | Performance Monitor from any Windows NT machine. Windows 2000/XP machines call the option simply "Performance."

Once you access Performance Monitor, you need to configure it to display data. The process of configuring Performance Monitor requires you to understand the concept of objects, counters, and views. An object in Performance Monitor relates directly to the component of your system that you want to monitor, such as the processor or memory. Each object has different measurable aspects, called *counters*. Counters, in other words, are the portions of an object that you want to track. As you decide which object(s) to monitor in your system, select one or mul-tiple counters for each object. Add these counters to whichever view you need to use. Performance monitor can display selected counter information in a variety of views, with each view imparting different types of information. The Log view, for example, lets you store data about your systems to be reviewed later. This is the view used to create a baseline, and is the only one discussed here, although the other views (Chart, Alert, and Report) are useful for troubleshooting problems as they arise.

To access the Log view, either click the Log view button or choose View | Log. To add objects to the Log view, either click the Add To button (the plus sign) or choose Edit | Add to Log. In the Add to Log dialog box, first select the computer to monitor. Choose either the local machine (the default) or a remote machine. To monitor a remote machine, type in the computer name using Universal Naming

Convention (UNC). To monitor a machine named HOUBDC1, for example, you would type **\\HOUBDC1** in the Computer field. You can also use the Select Computer button (at the right end of the Computer field) to view the available machines and select the one you want to monitor, as shown in Figure 11-1.

While it is often easiest to monitor a machine locally, it is often more accurate to monitor the machines remotely. Performance Monitor running on a machine uses a certain amount of resources to take the measurements and to display the data graphically. Especially when you troubleshoot issues with disk performance, memory and paging, or processor use, you should not corrupt your results by monitoring locally. There are some cases where monitoring locally is preferred or required. If you are monitoring network access or networking protocol objects, for example, monitoring locally will affect the readings less than monitoring remotely. Similarly, you must monitor a system locally if you cannot access that system over the network. Finally, when you monitor objects created by a specific application, such as Exchange, you should monitor locally, as the objects related to this application are only created locally and will not be available from another system.

Once you have selected a system to monitor, either locally or remotely, you must select the object to monitor. Select one or more objects to monitor from the list in the Object field. Note that the Log view is somewhat different from the other views in that you only add objects to the view, not the specific counters for the objects, as shown in the Add to Log dialog box in Figure 11-2.

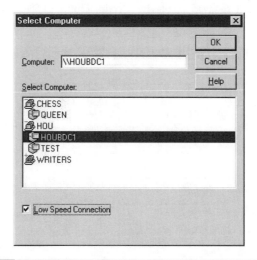

FIGURE 11-1 *Select Computer* in Performance Monitor

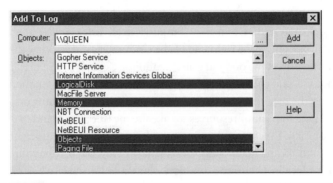

FIGURE 11-2   The Add To Log dialog box in Performance Monitor

After you select the objects for Performance Monitor to track and log, select Options | Log Options to save the data to a log file and to start the logging by clicking the Start Log button, as shown in Figure 11-3. This dialog box also gives you the opportunity to select the update method and time.

After you have configured the log to save to a particular file, you can see the log file name, status of the logging process, log interval, and file size of the log in the Performance Monitor dialog box. To stop collecting data in a log, open the Log Options dialog box again and click Stop Log. You can then choose to create a new log file and begin logging again, if necessary. You will also have the ability to view data from one of these saved log files by selecting Options | Data From. In the Data

FIGURE 11-3   The Start Log button in Performance Monitor

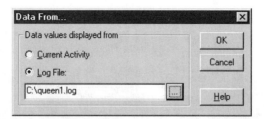

FIGURE 11-4 The Data From dialog box in Performance Monitor

From dialog box, shown in Figure 11-4, you can choose to continue obtaining data from the current activity or to obtain data from a particular log file.

When you choose to obtain data from a saved log, you go back to that frozen moment in time and add counters to the other views for the objects you chose to save in the log. In our log options, we selected to store data for the Logical Disk object, for example. After we have loaded that particular log file, we can change to the Chart view, add counters for the Logical Disk object, and view a static chart for that moment in time, as shown in Figure 11-5. You may want to select a wide variety of objects, so that when you open the log to display in any of the other views (Chart, Alert, and Report), you can add any counters necessary.

The Performance Monitor utility described here is specific to Windows NT systems, but you should create a baseline on whatever types of systems you have

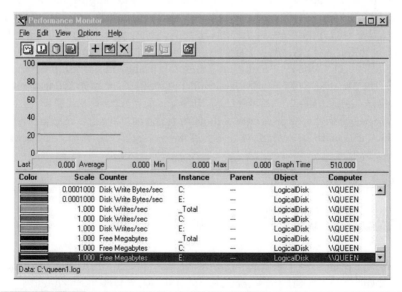

FIGURE 11-5 Viewing a static chart in Performance Monitor

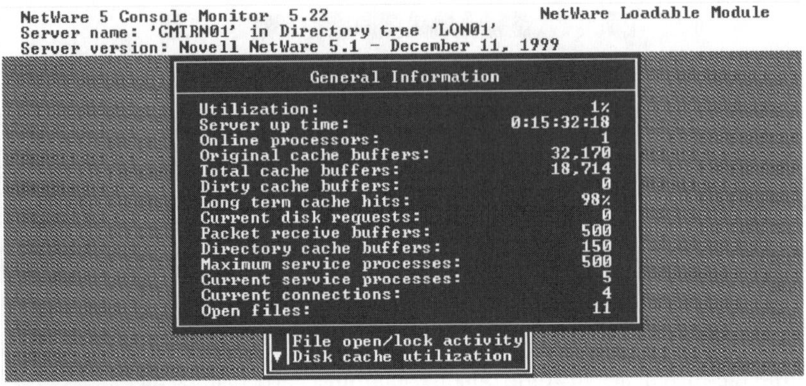

```
NetWare 5 Console Monitor  5.22                    NetWare Loadable Module
Server name: 'CMTRN01' in Directory tree 'LON01'
Server version: Novell NetWare 5.1 - December 11, 1999
```

```
                        General Information
        Utilization:                              1%
        Server up time:                    0:15:32:18
        Online processors:                         1
        Original cache buffers:               32,170
        Total cache buffers:                  18,714
        Dirty cache buffers:                       0
        Long term cache hits:                    98%
        Current disk requests:                     0
        Packet receive buffers:                  500
        Directory cache buffers:                 150
        Maximum service processes:               500
        Current service processes:                 5
        Current connections:                       4
        Open files:                               11

              File open/lock activity
            ▼ Disk cache utilization
```

FIGURE 11-6   NetWare 5 Monitor general information screen

and for all aspects of your network. Be certain to create multiple baselines, to show both the systems at rest and in use, using Performance Monitor as well as other systems management or network sniffer tools.

NetWare Monitor

On a NetWare server, most of the critical information you might need to see and document to establish your baseline can be obtained by loading the *Monitor* application (see Figure 11-6) on the server itself (you can view the program remotely on a client PC, but it runs on the server). Novell calls a program that runs on the server in this way a NetWare *Loadable Module* or NLM, and you issue the command 'LOAD MONITOR' at the server's console prompt to start the program.

The Monitor NLM can display a wide range of information, from memory usage to individual statistics about the NICs installed in the server. Many system managers leave Monitor running all the time so that they can keep an eye on things; it can also be used to kick users off the server and see which files they are accessing!

Objective 11.03 Problem Analysis

All the planning and documenting we discussed in Chapter 10 comes in handy when the network (or something on it) stops working like it should—you now need to go from planning and prevention mode to troubleshooting mode. When you move into troubleshooting mode, your purpose is to figure out what the problem really is. This can be challenging, as you can imagine, when a user calls you complaining that he or she cannot log on to the server. This symptom could be traced to a variety of causes, including (but not limited to) user error, broken or unplugged cable, server crash, or incorrect protocol configuration. The trick is to figure out which one. This requires a troubleshooting model or method that helps you to keep your mind open while ruling out things that are obviously not causing your problem. With this troubleshooting model, it also helps to know which tools to use to diagnose problems. There are a variety of both software and hardware tools that can aid in ruling out your wild guesses.

Troubleshooting Model

No matter how complex and fancy we decide to make it, any troubleshooting model can be broken down into simple steps. Having a sequence of steps to follow makes the entire troubleshooting process simpler and easier because we have a clear set of goals to achieve in a specific sequence. The most important steps are the first three that help us to narrow down the cause of a problem to a specific item. These steps carry so much weight because when you figure out what's wrong, you've probably also figured out how to fix the problem and how to prevent it from happening in the future. The basics of any troubleshooting model should include the following steps:

- Establish the symptoms.
- Isolate the cause of the problem (identify the scope of the problem).
- Establish what has changed that might have caused the problem.
- Identify the most probable cause.
- Implement a solution.
- Test the solution.
- Recognize the potential effects of the solution.
- Document the solution.

Establish the Symptoms

If you are working directly on the affected system and not relying on someone over the telephone to guide you, establishing the symptoms will come down to your observation of what is (or isn't happening). Over the telephone, you will need to ask questions based on what the user is telling you. These questions can be either *closed-ended*—to which there can only be a "yes" or "no" type answer such as, "Can you see a light on the front of the monitor"—or they can be *open-ended*, such as, "Tell me what you see on the screen." The type of question you use at any instant will depend on the information you need and the abilities of the user—if, for example, the user seems to be technically oriented, you might be able to ask more closed ended questions because they will know what you are talking about. If, on the other hand, they need a little encouragement, open-ended questions will allow them to explain what is going on in their own words.

Isolate the Extent of the Problem

One of the first steps in trying to determine the cause of a problem is to understand the extent of the problem; find out if it is specific to one user or if it's network-wide. Sometimes, this entails trying the task yourself—from a user's machine and from your own machine.

For example, if a user is experiencing problems logging in to the network, you might need to go to that user's machine and try to use their user name to log in. This lets you determine if the problem is a user error of some kind, as well as enabling you to see the symptoms of the problem yourself. Next, you probably want to try logging in with your own user name from that machine or try having the user log in from another machine. In some cases, you can ask other users in the area if they are experiencing the same problem—this helps you determine if the problem is affecting more than one user. Depending on the size of your network, find out if the problem is occurring in only one part of your company or across the entire network. What does all of this tell you? Essentially, it tells you how big the problem is. If nobody in an entire remote office can log in, you may be able to assume that the problem is the network link or router connecting that office to the server. If nobody in any office can log in, you may be able to assume that the server is down or not accepting logins. If only that one user in that one location can't log in, it may be a problem with that user, that machine, or that user's account.

> **Exam Tip**
>
> Eliminating variables is one of the first tools in your arsenal of diagnostic techniques.

Isolate the Cause of the Problem

After determining the extent of a problem, the next step requires eliminating all the extra variables—all the other possible causes of the problem. If you have determined that the problem is specific to that user on that machine, you have already learned a great deal. First, you have learned that it is not a user account problem, because you tested that user's ability to log in from another machine. You have also determined that it isn't user error, because you've tried it yourself. By having other users try the task, you have also eliminated the possibility that the server is down.

Ask Isolating Questions

The goal of this step is to isolate the problem to a specific item (hardware, software, user, and so forth) or to identify what has changed that might have caused the problem. You may not have to ask many questions before the problem is isolated, or it might take some time and involve further work "behind the scenes." Isolating questions are designed to "home in" on the likely cause of the problem—here are some examples:

- "Tell me what you were doing when the problem occurred."
- "Has anything been changed on the system recently?"
- "Has the system been moved recently?"

Notice the way we've tactfully avoided the word "you," as in "Have *you* changed anything on the system recently?" This avoids any implied blame on the part of the user and makes the whole troubleshooting process more friendly.

Some isolating questions might be asked "internally" by yourself to yourself, such as, "Was that machine involved in the software push last night?" or "Didn't a tech visit that machine this morning?" As you can see, these questions can only be answered if *your* documentation is up to scratch. Sometimes, isolating a problem may require you to check system and hardware logs (such as those stored by some routers and other network devices), so make sure you know how to do this.

While working through the process of determining the cause of a problem, you will need to use many tools. Some of these tools, as mentioned above, are difficult to quantify–such as asking questions, referring to your network baselines and documentation, and synthesizing all your network knowledge. Other tools are easier to describe—these are software and hardware tools that enable you to gain more information about your network. Some of the tools that fall into this category have been described already, and others are covered in Chapter 12—the trick is in knowing how to apply these tools to solving your network problems.

Identify the Most Probable Cause

This one's down to experience (or good use of the support tools at your disposal, such as your knowledge base); you need to decide from the *possible* causes which one is the most *probable*—we're trying to ensure that the solution you subsequently choose fixes the problem the first time. This may not always happen, but in any event, we don't want to spend a whole day "stabbing in the dark."

Implement a Solution

Once you think you have isolated the cause of the problem, you should decide what you think is the best way to fix it and then try your solution. This may be advice over the phone to a user, a replacement part, or a software patch. All the way through this step, document what you are trying and try one likely solution at a time—there's no point installing several patches at once, because this doesn't tell you specifically what fixed the problem; similarly, there's no point in replacing several items of hardware (such as a hard disk and its controller cable) at the same time, because this won't tell you which part (or parts) actually failed. Although it may take longer to be methodical, it will save time the next time—or perhaps allow you to pinpoint what needs to be done to stop the problem from reoccurring at all, and so reduce future call volume to your support team—that's got to be worth the effort!?

Test the Solution

This is the bit everybody hates. Once you think you have fixed a problem, try and make it happen again. If the problem doesn't reoccur, great! If the problem hasn't gone away, you know you've not finished the job in hand. Many techs want to slide away quietly when everything seems to be fine, but it doesn't impress your customer when the problem starts up again 30 seconds after you've left the building—and who wants to make another two-hour car trip again the next day to "fix" the same problem? The other issue here is where you are providing support to someone else rather than working directly on the problem—in this case, you want *them* to try and re-create the problem. This will confirm that they understand what you have been telling them and will educate them at the same time so that they don't have to call you back later and say "Can we just go through that again?"

Recognize the Potential Effects of the Solution

OK, now *you* have changed something on the system—think about the wider repercussions of what you have done. If you've replaced a faulty NIC in a server, will the fact that the MAC address has changed (remember, it's built in to the NIC) affect anything, such as logon security controls or your network management and inventory software? If you have installed a patch on a client PC, will this change the default protocol or any other default settings that may affect other functionality? If you have changed a user's security settings, will this affect their ability to access other network resources? Partly, you are still testing the solution to make sure it works properly, but you are also making yourself think about the effects of your work on the system as a whole.

Document the Solution

It is *vital* to document the problem, symptoms and solutions to all support calls for two main reasons: Firstly, your support database becomes a knowledge base for future reference, allowing everyone on the support team to learn how to identify new problems as they arise and know how to deal with them quickly, and without having to duplicate someone else's research efforts. Secondly, the documentation allows you to track problem trends and anticipate future workload, or even to identify where a particular brand or model of an item such as a printer or a NIC seems to be more unreliable (or causing you more work) than others. Don't skip this step—it *really* is essential!

Exam Tip	
Remember these problem analysis steps!	

Objective 11.04   Checking System Logs

Most network operating systems and modern client systems maintain their own log files, and it is important to check these logs on a regular basis—once a day is a good idea, especially for servers. Checking the logs achieves two things: It can tell you *why* a certain problem has occurred, and it can alert you to a problem that may get worse if not treated—for example, a log file can alert you to "timeout errors" from a hard disk that's having problems reading or writing data—*before* it becomes another blip on the bathtub curve!

With a fault-tolerant server, examining the system logs regularly is vital because some component failures will be logged but, because the system has redundant items, the server may still run as if nothing has happened—it's both good and bad to discover that one of your mirrored drives actually failed several weeks ago without anyone noticing: good that the system kept running, bad that no one realized that a disk replacement is needed to maintain full fault tolerance.

Windows' Event Viewer

Windows' Event Viewer (NT/2000/XP) displays any errors or problems that have occurred in your system (see Figures 11-7, 11-8, and 11-9). If a user repeatedly failed at their logon, for example, this might be recorded in the appropriate view in the Event Viewer tool. That information could be the clue you need to determine that a user is locked out, either because they forgot their password or because someone has been trying to hack in to that account. The three main logs managed by NT/2000/XP are as follows:

- **The System Log** This tracks three main types of events: information (noncritical system events), warnings (events that might need checking), and errors (software or hardware component failures).
- **The Security Log** This tracks security events based on a domain's audit policy—these events include successful or unsuccessful login attempts, files accessed, and resources used. This log can be especially useful when someone can't access a network resource.

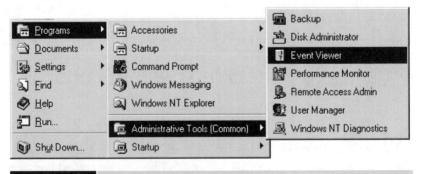

FIGURE 11-7   Starting Windows NT Event Viewer

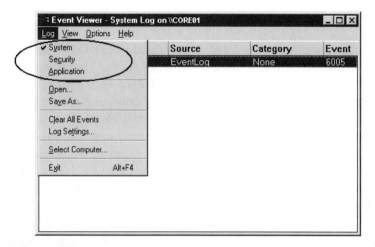

FIGURE 11-8 Windows NT Event Viewer log file types

- **The Application Log** This log tracks events for network services and applications (for example, DHCP and WINS events and events from other BackOffice products, such as SQL Server).

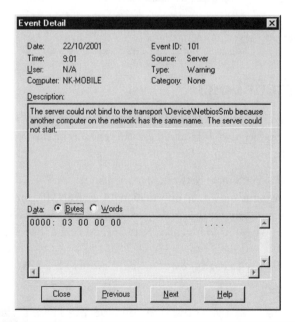

FIGURE 11-9 An error event

Novell NetWare Server Error Log

The General Error log on a NetWare server is called SYS$LOG.ERR and can be found in the \SYSTEM folder on the main (SYS) volume. Although the file is in plaintext format and can be viewed in any editor that you want, it is easily accessed through menus in the main system administration tools—SYSCON for NetWare 2.*x* and 3.*x* or the NetWare Administrator (NWADMIN) for NetWare 4 and up.

NetWare gives each event in the error log a *severity* number from 0 to 6 (0 to 5 on older versions of NetWare) that indicates how serious the logged event might be—a severity of 0 is an informational message. A severity of 3+ is usually worth immediate investigation. Figure 11-10 shows the error logged when a NetWare server needs more RAM fitted.

The locus and class numbers attempt to isolate the error to a specific function of the server; locus 19, class 2 indicates a problem with the cache memory (19) that is a temporary issue (2)—the last bit means that something hasn't actually broken, but needs attention all the same.

> **Exam Tip**
>
> Remember what error logs are available on NT/2000 and NetWare and that they should be inspected regularly. Do not worry about the specifics of how the logs are formatted.

Equipment Logs

As well as servers, a great deal of networking equipment (hubs, routers, and so forth) maintain their own logs, and these can generally be checked using several methods—the most common being the following:

- **SNMP**   The Simple Network Management Protocol. This allows you to retrieve status and logged information using an SNMP-compatible management program such as HP OpenView, Sun NetManage, Novell ManageWise (previously called NetWare NMS), and IBM NetView. Using

```
23-10-99   4:16:34 am:     SERVER-4.11-2324
   Severity = 5  Locus = 19  Class = 2
   Cache memory allocator out of available memory.
```

FIGURE 11-10   A NetWare error log entry

a management program can automate the process of checking devices. It also allows error conditions and alarm thresholds to be defined, and alerts can be sent to on-duty techs via e-mail, pager, and cell phone. This type of access to a device (via the LAN) is known as *in-band management*.

- **Terminal** Some devices have a built-in serial port to which a terminal (or a PC running something like HyperTerminal) can be connected. It is useful for when the network's not working properly and you need to check the device—but not so flexible for general checking, because you have to visit the device. This type of access to a device (not using the LAN) is known as *out-of-band management*.

- **Web interface** This is a popular way of accessing devices across the network for setup and management because all it needs is a web browser rather than (possibly) an expensive SNMP management tool (see Figure 11-11).

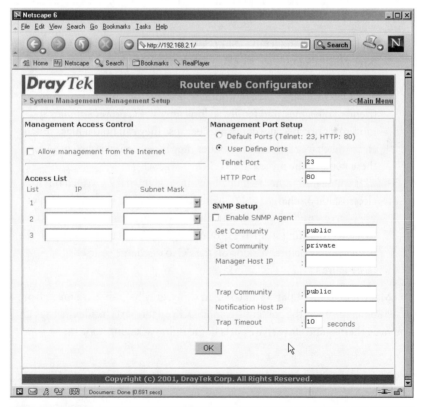

FIGURE 11-11 Setting up in-band management on an ISDN router via its web interface

Hardware Troubleshooting and Safety

Objective 11.05

One of the troubleshooting techniques used for hardware is testing by substitution—once you think you have identified a faulty item, you replace it and see whether your diagnosis is correct. You might also want to remove a hardware component and replace it to make sure that it is seated properly, or to clean its connectors. The simple premise that must be understood when ripping apart pieces of hardware (err, sorry, performing diagnostic substitution!) is that you only do such things *if you know what you are doing.* Prodding haphazardly round an expensive server with a screwdriver can be costly to both equipment and yourself. The Network+ exam doesn't expect you to have an in-depth knowledge of service techniques (that's the job of the A+ certification), but it's not a bad idea to understand the basics:

- **Electricity is dangerous**   Shut down, switch off, and disconnect all power leads before even thinking about opening up a computer or any other piece of equipment—it's the thing to do before you do *anything* else. Electrical safety is paramount; your life is precious to you, your friends, colleagues, and family, so look after it. PC power supplies and monitors are especially dangerous because they can hold a high-voltage electrical charge for some time after they have been switched off. Leave these items to the professionals.

- **Electronic components don't like static electricity**   Watch out for electrostatic discharge (ESD)—also known as static electricity. Always use proper grounding techniques when working inside the PC. Try to use a grounding strap. If a grounding strap is not available, touch the power supply before working on the PC to discharge yourself (see Figure 11-12).

Many replacement parts will come in shiny, gray bags that are made from a material that protects the contents from ESD. Keep the parts inside the bags until you need them—and store spare parts in the right packaging, too.

FIGURE 11-12 Touching the power supply

CHECKPOINT

✔ **Objective 11.01: General Network Troubleshooting** Troubleshooting is a mix of knowledge, intuition, and common sense. The knowledge bit we can help you with to a degree, but you only gain the *right* kind of knowledge by working "out in the field" and speaking to your peers, making use of their experience and learning from their (and your) mistakes.

✔ **Objective 11.02: Establishing a Baseline** You can sometimes only tell when things are not as they should be because you *know* how the system should work under normal circumstances. This makes it important to establish a *baseline*—a documented, static picture of your network and servers working correctly. For NT/2000 servers, the Performance Monitor is one tool that you can use to monitor real-time and historical data. On a NetWare server, you can see most of the server's operational parameters through the MONITOR application that's run on the server (it's classed as a NetWare Loadable Module , or NLM).

✔ **Objective 11.03: Problem Analysis** It is important to approach any troubleshooting in a methodical way—what needs to be done to solve a specific problem will vary according to the nature of the problem, but the general chronology of how things must happen is reasonably generic: establish the symptoms, isolate the cause of the problem (identify the affected area), establish what has changed that might have caused the problem, identify the most probable cause, implement a solution, test the solution, recognize the potential effects of the solution, and document the solution.

✔ **Objective 11.04: Checking System Logs**   Don't forget that a server can tell you a lot about what's going on (or going wrong) if you take a look at its error logs. The logs can also be used to preempt some problems and stop them from becoming reality. As well as being troubleshooting tools, the logs also help you manage the health of your server before something nasty happens, so checking them should be a standard operating procedure.

✔ **Objective 11.05: Hardware Troubleshooting and Safety**   Before *any* hardware troubleshooting it attempted, make *sure* you know what you are doing—electricity can kill, so check and double check that the equipment you are planning to open is completely isolated from the power source before starting work. Electronic components (memory, hard disks, NICs, and so forth) can be damaged by incorrect handling procedures because they are sensitive to static electricity, so always use the proper service tools (a wrist strap and ground cord), or take steps to minimize the potential to zap your expensive kit.

REVIEW QUESTIONS

1. Which of the following helps to identify some problems before they occur? (Select all that apply.)

   A. Establishing a baseline
   B. Checking system logs daily
   C. Testing solutions thoroughly
   D. Using isolating questions

2. Which of the following is not part of the troubleshooting model? (Select one answer.)

   A. Identify the most probable cause.
   B. Test the solution.
   C. Establish a baseline.
   D. Establish the symptoms.

3. Susan cannot log on to the network. Which of the following would be the best question to ask first? (Select one answer.)

   A. "Tell me exactly what happens when you try to log on."
   B. "Is anyone else nearby having problems logging on?"
   C. "What protocols are installed?"
   D. "What operating system are you using?"

4. Which of the following commands or programs could be used to establish a baseline? (Select all that apply.)

   A. NETSTAT
   B. MONITOR.NLM
   C. PFMON
   D. PerfMon

5. Which of the following is a closed-ended question? (Select all that apply.)

   A. "Has anything been changed on the system recently?"
   B. "Can you see a power light on the monitor?"
   C. "What lights can you see on the monitor?"
   D. "Tell me what happens when you move the mouse"

6. Which of the following programs can be used to view the error logs on a NetWare Server? (Select all that apply.)

   A. Notepad
   B. Event Viewer
   C NWADMIN
   D. SEVERITY

7. Which of the following programs can be used to view the error logs on an NT Server? (Select all that apply.)

   A. Event Viewer
   B. PerfMon
   C. APPLOG
   D. MONITOR.NLM

8. Which of the following steps should be first in a troubleshooting model? (Select one answer.)

   A. Isolate the cause of the problem.

   B. Establish what has changed that might have caused the problem.

   C. Establish the symptoms.

   D. Recognize the potential effects of the problem.

9. What is the first step to be taken before installing a new NIC in a server? (Select one answer.)

   A. Clear the error logs.

   B. Remove the NIC from its packaging.

   C. Fill in the guarantee/warranty card.

   D. Shut down and isolate the server from its power source.

10. Kevin in marketing cannot log in to his company's TCP/IP network. What should you do to identify the scope of the problem? (Select one answer.)

    A. PING Kevin's workstation.

    B. Check whether other users in Kevin's area can log in.

    C. Check whether users in other offices can log in.

    D. Ask Kevin to run WINIPCFG.

REVIEW ANSWERS

1. **A B** Establishing a baseline gives you a standard by which network operation can be compared at any time (A). Checking system logs daily (B) will alert you to recoverable events that haven't caused the system to crash but are still not normal and so need investigation before something worse happens.

2. **C** Establishing a baseline is not part of the troubleshooting model—it's a separate activity that should come before you have any problems.

3. **A** The first step in the troubleshooting process is to establish the symptoms.

4. **B D** Monitor (B) will help you establish baselines for a NetWare server. PerfMon (D) will do the same for NT/2000 servers.

5. **A** **B** Closed-ended questions can usually only be answered either "yes" or "no."

6. **A** **C** NetWare error logs can be viewed using the administration utility (C), but since they are in pure text you can also open them with Notepad (A).

7. **A** The Event Viewer is used to view the logs on an NT server.

8. **C** Establishing the symptoms is the first step of the troubleshooting process.

9. **D** Always shut down and isolate equipment from its power source before attempting any form of internal activity.

10. **B** Checking whether other users in Kevin's area can log in will identify the immediate scope of the problem. Answer C would come next just to make sure it's not a network-wide problem and then you might PING his machine to see if it can be "seen" from your location.

Configuring and Troubleshooting Hardware and Software

	NEWBIE	SOME EXPERIENCE	EXPERT
ETA	3 hours	2 hours	1 hour

Previous chapters have given you insight into many aspects of networking and network technologies. Here's where you bring some of that knowledge together and apply it to some specific hardware and software configuration and troubleshooting issues. Bear in mind that the best way to learn about this kind of thing is to actually do it; CompTIA states that the Network+ exam is suitable for persons with at least nine months of experience in the field. You can learn most of what you need from a book (such as this one!), but it's the practical experience that counts when you're out there faced with a dead server and an IT manager pacing up and down outside the computer room door!

Objective 12.01 Troubleshoot Network Media

Symptoms of network media faults can range from the inability of a single client to connect to the network to the failure of an entire system. The topology of your network determines the extent of a problem caused by a single failure, and how you troubleshoot media-related problems. On a bus-based network, a single cable break will shut down the entire segment, but with a UTP-based star-bus topology, a cable fault may affect only one client, unless it's the cable between two hubs or to a server.

Media faults can generally be categorized as follows:

- Cable breaks
- Cable shorts
- Incorrect wiring to connectors
- Badly fitted or damaged connectors
- Incorrect or over-long cables or segments
- Cables located near sources of interference
- Environmental effects (heat, cold, water, and so on)

Most network cable installers carry an arsenal of tools to help them install and test new structured cabling systems. These tools range from inexpensive crimpers (the tools that put the connectors on the ends of the cables) and punch-down tools (the tools that push UTP wiring into the connectors on wall plates, or into punch-down connectors on patch panels like those shown in Figure 12-1) to multi-thousand-dollar cabling testers that plug into two ends of a cable. The higher-end testers provide acres of detailed information to ensure that the electrical

FIGURE 12-1   Punch-down connectors on the back of a patch panel

properties of a cable pass a battery of EIA/TIA standards. These tools are indispensable to the folks who install cable, and most of them require significant training to use and to understand.

Visual Indications of Problems

Apart from the obvious—a completely severed cable, for instance—look for help from indicator lights on NICs and hubs. A broken coax Ethernet segment will often cause the collision light on a hub to stay on permanently, and there may also be a partition light to indicate that a faulty segment has been isolated from the rest of the LAN. Broken UTP cables tend to cause LINK lights on NICs and hubs to go off. Inspecting connectors for signs of damage is not always easy because the fault may be internal to the connector; testing by substitution is an easier option.

> **Travel Advisory**
>
> Some network techs tie a knot at one end of a known faulty cable, as close to the connector as possible. This ensures that the cable doesn't get placed back with good cable stock and, even if it is, it will be easy to see that the cable shouldn't be used.

Testing Equipment

Because bad versus good cables and working versus faulty network topologies have specific, measurable characteristics, test equipment can often save a great deal of time when you're looking for faults, especially when you have narrowed the problem down to a specification issue, such as an over-long segment, or poorly installed UTP cabling that's laid too close to a power cable. These types of faults do not generate any physical symptoms, and they can be found only by performing a range of tests. The most common types of test equipment are described here.

Simple Test Meters (Multimeters)

A multimeter, shown in Figure 12-2, can be used to test a cable or bus segment for open or short circuits by testing an electrical characteristic called *resistance*, measured in *ohms*. A good cable will have close to zero resistance (zero ohms) between its ends (pin 1 to pin 1 on a UTP cable, or core to core on a piece of coax). A faulty or broken cable will show a higher than normal resistance—anything above a few ohms to infinity, which is written as ∞.

You might remember that a bus-based network needs to be terminated at either end for correct operation. These terminators have a resistance of 50 ohms, and when they are placed correctly as a pair, their effective resistance is seen as half this value. So if you use a multimeter to probe a good segment of coax (at the NIC connector on a T-piece), you should get a reading of around 25 ohms, plus the resistance of the cabling (see Figure 12-3). The reading may be a few ohms higher on a very long run of cable. If you see a higher value, say above 50 ohms, then you have a break in one direction or another along the bus (see Figure 12-4). A reading of lower than 25 ohms indicates a short circuit somewhere.

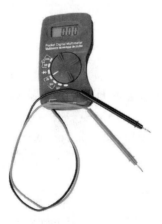

FIGURE 12-2   Simple multimeter

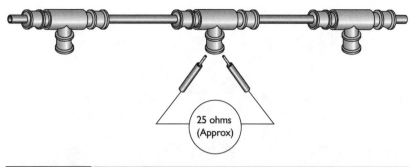

FIGURE 12-3   Probing a good Ethernet bus

Tone Locators

Even in the best of networks, labels fall off ports and outlets, mystery cables disappear behind walls, and new cable runs are added. Most networks require you to be able to pick out one particular cable or port from a stack. A *toner* is a generic term for two separate devices that are used together: a tone generator and a tone probe. These two devices are often referred to as *Fox and Hound*, the brand name of a popular toner made by Triplett Corporation. The tone generator connects to a cable with alligator clips, tiny hooks, or a network jack, and sends an electrical signal along the wire at a certain frequency. A tone probe emits a sound if it comes close to the cable to which the tone generator is connected (see Figure 12-5).

To trace a cable, the tone generator is connected to the cable, and the tone probe is moved next to all of the possible cables. The tone probe then makes a sound when it is next to the right cable. More advanced toners include phone

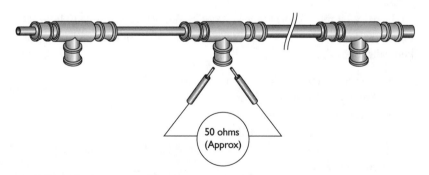

FIGURE 12-4   Probing a broken Ethernet bus

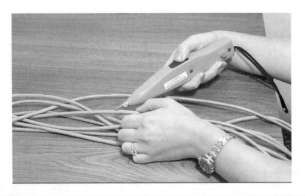

FIGURE 12-5   Tone locator in use

jacks, enabling the person manipulating the tone generator to communicate with the person manipulating the tone probe: "Jim, move the tone generator to the next port!" Some toners have one probe working with multiple generators. Each generator emits a different frequency, and the probe emits a different sound for each frequency. Good toners cost around US$75. Bad toners can cost less than US$25, but usually don't work very well. If you want to support a network, you'll need to own a toner.

Together, a good, medium-priced cable tester and a good toner are the most important tools used by folks who support, but don't install, networks. Be sure to add a few extra batteries—avoid the frustration of sitting on the top of a ladder holding a cable tester or toner that has just run out of juice!

Cable Testers

As the names implies, cable testers test cables. But before we can talk about cable testers, we have to determine what makes a cable bad. Most network techs want to know the following:

- How long is this cable (is it over its rated length)?
- Are any of the wires broken?
- If there is a break, where is it?
- Are any of the wires shorted together?
- Are any of the wires not in the correct order (that is, are there any split or crossed pairs)?
- Is there too much electrical or radio interference?

Cable testers are designed to answer some or all of these questions, depending on the amount of money you are willing to pay. The low end of the cable tester market consists of devices that test only for broken wires; these testers are often called *continuity testers*. Some cheap testers will also test for split or crossed pairs and shorts (see Figure 12-6).

These cheap testers usually require you to insert both ends of the cable into the tester. That can be a little bit tough if the cable is already installed in the wall!

Medium-priced testers add the ability to tell you the length of the cables. They also tell you where a break or short is located. These are generically called *Time Domain Reflectometers*, or TDRs (see Figure 12-7).

The medium-priced testers will have a small loopback device that gets inserted into the far end of the cable, enabling the tester to work with installed cables. This is the type of tester that you want. With a basic unit, you can plug in both ends of a patch lead, and the tester will check for correct wiring and open or short circuits. If you are testing a wall port, you generally fit a loopback plug into the socket at the other end to complete the circuit and enable testing.

Exam Tip

Most UTP wiring schemes specify a maximum segment length of 100 meters, but the full EIA/TIA 568 specification allows a fixed (horizontal) cable length of only 90 meters. The remaining 10 meters is to account for the length of the patch cables.

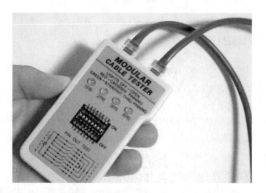

FIGURE 12-6   Simple cable tester

FIGURE 12-7   Time Domain Reflectometer (TDR)

A combination of troubleshooting methodology and test equipment will enable you to determine whether a particular cable is bad. In most troubleshooting situations, you will use other clues to determine whether you have a hardware or software problem. In the "I can't log on" scenario, for example, if you have determined that everyone else in the area can log on, and that this user can log on from another location, you have narrowed the problem to either a configuration or hardware issue. If all network activity is broken (that is, if nothing is available in Network Neighborhood, or you can't ping the default gateway), you may choose to test cables connecting the PC to the server. This is not the only option, but it is one variable that can be tested and eliminated.

Protocol Analyzers

Things are getting a bit heavy when you reach for a protocol analyzer because this means that you're checking out your network at a very fundamental level by analyzing individual data packets on the network. Software-based protocol or network analyzers (also called *packet sniffers*) include applications such as the Network Monitor (NetMon) provided with Windows NT/2000/XP. Use these tools when unexplained slowdowns occur on your network, to help determine which machines are possibly sending rogue or malformed packets. A protocol analyzer enables you to determine whether there is a broadcast storm (or just too much broadcasting in general), or whether you are the victim of a hacker attack, for example. Protocol analyzers can serve many purposes; in addition to identifying faulty hardware, they can help determine whether there's any faulty software on the network that might be sending out dodgy data, and sometimes they can even help trace intermittent faults, such as cabling problems (though other, simpler diagnostic steps can usually be taken first, employing some of the troubleshooting methods and tools discussed earlier).

Objective 12.02   Configure and Troubleshoot Software

Throughout the book, you have read about software tools that can be used when configuring your network and that can also be applied to troubleshooting. Since most of these have been described elsewhere in this book, this section presents just a review of the basic purpose of these tools and the circumstances under which they may be used.

I Can't See Anything in Network Neighborhood!

When a user is completely cut off from the network, the problem is usually limited to that user's workstation or network connection. When Suzy Tech gets a call from Johnny saying that his Windows 2000 machine is on, but he can't log in and he can't see any other machines on the company's TCP/IP network, Suzy goes to Johnny's office to run some tests. The first test that Suzy runs is a PING command on an external machine. She doesn't expect this to work, but she tests just to be certain. Next, she tries a ping of Johnny's machine by using either PING Localhost or PING 127.0.0.1. When the ping of the local machine does not work, as shown in the next example, Suzy guesses that the problem is in the TCP/IP configuration.

```
C:\>PING 127.0.0.1
Unable to contact IP driver, error code 2
```

To view the machine's TCP/IP configuration, Suzy uses IPCONFIG (see the example that follows), and this command tells her that there's something wrong with the machine's setup. After checking the network configuration, she notices that the only protocol installed is NetBEUI (needed for a couple of systems not running TCP/IP). Suzy installs TCP/IP, and Johnny is now able to connect to the network.

```
C:\>IPCONFIG
Windows 2000 IP Configuration
Error: TCP/IP is not running on this system
```

Exam Tip

To view the TCP/IP configuration of a Windows 9x machine, use
WINIPCFG. To view the TCP/IP configuration of a UNIX/Linux
system, use IFCONFIG.

If Suzy's PING 127.0.0.1works, she must assume that the TCP/IP and networking configuration of Johnny's machine is correct. She now moves to checking hardware, using a network card utility to verify that the NIC itself is working correctly. She uses a cable tester to verify that the cable from Johnny's workstation is working correctly. When the cable tester shows that the cable is bad, she replaces the cable between Johnny's workstation and the patch panel and is able to connect.

I Can't Get to This Web Site!

Reaching external web sites requires that a variety of components be configured correctly. Some of these components are within your company's internal control; many of them are not. When Fatima calls and tells Suzy Tech that she cannot reach http://www.comptia.org, Suzy's first step is to try to reach that site herself. In this case, Suzy is also unable to get a response from the comptia.org site. One of her next steps is to try to ping the site, first by name and then by IP address. She gets no response by name, but she does get a normal response when she tries to ping the site by IP address (see the example that follows). This immediately indicates to her that the problem lies with name resolution: in this case, DNS.

```
C:\>PING www.comptia.org

Pinging www.comptia.org [216.119.103.72] with 32 bytes of data:
Reply from 216.119.103.72: bytes=32 time=28ms TTL=105
Reply from 216.119.103.72: bytes=32 time=27ms TTL=105
Reply from 216.119.103.72: bytes=32 time=27ms TTL=105
Reply from 216.119.103.72: bytes=32 time=26ms TTL=105
Ping statistics for 216.119.103.72:
```

```
    Packets: Sent = 4, Received = 4, Lost = 0 (0% loss),
Approximate round trip times in milli-seconds:
    Minimum = 26ms, Maximum =  28ms, Average =  27ms
```

If Suzy is unable to ping with either the IP or host name, she might consider two things. First, if her company uses a firewall or proxy server to reach the Internet, she would want to ping that machine. This is usually the same IP address as the default gateway TCP/IP setting. If Suzy can successfully ping her default gateway, the problem is almost certainly not something she or her company has any control over. To verify this, Suzy should attempt to reach some other external sites, both by pinging and by using a browser. If she can reach other sites successfully, the problem is most likely with the comptia.org site or gateway.

Exam Tip

Some web sites block PING requests because they get so many of them! If you can't ping a site, this does not always mean there's a problem, but as far as the Network+ exam goes, assume that every web site on the Internet is pingable.

If pinging the web site by DNS name and IP address proves unsuccessful, but pinging the network's default gateway is successful, Suzy can also try using the TRACEROUTE (TRACERT) program to check the routing of data between the local network and www.comptia.org. If a routing problem exists anywhere along the line, TRACERT will indicate a timeout error at that router hop.

Travel Advisory

For a tool set that includes tools to look up a web site's IP address, visit http://www.samspade.org.

Our Web Server Is Sluggish!

A slow response from a server can be related to a variety of factors. Usually, however, the culprit is either a connection to the server or the server itself. When Wanda, who is working at home, calls and tells Suzy Tech that she's getting a very slow response from their company's web site, Suzy leaps into action. She tries to reach the offending server and is immediately connected, which indicates that it may be a connectivity problem for that user. She asks Wanda to try a TRACERT command from her workstation to the slow server. This reveals to Suzy that the slowdown happens at one of the intermediate steps that Wanda connects through. This problem is out of Suzy's hands, unless she can offer a direct dial-up option for Wanda.

If Suzy finds that she cannot reach the offending server quickly when she tries from her workstation, however, then the problem may lie with the server itself. Suzy checks the Change Log for the web server, to see if anyone has changed anything recently. If she finds that, say, a new antivirus component was recently added, she should check the vendor's web site to make sure that there are no known problems or patches for that piece of software. She would also use Performance Monitor to compare the server's current responses to the baseline that she has. This would help her determine that the bottleneck is related to excessive paging (using slow disk space to supplement the main RAM), indicating that the server may need more physical memory.

General Software Configuration Issues

One simple trick of the trade when you are experiencing networking problems that you can't quite pin down is to ensure that you are using the latest drivers and modules for every piece of hardware and software possibly (and sometimes not possibly!) related to the problem. For example, if you cannot pin down why a machine is running slowly, visit the web site of the NIC manufacturer and see whether a more recent driver is available for the card. Check out whether newer disk and screen drivers are available for your OS. Bear in mind that, for example, if you're running Windows 98, the drivers supplied on the original CD will be several years old. Remember, too, that newer drivers may fix the problem that's currently giving you a problem, but it may also introduce new ones, so always be prepared to go backward and reinstall older drivers. Make sure you either make a backup before you install the new drivers, or check that you have a copy of the old ones on a CD or floppy disk. Don't just keep a copy in a network folder—if you have network problems, how are you going to get at them?

Travel Advisory

A useful jumping-off point for getting new drivers for almost anything is www.drivershq.com.

Objective 12.03   Configure Hardware

A desktop computer or server contains a lot of hardware—lots to go wrong! Obviously, the Network+ exam's focus is on networking, so that might lead you to think that all you have to worry about is the NIC. That would be a big mistake! Sure, the NIC may develop a fault, and you may need to confirm this by running the diagnostics software that came with it (you *did* buy a decent NIC that came with such stuff, didn't you!?), but your troubleshooting skills also need to cover *installing* NICs—along with tape units, CD-ROM drives, new hard disks, modems, and so on. The Network+ exam doesn't assume that you're a super tech or that you know the ins and outs of everything—that's the focus of the A+ exam—but it pays off in real life (and for the exam) to know the basics. This section contains all you need to know, in super-condensed format.

Configuring System Resources

Modems and NICs require system resources to function properly. Don't worry about how to set these resources at this point; just be aware that they exist.

System resources is a Microsoft term (now part of the tech vernacular) that describes four totally different PC elements: IRQs, I/O addresses, DMA channels, and memory addresses.

IRQs

Interrupt Requests (IRQs) are used by devices to tell the CPU that they need some attention. This approach is more efficient than having the CPU keep checking every device one by one. Virtually every device in the PC uses an IRQ. Certainly, a NIC will require an IRQ, and so will a modem if it plugs straight into the PC's expansion bus; if it's plugged into a serial port, the IRQ is taken care of.

A standard PC has 16 numbered IRQs, but many of these are already taken up by devices such as the hard drives and floppy drive. Table 12-1 lists all of the IRQs and the devices that use them.

As you can see, realistically, a PC has only a few spare interrupts that can be used for a NIC and other plug-in devices. The most likely candidates are 10, 11, 5 (unless you have a second printer port fitted), and 2/9. IRQ 12 may be available if you have your mouse plugged into a serial port *and* you disable the onboard (PS/2 style) mouse interface; this is usually an option in the PC's setup program.

TABLE 12.1	PC IRQ Assignments	
IRQ	**Default Function**	**Available?**
IRQ 0	System timer	No
IRQ 1	Keyboard	No
IRQ 2/9	Open for use	Yes
IRQ 3	Serial ports	Yes
IRQ 4	Serial ports	Yes
IRQ 5	Second parallel port (if fitted)	Maybe
IRQ 6	Floppy drive	No
IRQ 7	Primary parallel port	No
IRQ 8	Real-time clock	No
IRQ 10	Open for use	Yes
IRQ 11	Open for use	Yes
IRQ 12	Mouse port	Maybe
IRQ 13	Math coprocessor	No
IRQ 14	Primary hard drive controller	No
IRQ 15	Secondary hard drive controller	No

Just in case you're wondering, IRQ 2 and IRQ 9 are tied together. It's an historic thing, and they're called the *cascaded* interrupts. Don't worry too much about this, but you might like to know that they're free for use by NICs and other hardware, although they don't work too well under some circumstances. Most techs treat them as available only as a last resort.

Things get a bit confusing when you consider client PCs because Windows 9*x*, 2000, and ME *do* allow interrupts to be shared under the watchful eye of the *Plug and Play (PnP)* configuration environment. PnP is a system that avoids all the hassle of manually configuring all four system resources for NICs and other plug-in cards, by having the PC and the operating system work out everything for themselves. The

> **Exam Tip**
>
> The golden rule for the Network+ exam is that interrupts cannot be shared. For example, if you have a tape streamer in a server with its expansion card configured to use IRQ 10, you wouldn't try to use this IRQ for a NIC.

best line to take is that if an exam scenario raises the possibility of any resources being accidentally shared, this sharing is likely to cause problems: either the PC will crash, or the NIC (or whatever is clashing) won't work properly.

If PnP is so great, you might be wondering why we're even discussing system resources. Three issues require network technicians to have a thorough understanding of resources. First, and perhaps most shocking, PnP does not always work perfectly and occasionally requires a little manual configuration. Second, millions of older devices came out before PnP. These *legacy* devices require you to understand system resources in detail. Third, and possibly most important, Network+ tests you on system resources. Know your resources!

I/O Addresses

The second system resource is the *I/O address*, or port address. *Every* device in the PC has an I/O address, or a range of them. Think of them as phone numbers for the devices—you generally use the I/O address to communicate with a device. I/O addresses are specified by four-digit hexadecimal numbers. Here are a few examples of common PC I/O addresses:

- **0060**   Keyboard
- **01F0**   Primary hard drive controller
- **03F0**   Floppy drive controller

There are dozens of other I/O addresses in use or allocated to other devices and, just like with IRQs, some I/O address ranges are free for expansion cards. The golden rule remains the same: you can't have two devices sharing I/O addresses. Not even Plug and Play can get around that.

DMA Channels

If an add-in card (or internal device) supports *Direct Memory Access* (DMA), then it can use the features of a chip called a DMA controller to whiz data from place to place much faster than it could be sent through the I/O route. Some NICs, sound cards, and disk controllers support DMA, but most internal modems don't. Many years ago, DMA was a popular method for speeding up devices, but with today's very fast computers, it is rarely used (aside from the exceptions already noted).

A *DMA channel* is a signal used to start a DMA data transfer. A PC has seven DMA channels, as listed in Table 12-2.

Exam Tip

Be aware that DMA is a system resource, and that a NIC may need to have a DMA assigned when it is installed.

DMA channels should be treated exactly like IRQs: no two devices should ever share a DMA channel.

Memory Addresses

The fourth and last system resource is the *memory address*. Some NICs (and various other add-ins) require a range of RAM to be set aside for their own use. This is defined by memory addresses, which are generally specified in pairs as the start and end locations for the allocated RAM: for example,

```
000A0000-000AFFFF_Video Memory
```

TABLE 12.2   DMA Channels

DMA Channel	Default Function	Available?
DMA 0/4	System	No
DMA 1	Open for use	Yes
DMA 2	Floppy drive	No
DMA 3	Open for use	Yes
DMA 5	Open for use	Yes
DMA 6	Open for use	Yes
DMA 7	Open for use	Yes

Often the leading zeroes are omitted, and because of the way the Intel microprocessor architecture allows memory addresses to be specified using two different techniques (don't ask, as you don't need to know for the Network+ exam, thank goodness!), the last digit is often ignored. For this reason, you might find the preceding abbreviated as follows:

```
A000-AFFF_Video Memory
```

The numbers are written in the ever-popular hexadecimal (base 16) notation, and—guess what?—having two devices competing for the same memory area is a no-go.

Assigning Resources

When IBM designed its PC, it defined industry-standard combinations of system resources for many of the built-in devices and functions. The Network+ exam doesn't expect you to know *all* of these resource allocations, but you *might* get a question or two about the serial (COM) and parallel printer (LPT) ports, so memorizing Table 12-3 is a good idea.

Notice that COM1 and 3 and COM2 and 4 both share interrupts. This breaks the Network+ rule about sharing IRQs—but that's the way IBM did things, and who are we to argue with IBM?

External modems often plug into a COM port (there are a few parallel port modems, and USB modems are becoming increasingly popular), so an external

TABLE 12.3   Common Port Settings

Port Name	I/O address	IRQ
COM1	03F8	4
COM2	02F8	3
COM3	03E8	4
COM4	02E8	3
LPT1	0378	7
LPT2	0278	5

modem will effectively use one of the I/O and IRQ pairs listed in the table. Internal modems come with their own built-in serial port and so will use a pair of resources according to how you configure them.

Although good old IBM allowed serial ports to share IRQs, it's not a good idea to push this idea too far in the real world. If, for example, you have a mouse connected to COM1 (address 03F8, IRQ 4), you should avoid configuring an internal modem to COM3 (address 03E8, IRQ 4). The best option here would be to configure the modem to COM2 or COM4. If your PC has a built-in COM2 (most PCs these days have two serial ports), then you could possibly disable it using the PC's built-in setup program. If you *do* configure an internal modem so that it shares an interrupt with another serial device, it *might* work, but more often than not the system will lock up or run very s-l-o-w-l-y.

It's not critical that you understand exactly what a system resource is. Just remember that there are four of them—I/O addresses, IRQs, DMAs, and memory addresses—and that all NICs and modems will need an I/O address and an IRQ; only NICs may also need a DMA channel or a memory address.

Plug and Play Resource Assignment

If the system, card, and operating system are all PnP, assigning system resources is automatic (hooray!). The system will boot, recognize the PnP device, and prompt for the driver disk (see Figure 12-8). The rest is automatic, although you will probably need to reboot.

| **FIGURE 12-8** | Plug and Play helping to configure a NIC |

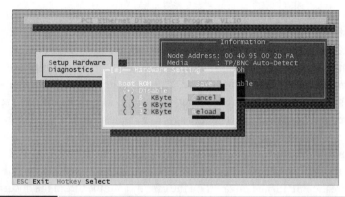

FIGURE 12-9   NIC configuration utility

Manual Resource Assignment

If the card is non-PnP, then you have still more work to do. You need to set the resources on the utility that came with the disk. These utilities are almost always DOS programs. Figure 12-9 shows a typical utility.

Setting resources for a non-PnP NIC requires a two-step process. First, install the DOS driver and configure the card resources with the setup utility. Second, boot to Windows, go to the Device Manager, and set the system resources. The setup utility configures the card; you also need to tell Windows what resources that card requires.

Objective 12.04   Install NICs and Modems

Installing a device in a PC is a three-step procedure: First, you must physically install it. Second, it must be assigned unused system resources, either by Plug-and-Play or manually. Third, you (or PnP) must install the proper drivers.

Physical Connections

First, plug in the card. One thing is for sure; if you don't plug the NIC or modem into the computer, it just isn't going to work! Fortunately, physically inserting the modem or NIC into the PC is the easiest part of the job. If the card is not PnP, however, you must determine the available system resources and then determine how to set the resources before you install the card. The best way to determine available unused resources is with a third-party utility such as Touchstone's CheckIt. If you are installing a card on a Windows 9x system, use the Device Manager to determine open resources by clicking on the Computer icon, as shown in Figure 12-10.

After settling on the open resources you want to use, determine how to set those resources for your non-PnP card. This normally is done with a special software utility on the driver disk or through tiny jumpers on the card, which place a shorting link (sometimes called a *strap*) over a pair of jumpers to complete an electrical circuit and set a corresponding configuration, such as a specific IRQ (see Figure 12-11).

If the card is PnP, you may still need to deal with jumpers. Many PnP cards can have the PnP turned on or off on the card by a jumper. Read the documentation to be sure about jumpers before you install the card.

Most PCs today have two types of expansion slots in the PC. The first, and most common, of the two expansion slots is the Peripheral Component Interconnect (PCI) type (see Figure 12-12). These are 32-bit, fast, self-configuring expansion slots; virtually all new NICs sold today are of the PCI type, and with good reason. PCI's speed enables the system to take full advantage of the NIC.

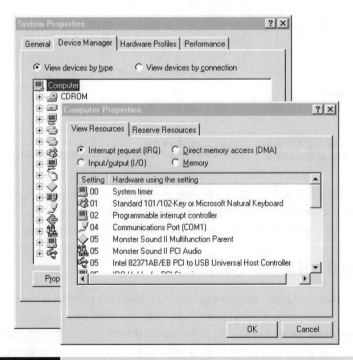

FIGURE 12-10   Windows 9x Device Manager

FIGURE 12-11   An old network card that uses jumpers for configuration

Still present are the old Industry Standard Architecture (ISA) slots (see Figure 12-13). These slots date back to the old 80286-powered IBM AT computer and have not changed at all since then. They are 16-bit and very slow. Most modern PCs still have a few of these old expansion slots, because lots of devices still do not need the speed of PCI, and having a few slots ensures compatibility. Most modems continue to be ISA, although every modem manufacturer now has PCI modems, plus, there are still a number of ISA NICs manufactured. ISA is definitely going, but not it's not yet gone.

Many techs disagree about whether to buy PCI or ISA. The general consensus is to try to buy PCI NICs. Modems' relatively slow speeds make them good candidates for ISA, although many people worry that ISA will fade away soon, and unless they buy a PCI modem, they will be stuck with outdated technology if their next PC doesn't come with ISA slots.

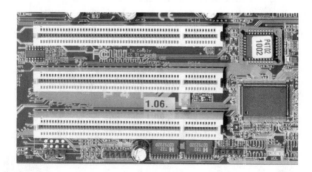

FIGURE 12-12   PCI slots

FIGURE 12-13 ISA slots

Objective 12.05 — Troubleshoot NICs and Modems

If a PC can't access a network, it's prudent to look in the back and be sure that the cleaning person didn't accidentally unplug the card during the night.

Don't laugh! When a network problem arises, especially a problem with a networked PC that ran well previously, the first thing to check (depending on the symptom) is whether it is plugged in. There have been too many situations where some fancy-pants, overly certified network guru doesn't have the common sense to check such basic things as whether the LINK light is on!

Troubleshooting NICs

If you do feel that the NIC may be faulty, reach for a copy of its driver disk. Every (decent) NIC's driver disk has a handy utility to test the card; sometimes it's the same utility used to set system resources. Poke around on the driver disk and find it. Like the configuration utility, the testing utilities are usually DOS programs. Figure 12-14 shows an example of a diagnostic program in action.

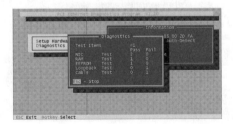

FIGURE 12-14 NIC diagnostics in action

The NIC diagnostics may help you pinpoint the problem, but if the card has a blown transceiver (the bit that carries data between the media and the NIC itself), the NIC's card-checking diagnostics may not pick this up. Knowing this, most NIC diagnostics include a test-the-network diagnostic function that makes the card send or receive test packets. You usually need another identical NIC in another system running the same diagnostic function to do this test.

Another device that is often used to confirm that a NIC is functioning correctly is a hardware loopback device. This device usually plugs directly into the NIC and bounces back any transmitted test packets so they can be picked up and verified by the diagnostics software.

If you really have exhausted all possibilities and still believe that the NIC is faulty, the next thing to do is to test by substitution, but be careful to ensure that the replacement NIC is 100 percent identical to the suspect one. If you're not sure, or if it's definitely not the same, then you will have to remove the existing NIC drivers and install ones for the replacement card.

Troubleshooting Modems

Modems rarely have a diagnostic disk, but all versions of Windows 9*x*, ME, and 2000 have a basic communications check built into the Modem applet in the Control Panel. This function attempts to send some basic commands to the modem and then displays the responses. The responses will vary from modem to modem, but if you *do* get something back, at least you know that your PC seems to be connected correctly to the unit.

You can also use the Windows' HyperTerminal program to talk directly to your modem; simply configure the program to communicate with the *Direct to Comx* option and specify the COM port to which the modem is connected or configured. You can then pretend that you are Dial-up Networking and send your modem command strings that should elicit a response. A typical test sequence works like this:

Action	Description/Notes
Configure HyperTerminal and connect to your modem.	Besides choosing the Direct to Comx option, don't forget to specify the COM port.

(Continued)

Action	Description/Notes
When the terminal screen appears, press ENTER a couple of times.	This allows the modem to sense your connection speed.
Type ATE1V1 and press ENTER.	This command ensures that your modem echoes commands back to the screen so you can see what you are doing. You may have to blind type this if command echoing is currently off.
Type AT and press ENTER.	If you are communicating with your modem, it should respond with OK.
Type ATDT followed by valid phone number (maybe your cell phone number or a nearby internal extension): for example, ATDT5551234567.	If your phone system uses pulse dialing instead of tone dialing, use ATDP. If you need to dial 0 or 9 for an outside line, add this with a comma before your telephone number: for example, ATDT9,5551234567.
If your phone rings, press ENTER to cancel the call.	See the next sequence if your phone doesn't ring.

The preceding sequence either should ring your phone (press ENTER to cancel the call; you don't have to pick up), or you will see one of the following responses:

Response	Diagnosis
BUSY	Check the phone you are calling. Maybe the cell phone network is busy; try again.

(Continued)

Response	Diagnosis
NO DIALTONE	The modem can't sense a dial tone. Check the modem phone lead and/or plug a real phone into the outlet to check that it's live.
NO ANSWER	Did your phone ring? If not, try again. If you are calling your cell phone, maybe your call went through to your messaging service. Are you in a service area? Does the modem's phone line have a bar on cell phone numbers? You may need to find a local number or extension to call.

The response should give you a basic indication of the state of the modem (Figure 12-15).

Sometimes a fault occurs because the internal interface between the modem and the phone line gets fried by an electrical surge down the line caused by an

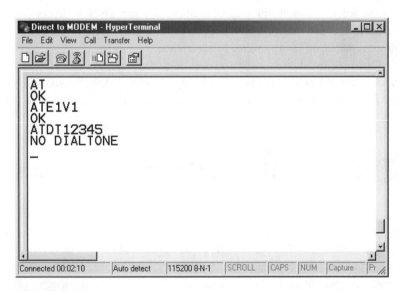

FIGURE 12-15   Having a chat with a modem

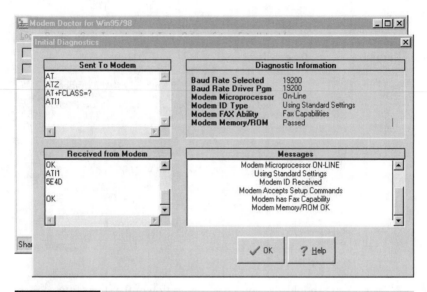

FIGURE 12-16   Modem Doctor

electrical storm. In this case, your PC can communicate with the modem, but the modem will never see the phone line again, so all you get is NO DIALTONE. If you verify that the modem itself is faulty, it's usually cheaper to replace it than to have it repaired, unless it's covered by a warranty.

To simplify modem checking, you could also use the popular shareware application Modem Doctor, written by Hank Volpe. Modem Doctor comes in a DOS and a Windows version and is the best modem tester available (see Figure 12-16).

Objective 12.06   Basic PC Connector Types

Most external modems connect to the PC through an available serial port, and almost all PCs come with two serial ports, often with male nine-pin connectors (sometimes called DB-9M connectors). It's important to know what connector types you are likely to see on a PC, especially because some are used for several different purposes, and if you plug the wrong thing into the wrong port, you may do some damage!

Exam Tip

The Network+ exam does test on connectors! You have to know which ones are used for what purpose.

Because the Network+ exam throws in the odd connector-based question, here's an overview of what you need to know.

DB Connectors

DB connectors are the D-shaped connectors used for hundreds of different connections in the PC and network world. DB connectors come in a number of different forms. DB connectors can be male (pins) or female (sockets); they can have different numbers of pins or sockets (9-, 15-, and 25-pin are most common); and they usually have two rows of pins, although there are a few exceptions. Figure 12-17 shows a 25-pin female DB connector. This is called, appropriately, a female DB-25 or a DB-25F. Figure 12-18 shows a DB-25M (male) connector.

The most common DB connectors used in the networking world are the DB-15F connector used on 10Base2 Ethernet networks and the DB-9F used on older Token Ring cards. The Network+ exam assumes that you know these connectors as well as the standard connectors used on the back of PCs (see Figure 12-19), such as the DB-25F (parallel ports) and the DB-9M or DB-25M (serial ports).

Be aware that the multifunction aspect of DB connectors can lead to confusion because totally different devices could use the exact same DB connector. 10Base2 NICs, joysticks, and Musical Instrument Digital Interface (MIDI) cards (a digital interface for musical instruments and other equipment), for example, all use the DB-15F connector. If you see a DB-25F, it might be a parallel port or a SCSI connector (see "SCSI Connectors" later in this chapter).

FIGURE 12-17   DB-25F connector

FIGURE 12-18   DB-25M connector

How can you tell the function of one of these connectors? The trick is, first, to remember that DB-25F and DB-15F connectors are widely used in the IT world for various ports and interfaces, so it's never safe to think, "Ah, a DB-25F—must be a parallel port!" Second, know the functions of the various connectors on each expansion card. For instance, almost every PC has a sound card, and that sound card will have a DB-15F connector for a joystick or MIDI port, as well as microphone and speaker connections. Figure 12-20 shows a typical sound card with a DB-15F connector and audio jacks. If you can identify the card, you also know the DB type! Figure 12-21 shows a 10Base5 card. Will a 10Base2 have speaker connections? Of course not! If you know the functions of the NIC card's connections, it takes little more than some common sense to determine which connector is which. Finally, use a process of elimination based on the cards/connectors you can identify on the back of the PC.

Centronics Connectors

Another connector to watch for is the *Centronics* connector. These are not DB connectors, but tend to get lumped in with DB when techs discuss connectors.

FIGURE 12-19   Serial and parallel ports on the back of a PC

FIGURE 12-20   Sound card connectors with audio jacks and a DB-15F connector for a joystick or MIDI device

Centronics connectors are the D-shaped connectors on the backs of printers. They do not have true pins. Instead, they use a single blade that contains some number of flat tabs that make the connection. Although Centronics connectors do not truly have pins, the term *pins* is still used with these connectors to reflect the number of tabs. Centronics connectors come in both female and male versions, and in only two common sizes: the famous 36-pin Centronics connector on the backs of printers, and the increasingly rare 50-pin connector used with SCSI devices. Figure 12-22 shows the female 36-pin Centronics printer connector.

SCSI Connectors

Fortunately, the Network+ exam isn't interested in your ability to configure SCSI. However, the exam does demand that you know the many connections unique to SCSI devices. No other one class of devices has as many connections as SCSI. SCSI

FIGURE 12-21   10Base5 card with a DB-15F AUI port

36-pin Centronics printer connector

has been in existence for a long time and has gone through four distinct standard upgrades, plus many variations within each standard over the years.

SCSI devices can be either external (outside the PC) or internal (inside the PC). This gives SCSI drives an advantage over EIDE drives. There are two types of internal SCSI connections. Both of these connections are inserted into a ribbon cable, just as with EIDE: the 50-pin *narrow* connection and the 68-pin *wide* SCSI. Figure 12-23 shows a typical 50-pin narrow connection with a ribbon cable attached.

The oldest external SCSI connector is a 50-pin Centronics connector (see Figure 12-24). Although it is dated, a large number of SCSI devices still use this connector. It looks like a slightly longer version of the printer Centronics connector.

Many older host adapters use a DB-25F connector. This SCSI connector is identical to that for a PC parallel port; however, if you plug your printer into the

50-pin narrow SCSI connection

FIGURE 12-24   50-pin SCSI Centronics connector

SCSI port, or a SCSI device into the printer, it definitely will not work, and in some cases you may damage something!

Most modern SCSI devices now come with special, SCSI-only, high-density DB connectors. High-density DB connectors look like regular DBs at first, but they have much thinner and more densely packed pins. High-density DB connectors come in 50-pin and 68-pin versions. The 50-pin version is much more common (Figure 12-25).

Make sure you know all of the different connector types, even those that are not used for network connections. The Network+ exam writers love to make up questions that include bizarre combinations such as DB-36M in an effort to catch those who don't know their connectors. DB and Centronics connectors are very common and can have multifunction aspects that provide the basis for some absolutely excellent (or tricky, depending how you look at it) questions, which you will get wrong if you are not comfortable with connectors.

FIGURE 12-25   High-density DB-50 connector

CHECKPOINT

✔ **Objective 12.01: Troubleshoot Network Media**   Experience counts when troubleshooting anything, and this is true for networks as well. Knowing the typical faults and their symptoms within the framework of the network topology in use will help you pinpoint a fault quickly. There are a number of tools available to help fix problems, from simple hand tools to expensive Time Domain Reflectometers (TDRs), but it's your knowledge that helps you decide what tools to use and when. Your knowledge also determines whether you can make meaningful use of test results. At the simplest level, the basic tools will help you reconnect or fix a faulty cable. When things get heavy, TDRs and protocol analyzers can help you fix the most obscure problems.

✔ **Objective 12.02: Configure and Troubleshoot Software**   The simplest, and often the most effective, software tools are the freebies that come with the various operating systems. You can do a lot with PING and TRACER-OUTE (and the rest) to diagnose network problems. Many common faults are protocol related; if you don't have the right protocols installed, or if they are misconfigured, then you are not going to see all systems (or maybe anything) on your network. Once again, start simple and look for the obvious, rather than dashing straight into supertech mode.

✔ **Objective 12.03: Configure Hardware**   The key to getting hardware working correctly is ensuring that it is allocated nonconflicting resources. Plug and Play should make this an easy task, but it's not 100 percent reliable, and there's still some legacy hardware out there that doesn't support it. Knowing how to set IRQs, I/O addresses, DMA channels, and memory addresses manually is essential. Knowing what resources are already in use is also important.

✔ **Objective 12.04: Install NICs and Modems**   Knowing each step in the installation process will help you get things right. You should also be aware that there are different expansion bus technologies (PCI and ISA being the main two), and that it's important to ensure that the NIC or (internal) modem you're about to install matches the available slot(s).

✔ **Objective 12.05: Troubleshoot NICs and Modems**   I never get tired of saying that a methodical approach to troubleshooting pays dividends. (Hey, did you see that? I've just said it again!) Looking for obvious symptoms of faults is a good start: check NIC LINK lights and look for broken or disconnected modem phone line cables first, rather that suspecting some deeply technical problem. The problem may well turn out to be not so simple after all, but check the basics first and use the (free) diagnostic tools at your disposal, such as the software that came with the NIC and the testing features built into most modern versions of Windows.

✔ **Objective 12.06: Basic PC Connector Types**   If you have been working in a technical environment for any length of time, you will surely know what plugs in where, but you may not always know what all the connectors are called. Knowing your DB-9Fs from your Centronics 36s will help when you read information and instructions. It will also add up to Network+ exam points.

REVIEW QUESTIONS

1. Which of the following tools can identify a cabling fault due to an over-long segment? (Select all that apply.)

   A. Multimeter
   B. TDR
   C. Tone locator
   D. Punch-down tool

2. Isabel suspects that electrical interference is affecting a segment of network cabling. What should she do first to test her diagnosis? (Select one answer.)

   A. Use a TDR.
   B. Use a protocol analyzer.
   C. Install a length of optical fiber.
   D. Reroute the media.

3. Which of the following commands will specifically confirm that TCP/IP has not been installed correctly on a client PC running Windows 98? (Select all that apply.)

   A. ATDT 123
   B. PING 127.0.0.1
   C. IFCONFIG
   D. NBTSTAT

4. Which of the following commands will display the TCP/IP configuration of a system running UNIX/Linux? (Select one answer.)

    A. WINIPCFG
    B. PING 127.0.0.1
    C. IFCONFIG
    D. IPSTAT

5. Stella complains that her modem won't make a connection. What would be the best first step in the troubleshooting process? (Select one answer.)

    A. Ask Stella what exactly happens when she tries to use the modem.
    B. Run HyperTerminal and issue the command AT and press ENTER.
    C. Replace the phone cord.
    D. Check the phone line.

6. John can connect to the local Internet server using its IP address, but not using its URL (www.acmeintra01.com). What is the most likely cause? (Select one answer.)

    A. The server is down.
    B. WINS is not configured properly.
    C. The default gateway is faulty.
    D. DNS services are not available, or DNS has not been set up properly on John's PC.

7. Which of the following configurations is used by COM1? (Select one answer.)

    A. Port 02F8, IRQ 4
    B. Port 03F8, IRQ 3
    C. Port 03F8, IRQ 4
    D. Port 0378, IRQ 3

8. Which of the following configurations is used by LPT2? (Select one answer.)

    A. Port 0278, IRQ 5
    B. Port 0378, IRQ 7
    C. Port 02F8, IRQ 5
    D. Port 0278, IRQ 7

9. Which of the following connectors are *not* used for a SCSI port? (Select all that apply.)

   A. Centronics 50-pin
   B. DB-25F
   C. DB-9M
   D. High-density DB-36

10. Which of the following systems resources are *not* generally used by an internal modem? (Select all that apply.)

    A. IRQ.
    B. I/O address.
    C. Memory address.
    D. All of the above are used.

REVIEW ANSWERS

1. **B** From the list, only a TDR will accurately determine segment length. A multimeter (A) will be able to measure resistance, but this measure cannot really be translated into length.

2. **D** Keep it simple. Move the affected cable and see what happens. If this doesn't work, then it's time to think about a protocol analyzer.

3. **B** Only the PING command will check whether the local TCP/IP configuration is working. IFCONFIG (C) is a UNIX command, and the question addresses Windows 98. ATDT (A) is a modem command, and NBTSTAT (D) is not a TCP/IP-related command.

4. **C** IFCONFIG is the command that displays TCP/IP configuration information on a UNIX/Linux system.

5. **A** Good methodology says that you should identify the symptoms first.

6. **D** You know that you can connect to the server, so you're communicating over the network, ruling out A and C. Since you're communicating with a web server via its URL, it's not a NetBIOS name problem, so (B) is irrelevant (WINS resolves NetBIOS names and has nothing to do with URLs).

7. **C** COM1 uses port 03F8 and IRQ 4.

8. **A** LPT2 uses port 0278 and IRQ 5.

9. **C** **D** SCSI ports can use Centronics 50-pin connectors or DB-25F connectors, among others. The high-density connector used is also a 50-pin connector, not a 36-pin connector (D).

10. **C** Internal modems don't need memory address resources.

About the CD-ROM

Mike Meyers' Certification Passport CD-ROM Instructions

To install the *Passport* Practice Exam software, perform these steps:

1. Insert the CD-ROM into your CD-ROM drive. An auto-run program will initiate, and a dialog box will appear indicating that you are installing the Passport setup program. If the auto-run program does not launch on your system, select Run from the Start menu and type *d*:\setup.exe (where *d* is the "name" of your CD-ROM drive).
2. Follow the installation wizard's instructions to complete the installation of the software.
3. You can start the program by going to your desktop and double-clicking the Passport Exam Review icon or by going to Start | Program Files | ExamWeb | Network+.

System Requirements

- **Operating systems supported:**   Windows 98, Windows NT 4.0, Windows 2000, and Windows Me
- **CPU:**   400 MHz or faster recommended
- **Memory:**   64MB of RAM
- **CD-ROM:**   4X or greater
- **Internet connection:**   Required for optional exam upgrade

1

Technical Support

For basic *Passport* CD-ROM technical support, contact Hudson Technical Support:

- Phone: 800-217-0059
- E-mail: mcgraw-hill@hudsonsoft.com

For content/subject matter questions concerning the book or the CD-ROM, contact MH Customer Service:

- Phone: 800-722-4726
- E-mail: customer.service@mcgraw-hill.com

For inquiries about the available upgrade, CD-ROM, or online technology, or for in-depth technical support, contact ExamWeb Technical Support:

- Phone: 949-566-9375
- E-mail: support@examweb.com

Career Flight Path

Network+ Certification generally serves as the follow-up to the immensely popular A+ Certification and is an important cornerstone for any number of career flight paths. Many IT companies see Network+ Certification as the foundation for networking expertise. After Net+, you have a number of certification options, depending on the types or specific brands of network hardware you choose to support. Look at these four in particular:

- CompTIA Server+ Certification
- Microsoft Certified Professional Certifications
- Novell NetWare Certifications
- Cisco Certifications

CompTIA Server+ Certification

Server+ Certification offers a more in-depth testing of your knowledge of PC and server-specific hardware and operating systems. If you plan to follow the path of the high-end hardware tech, Server+ is a good next step—plus Server+ is a natural lead-in to Cisco certifications (see the section that follows).

Microsoft Certified Professional Certifications

Microsoft NT, 2000, and XP operating systems control a huge portion of all installed networks, and those networks need qualified support people to make them run. Microsoft offers a series of certifications for networking professionals that naturally follow the CompTIA certifications. Microsoft offers a whole slew of

1

tracks and exams, but here's what I suggest. First, take either the Microsoft 70-210: Installing, Configuring, and Administering Microsoft Windows 2000 Professional or the 70-215: Installing, Configuring, and Administering Microsoft Windows 2000 Server exam. Either one gives you the first certification, Microsoft Certified Professional (MCP).

Once you've taken either 70-210 or 70-215, take the other one, because if you've followed the path I've suggested, you're well on your way to attaining the Microsoft Certified Systems Administrator (MCSA) certification. To become an MCSA, you need to pass three exams (most folks take 70-210, 70-215, and 70-218: Managing a Microsoft Windows 2000 Network Environment) and one elective. The cool part is that you can substitute A+/Network+ or A+/Server+ for that elective exam. You're almost there already!

Finally, if you want to stay the course, Microsoft's ever-popular Microsoft Certified Systems Engineer (MCSE) certification holds a lot of clout for those looking to work in the networking field. The MCSE consists of seven exams—four core and three electives—of which you'll already have at least three. Check out Microsoft's training web site at http://www.microsoft.com/trainingandservices for details.

Novell NetWare Certifications

Novell NetWare may not be the powerhouse it once was, but a huge installed base of NetWare networks is still out there! The surge of techs toward Microsoft certifications has created a bit of a shortage of good NetWare certified techs. The Certified NetWare Engineer (CNE) is the certification to go for if you want to get into NetWare networks. Novell has a number of tracks, but most techs will go for the 50-653: NetWare 5.1 Admin, and the 50-632: Networking Technologies exams. Check out Novell's certification web site at http://www.novell.com/education/cert-info/cne/ for more details.

Cisco Certifications

Let's face it: Cisco routers pretty much run the Internet, not to mention most of the world's intranets. Cisco provides three levels of certification for folks who want to show their skills at handling Cisco products. Nearly everyone interested in Cisco certification starts with the Certified Cisco Network Associate (CCNA). The CCNA is only one exam (640-507) and a darn easy way to slap the word Cisco on your resume! After the CCNA, you should consider the Certified Cisco Networking Professional (CCNP) certification. See the Cisco certification web site at http://www.novell.com/education/certinfo/cne/ for more details.

Index

INTERNATIONAL CONTACT INFORMATION

AUSTRALIA
McGraw-Hill Book Company Australia Pty. Ltd.
TEL +61-2-9417-9899
FAX +61-2-9417-5687
http://www.mcgraw-hill.com.au
books-it_sydney@mcgraw-hill.com

CANADA
McGraw-Hill Ryerson Ltd.
TEL +905-430-5000
FAX +905-430-5020
http://www.mcgrawhill.ca

GREECE, MIDDLE EAST,
NORTHERN AFRICA
McGraw-Hill Hellas
TEL +30-1-656-0990-3-4
FAX +30-1-654-5525

MEXICO (Also serving Latin America)
McGraw-Hill Interamericana Editores S.A. de C.V.
TEL +525-117-1583
FAX +525-117-1589
http://www.mcgraw-hill.com.mx
fernando_castellanos@mcgraw-hill.com

SINGAPORE (Serving Asia)
McGraw-Hill Book Company
TEL +65-863-1580
FAX +65-862-3354
http://www.mcgraw-hill.com.sg
mghasia@mcgraw-hill.com

SOUTH AFRICA
McGraw-Hill South Africa
TEL +27-11-622-7512
FAX +27-11-622-9045
robyn_swanepoel@mcgraw-hill.com

UNITED KINGDOM & EUROPE
(Excluding Southern Europe)
McGraw-Hill Education Europe
TEL +44-1-628-502500
FAX +44-1-628-770224
http://www.mcgraw-hill.co.uk
computing_neurope@mcgraw-hill.com

ALL OTHER INQUIRIES Contact:
Osborne/McGraw-Hill
TEL +1-510-549-6600
FAX +1-510-883-7600
http://www.osborne.com
omg_international@mcgraw-hill.com

ExamWeb is a leader in assessment technology. We use this technology to deliver customized online testing programs, corporate training, pre-packaged exam preparation courses, and licensed technology. ExamWeb has partnered with Osborne - McGraw-Hill to develop the CD contained in this book and its corresponding online exam simulators. Please read about our services below and contact us to see how we can help you with your own assessment needs.

www.examweb.com

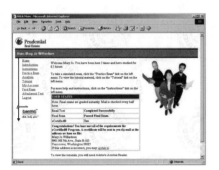

Corporate Assessment

ExamWeb can customize its course and testing engines to meet your training and assessment needs as a trainer. We can provide you with stand-alone assessments and courses or can easily integrate our assessment engines with your existing courses or learning management system. Features may include:

Technology Licenses and Partnerships

Publishers, exam preparation companies and schools use ExamWeb technology to offer online testing or exam preparation branded in their own style and delivered via their websites. Improve your assessment offerings by using our technology!

✓ Corporate-level access and reporting

✓ Multiple question types

✓ Detailed strength and weakness reports by key subject area and topic

✓ Performance comparisons amongst groups

Check www.examweb.com for an updated list of course offerings.

Coming soon:

CCNA™ Passport / A+™ Passport / Server+™ Passport / Network+™ Passport / Java™ 2 Passport
MCSE Windows 2000™ Professional Passport / MCSE Windows 2000™ Server Passport
MCSE Windows 2000™ Directory Services Passport
MCSE Windows 2000™ Network Infrastructure Passport

For more infomation, please contact corpsales@examweb.com or call 949.566.9375